HOW YOU CAN
TRADE
LIKE A PRO

HOW YOU CAN
TRADE
LIKE A PRO

BREAKING INTO OPTIONS, FUTURES, STOCKS, AND ETFS

SARAH POTTER

New York   Chicago   San Francisco   Athens   London   Madrid
Mexico City   Milan   New Delhi   Singapore   Sydney   Toronto

1 2 3 4 5 6 7 8 9 0 QFR/QFR 10 9 8 7 6 5 4

ISBN   978-0-07-182549-8
MHID 0-07-182549-5

e-ISBN   978-0-07-182418-7
e-MHID 0-07-181418-9

McGraw-Hill Education books are available at special quantity discounts to use as premiums and sales promotions or for use in corporate training programs. To contact a representative, please visit the Contact Us pages at www.mhprofessional.com.

This book is dedicated to every person who has ever said, "I wish I knew how to trade." If you believe in your own ability to learn the skill of trading and have the dedication to follow through with a trading plan, this book is written for you.

CONTENTS

ACKNOWLEDGMENTS

Writing a book, especially while trading, has been a very reflective journey. Even though trading can be quite solitary, this process has helped me to realize how fortunate I am to have such an amazing network of support.

Thank you to my husband, Tristan, and daughter, Claire, for being patient when I spent countless hours dedicated to writing this book. Tristan, I am forever thankful to have such an amazing partner. You have been incredibly patient as I have worked through many of the emotional lessons in the markets. I am grateful for your patience, your belief in my ability, and your support.

Everyone needs someone to help him or her get started publishing online. I am thankful to have worked with Kira Brecht. Kira, you helped me to take my first steps to publish articles and continued to be a great support.

John Carter, there are few traders who have put themselves out there in the markets and who are willing to share their knowledge as openly as you. I thank you for believing in other traders in the markets and sharing your experience. I thank you for your time, for believing in me, and for helping me to broaden my vision of what is possible.

To the many traders who are regular readers of www.shecantrade.com, I want to thank you for being loyal readers, asking questions, and sharing your stories. This blog is incredibly rewarding to write. I'm so glad that I can support other traders and help to break down barriers to enter the trading world.

To my parents, who from an early age encouraged our meetings on the front porch. Those meetings were really the beginning of my learning the importance of dreaming and then figuring out how to realize those dreams. Thank you for always listening and giving just enough advice.

Finally, I would like to thank Zachary Gajewski at McGraw-Hill for supporting this book concept. Zach, your feedback and guidance have made writing this book an enjoyable experience.

FOREWORD

When Sarah asked me to review her manuscript, I was excited to learn that she had taken her approach and consolidated it into a single, comprehensive book. When I first met Sarah, I was intrigued by the way she presented information in a unique and clear manner—something extremely difficult for many traders to do. She later informed me that she had received a master's degree in education. And I thought, "What a perfect combination." Take someone who knows how to trade, add in someone who has been specifically trained on how to take complicated information and explain it in such a manner as to accelerate the learning process, and presto—you have the book you are holding in your hands.

I love that Sarah covers trading options in this book. So many trading books either avoid options because the writers do not understand them or make options trading so complicated that people throw in the towel before they even try them out. Instead, an option trader herself, Sarah dives right in with clarity and even discusses one of my own favorite strategies—selling out-of-the-money call and put spreads. Who doesn't love a setup where you can be wrong on market direction and yet still make money on the trade? And the fact of the matter is, with all the high-frequency trading and market manipulation that goes on, basing a trading plan purely on market direction in today's market is insane. To have an edge in these markets, traders must learn how to sell option premia, that is, be able to make money without having to do anything but follow mathematically established probabilities regardless of market direction. It's a beautiful thing. If you decide not to take the time to learn about trading options, then good luck making money consistently in the markets—because you'll need it!

Sarah's book takes the newer trader through the myriad of market noise and cuts to the chase. She reviews the important markets a trader needs to be familiar with, covering stocks, options, and futures. She also discusses some of the main types of trading you should focus on—believe it or not, a large part of successful trading involves avoiding the strategies that essentially guarantee failure. And I love that she discusses finding the right type of trading that fits your personality. I've always believed this to be a key factor in successful trading.

Sarah's chapter on building a trading plan is one of the best I've ever seen. It's clear. It's concise. And it does one thing I've never seen another trader discuss, which is establishing one's motivation for placing a trade. Over time, this becomes incredibly important to clarify. Are you placing a trade because you are bored? Want to escape the trials and tribulations of corporate life? Want to show your parents a thing or two? Placing a trade for the wrong reasons always, not sometimes but always, leads to failure. Establish your motivations up front, and put them in the clear, concise plan Sarah has laid out—and trading success suddenly becomes a reality.

I've been trading for over 20 years now, and whenever a "newbie" approaches and asks me where to get started, I'm usually stumped for a good answer. What path to throw them down? Which shark-infested waters do they really want to explore? On the one hand, trading is the simplest thing a person will ever do in his or her life. Fund an account, turn on the computer, and a trader is born. On the other hand, as most traders learn all too quickly, it is also the most difficult way on the planet in which to make a consistent living. Yes, most people can make money on the next trade, just as most people can sink a 10-foot putt. But out of the next one-hundred 10-foot putts, how many can they sink? Just as out of their next 100 trades, how many of them will make money? And it's not just wondering how many of them will hit their profit targets. Markets are continually changing. The market doesn't care if you have a predefined target or not—it certainly has no obligation to hit that target for you. With the markets continually changing, the only consistency is change. The question, then, is out of 100 trades, how many were managed in such a way as to continually increase the potential for reward and decrease the potential for risk? Anyone can make money on the next trade. But to have a profit-and-loss (P&L) statement that's in the positive after 100 trades takes skill, training, patience, and a plan. And this is why traders shouldn't start risking their money until they know how the markets really work and how to develop a trading plan that sets them up for success. Sarah's book does exactly that.

John F. Carter
Austin, TX
Author, Mastering the Trade
Founder, SimplerOptions.com

1

YOU TOO CAN TRADE

Illustrated by Noble Rains

Chapter Key Concepts

- *Most books explain the what about the markets; this book also includes the how.*
- *Successful traders trade like professionals.*
- *You need to understand the risks and respect the market.*
- *There are differences between intraday and swing trading.*
- *You need to understand the five styles of traders.*
- *You need to identify your motivation to trade.*

What many people don't realize is that professional traders earn their living by capitalizing on the market movement between the highs and lows of the day. These trading opportunities are often not what is reported in the news or what is shown in the movies. Unlike the typical "Hollywood-ized" versions of high-stress trades that occur only during market extremes, the trades that professional traders engage in involve multiple strategies to capitalize on the varying market conditions. Trades can be as fast as opening and closing a position in less than a minute or last several days or longer. Many people are seduced by the thought of making money in the markets, but few actually have access to the trading information used by professionals.

How to Trade Like a Pro shares real information from a professional trader's point of view, including insights into trading literacy, market analysis, trading setups, and it provides strategies aimed at overcoming the obstacles that new traders must confront. It is clearly explained information offered as a foundation for understanding and operating in the world of trading. This book will be a launching point to trading various markets to empower readers to make their own trading decisions and develop a MY TRADE plan that will either get them started in the trading market or allow them to refine an existing trading plan. If you have just begun your trading journey or are working on refining your existing trading strategy, this book will offer insights into how real traders make their living. By the end of this book, readers will have the tools to build a foundation to personalize a trading plan that helps them to reach their goals and maximize their trading potential.

This chapter will introduce you to the basics of the trading industry. It will discuss some insights into the world of trading from a professional's point of view.

You Too Can Trade

I want to begin with a clear message: *anyone can learn to trade.* Anyone is able to analyze and make rational decisions about the markets, provided that he or she has developed the skill to do so. I've written this book for you because I believe that anyone can learn to trade (I am one), and it's about time everyone felt empowered with trading literacy to make informed trading decisions.

There are many myths in the trading industry that for some reason or another limit average people from feeling that they can trade. Trading is a skill like any other; it is achievable with a solid trading plan, some foundational knowledge, and specific goals. In fact, many people have already developed specific skills that can help them to trade but often don't realize it. Whether you are someone who has played in a fantasy football league, watched *Survivor*, traded baseball cards, or participated in a seed exchange, you have developed skills that can be supportive in trading.

Trading requires a trading plan and the ability to follow through with that plan. Trading is about making smart decisions based on gathering information to form a trading assumption, then executing a clearly defined plan, including an entry and exit strategy. The more prepared you are when you enter a trade, the more empowered you will feel during and after the trade.

I also want to emphasize that trading can take your money as fast as it can make you money. Trading is lucrative only as long as it is treated with respect and approached responsibly. Just as with all investing strategies, there are risk parameters with which each individual must be comfortable. Most people who are new to trading will try trading by putting their money toward purchasing stock in one company, holding it over a period of time, and then hoping to sell it for a big payoff. The reality, though, is that most traders do not make their money in this way. There are many more ways to trade the markets.

As long as you have the desire to learn to trade, this book will help you to actually understand the *what*, *when*, *where*, *why*, and *how* of trading futures and options like a real trader.

Who Should Trade?

Whether you are a stay-at-home mom, someone looking to supplement your income, or someone desiring to be your own boss, trading can be an option for anyone with access to the Internet and a solid trading plan. Most people can trade as long as they learn some market fundamentals and trade within their means. Trading doesn't mean that you need to sit in front of a computer screen all day either (although I would argue that watching the markets is actually fun). There are many trading strategies that can match a trader's time commitment to the markets. As long as the trading strategies match the trading goals and the time that a person can commit to trading, anyone can trade.

Trade Like a Pro

What does it mean to trade like a professional?

In my mind, professionalism is more a state of mind. Professional traders have a plan and carefully pay attention to risk and reward. Professional traders are able to manage their risk and especially control any trading losses so that they don't blow out their trading account.

Professional traders have a mindset that allows them to make rational decisions about their trades and their market assumptions. Professional traders will rely on their own analysis and understand the ins and outs of their trading strategy.

Unfortunately, some people try dabbling in the world of trading without the knowledge and mindset of a professional trader. This experience usually results in a loss of money and a bitter taste for trading. However, if you place your trades in the same manner as a professional trader, you will be much more likely to be on the winning side of the trade. Table 1.1 lists some of the differences between a new trader and a professional trader.

TABLE 1.1 Differences between a new trader and a professional trader

What New Traders Do	What Professionals Do
• Put all their capital in one investment. • If an investment doesn't work the way they want, they just keep it forever. • They invest based on random information from random sources. • They do not understand what they are buying.	• They spread capital among many investments. • They have a plan, and if the plan doesn't work, they get out of the trade. • They understand what they are investing in and have a plan of what they are going to do with the stock. • They have reliable technical or fundamental analysis to support their trading decisions. • They know that stocks go up and stocks go down and have strategies to capitalize on both.

When professionals trade, they have a clear price they are targeting for entries, exits, and their expectations for profits and losses. Professional traders are well diversified in the markets. They place multiple trades or have multiple positions; they will not invest all their capital in one stock.

Once they have placed a trade, professionals do not hope that the trade works—they *react* to the movements in the markets in a rational manner. If the trade doesn't work out as planned, they simply react and get out, moving on to the next trading idea. Professionals do not take other people's random advice; they have a clear plan to trade that is based on information they have gathered and, most important, they only place trades they understand.

This book is written to help you trade like a professional with the same tools and setups used by real traders.

Sarah's Story

When people ask me what I do for a living, many people will innocently ask for some good stock tips or draw connections to the Wall Street movies. Everyone assumes that the only way to trade is to trade stocks. What most don't realize is that there are many markets and trading instruments available to trade. Most people are usually shocked when I explain that I trade only a small percentage of stocks. In fact, this strategy is the smallest part of my investing portfolio. I'm still working on the most effective way to explain what I do in a few sentences. Basically, what I respond with is something like: "There are many ways to trade, many time frames, many markets, and many trading instruments. I place trades in various markets, holding them for a short time frame."

The Best Way to Use This Book

This book not only will provide foundational knowledge about chart analysis, market overviews, and definitions of trading terms, but it also will help you to design your own trading plan and offer trading setups for both futures and options markets. I would encourage you to make reading this book an active process. Make notes for yourself, and apply them to your own MY TRADE plan as you read.

Once you have finished this book, you may choose to go out and open your own trading account and trade on your own. Or you may use the information contained herein when you speak with your investment advisor. My goal is to help you to feel like you are capable of understanding the markets and empower you to reach your potential as a trader. Once you finish reading this book, I hope that you will agree that you don't need to rely on a "knight in shining armor" or your investment advisor to feed you trading tips—you are capable of analyzing the markets and placing trades. Regardless of whether your goal is to earn a little extra income in the markets, trade part time, refine your trading plan, or use this book as a stepping stone to trading full time, it will provide valuable information to help you implement trading setups and a trading plan in various markets.

WHAT IS TRADING?

Trading has existed for centuries in many forms. Put most simply, it is a reciprocal agreement to buy and sell something. In order for a market to move, a trader will make a decision based on her market opinion and trade as a seller or a buyer of that market. The buying and selling of that particular trading instrument reflects its ever-changing value, and a trader profits from the buying and selling of that trading instrument. A trader is able to identify a trading opportunity based on a trading assumption and then place a trade accordingly. Even though most people will default to thinking about stocks as a trading instrument, there are many more markets that make up what is referred to as "the stock market."

There is often a misconception that "trading in the stock market" refers to one way to trade. In fact, this phrase is used loosely as an umbrella term that actually refers to many different ways to trade using many trading instruments. There is far more to trading than just buying stocks. There are many types of trading strategies and many types of trading instruments and markets to trade. Many professional traders have developed a trading plan that outlines trading strategies to be used in multiple markets and market conditions.

Regardless of the strategy or trading instrument, trading always must be treated with respect. Every trader must remember that for every winning trade, there is someone else in the market who has lost money. Obviously, every trader's goal is to be on the profitable side of a trade.

INTRADAY TRADING VERSUS SWING TRADING

Many people label all traders as the same, when, in fact, there are many different types of traders. The time frame within which a trader typically places trades, along with the markets and trading instruments that a trader uses, will distinguish one type of trader from another. One distinction among traders is based on swing trading versus intraday trading. Intraday trading is trading a few times during one trading session, commonly referred to as *day trading*, whereas the term *swing trading* means simply buying or selling a financial instrument such as a stock that can be held for longer time frames.

A trader should make the decision about the type of trading he will do based on the time commitment that he has to be able to monitor his trades. Any investment, whether it is for five minutes or five years, needs to be actively monitored and reevaluated periodically against a trading plan. Obviously, a trade that takes just five minutes will be monitored by the second, and a trade that is longer term, say, over a few months or years, will be monitored on a weekly or longer basis. Both types of traders participate in the same markets but will place trades with different timed goals.

FIVE STYLES OF TRADERS

Once traders differentiate themselves as intraday or swing traders, it's important that they determine a trading style that forms the basis of their trading assumptions. Most commonly, people will understand trading through the lens of someone who follows fundamental analysis because it is this type of analysis that is most commonly referred to in the mainstream media. Traders who trade for large institutions or mutual funds are the so-called experts media consult as experts of the stock market. The reality, though, is that there are probably five categories of traders who each trade at different scales and scopes. Each of these traders will have different opinions about the market.

Trades can be categorized by

1. Macro analysis
2. Quantitative trading
3. Fundamental based trading
4. Market makers or brokers
5. Technical analysis based trading

Each of these trading styles is based on various forms of analysis to create trading assumptions. One type of trading isn't better than another; each type of trader trades based on her personality and her own assumptions about the market. What is important to note is that each of these traders has different goals about the time frames traded in, the size of the accounts, and what is traded. Even though each of these traders fits under the umbrella of *trader*, some of their outlooks and advice will be relevant only to their type of trading.

Without an explanation of what type of trading someone is doing, there can be confusion for others who may not be immersed in the financial markets. Many times the differences are not discussed and lead to some confusion about what is expert trading advice or analysis. We all trade, but each of these types of trader will not trade the same way. Many traders will suggest that their methods of trading are the best and that others are less successful. This is all a matter of opinion. My goal in this book is to delve into technical trading because it is the type of trading that I use, the type of trading that I believe is most accessible to the average trader, and it makes the most sense to me. I prefer to avoid the debate about what trading style is the best because it honestly doesn't matter as long as you are making money with the style of trading that works for you. But what is important is that you understand that there are differences. Be aware of the differences so that you can know whether a trader's analysis is applicable and relevant to your trading goals.

One thing all five types of these traders will agree with is that you can't make millions with one and only one trade in your trading career. Anyone claiming to have a big "secret" to trading is probably treating the markets irresponsibly. Trading is a skill that will be developed and refined over time regardless of the type of trader you are.

The Five Types of Traders

Quantitative traders form their trading assumptions based on mathematical formulas. They attempt to find trading opportunities in the markets based on mathematical equations and calculations.

Macro traders employ a style that is related to most economists or mutual fund managers. They look at overall market trends and economic factors and trade on a very macro level. This type of trading is not for the average person because average people do not have the account size to trade this way.

A trader who uses *fundamental analysis* trades based on the financial health of a company. Such *fundamental* traders use accounting ratios and financial statements to create their ideas of a market's direction. This is the trading advice that is most often heard in the media. Most mutual funds rely on fundamentals to pick their stocks.

There are also traders who trade based on order size and volume; they are sometimes referred to as *market makers* or *brokers*. These traders work at the trading exchange, providing liquidity in the market. They trade with any other trader (like you or me) and make their profits based on the spreads they earn from the traders on the other side of a transaction.

Finally, there are *technical* traders. This is the type of trading that I think is most valid for traders, especially those who are trading small accounts, but this skill is rarely discussed until now. *Technical* traders will use chart patterns to find trades. They use interpretations of levels of support and resistance to develop their trading assumption. Technical analysis, as with any other form of analysis, can get very complicated quickly, but it doesn't have to. This book will discuss how to read charts using technical analysis in a practical way. This type of analysis keeps my opinions grounded in what is happening in the markets at the time and has served me well.

Every trader believes that her method of analysis is the best and most informative; it is, after all, the information on which that trader is relying to make money. I believe there is a role for each of these types of analysis, but it's important to realize that each type of analysis will be best for different types of trading, for different markets, for different account sizes, and for different trading goals. If a trader tries to apply the analysis from another trader without understanding the parameters around that trader's trading assumption, the outcomes may not be favorable. It can be a dangerous proposition to make trading or investing decisions based on what these experts have shared, especially if they are referring to trading assumptions based on an account size and trading goals that are different from your own. What might be good for one trader, based on his trading plan, may be devastating to another trader, based on her trading plan.

Luckily, there are many styles of trading, which means that there is one that should match your personality and goals. The key to trading is that that you need to find a style of trading, a trading instrument, and trading setup that match your risk parameters.

Sarah's Trading Tip

A 30-second television spot outlining market analysis should not be used as the sole point of information that you are using to make a trading decision. If you enjoy listening to or watching investment shows because you like to hear about other people's perspectives, that's great. I will on occasion watch them as well, but make sure that you listen with the understanding that these market experts may have different trading goals from yours. Take some of the information into consideration, but always apply your own trading analysis to your own trades.

WHY ARE YOU TRADING?

Every trader who trades professionally will have clearly defined guidelines that articulate the reasons why she is trading. The reasons why a trader trades will shape how aggressively she places trades, the time frame of her trades, and her trading outcomes. A professional trader has developed the ability to separate her emotional responses from rational decisions while trading. The ability to think rationally without the interference of emotions can be best established with a clearly articulated motivation to trade.

Clearly understanding your motivation to trade not only will help you to control your emotions while in trades, but it will also connect to your trading goals. As you continue to read, begin thinking about your motivation to trade. Your motivation is the starting point and the foundation of your trading plan.

In this chapter, I have just scratched the surface of trading. Even though it may seem simple, understanding some basic principles such as trading is not gambling, thinking of trading as a skill, and knowing your trading motivation will be a huge help as you move forward toward implementing your plan. The skill of trading requires focus on setups and being very aware of your emotional responses when you are involved in a trade. When you approach trading just like any other skill, you will realize that it is important to learn, refine, and reflect in order to create opportunities to meet your trading potential.

Keep your motivation and time commitments in mind as we move on to understanding some key trading terminology and the creation of a trading plan. In the following chapters I will begin to delve into understanding trading terminology, various trading instruments, and the various markets to trade.

Sarah's Story

A few years ago, I stumbled on the following quote: "The only difference between a dream and a goal is a timeline." I'm not sure who said it, but it is something that has remained with me. It is the statement that I will often reflect on when I'm making any big decision in my life. This is also the quote that I believe has supported my success in trading. It's important to remember that you can achieve your goals, but a timeline will be necessary to meet them. Dreaming big is good—it helps all of us stretch our realm of possibility—but it is a solid plan with a timeline that will help us actually to reach those goals. I encourage you to also be aware of what your dreams and goals are in life and to make sure that you spend time creating a timeline so that you can achieve what you desire. Understanding why you do what you do is very important. Establishing a clear goal for trading will help you to stay connected to your trading plan and guide your trading decisions.

My motivation to trade is clearly outlined in my trading plan. I trade for a few reasons. I trade because I like the flexibility during the day that trading offers. It provides time where I can focus on my work but also time for me to focus on my family. I enjoy getting up in the morning, engaging in my morning workout, reviewing the markets, potentially setting up some trades, and then spending some time in the middle of the day with my family before returning my focus in the afternoons to the markets.

I love the challenge that trading offers and its potential to work from home on a schedule that works for me. I am very motivated by a challenge and love the feeling of achieving a goal I have set out for myself.

Key Take-Aways

- An intraday trader refers to someone who is entering and exiting trades within one trading day, whereas a swing trader places trades and holds them over a longer time frame, usually a few days.
- The term *trader* is widely used in many contexts and can cause confusion about what someone is actually trading and using to form her trading assumptions.
- Five styles of trading include macro analysts, quantitative traders, fundamental traders, brokers and market makers, and technical traders.
- Be aware of your trading motivation to help you along your trading journey.

2

CHOICES TO MAKE

TRADING IS LIKE RUNNING A MARATHON. YOUR MENTAL FORTITUDE IS JUST AS IMPORTANT AS YOUR PHYSICAL PERFORMANCE.

Illustrated by Noble Rains

Chapter Key Concepts

- *Each market has its own personality. Find one that suits you.*
- *What are stocks, exchange-traded funds (ETFs), options, and futures? You have choices to make.*
- *How do basic trades in options and futures work?*
- *You must overcome the barrier of learning the language of trading.*
- *MY TRADE plan; Sarah's trading plan template.*
- *Introduction to the importance of identifying your trading personality and trading goals.*

As a new trader, you have many choices to make. One involves deciding on which market and trading instrument to trade. Since each market has its own unique feel, cost, and rate of return. When I coach new traders, they will often initially say to me that they want to buy stocks in large companies such as Apple and Facebook because of what they have seen or heard in the media. The reality is that there are many more ways to trade than just buying shares of stocks in a company, but these other markets are not discussed as widely in the mainstream media. Even though it is possible to make money buying and holding stocks, most traders will require a very large account and a long time frame to make this trading strategy profitable. This chapter will identify different markets and ways to trade beyond the "buy-and-hold-stock" type of trading. As we explore various markets we will uncover many definitions and terms. This chapter will help to break down some of the choices that traders will make related to the market in which they prefer to trade and begin to decode some "tradespeak."

Sarah's Story

My background is in education. Other than some elective economics courses in college, I don't come from a financial background. When I began to trade, it took me a long time to learn what all the terms in the trading industry actually meant. When I asked questions, I often found that I heard the same answers over and over again but didn't actually understand the root of the problem. Many traders, although I'm sure they are well-intended, have a tendency toward defining one trading term by using yet another trading term. Unfortunately, this doesn't lead to a clear understanding for some of us who don't come from a financial background. I found it very helpful to break down terms using analogies that made sense to me. Once I started relating trading terminology to things that made sense to me, I was able to apply my thinking to the language of trading. I would encourage you to do the same.

BACK TO THE BASICS

Going back to the basics helps to ground traders in the actual simplicity of the trade. In the market, there are people who are buying and selling a trading instrument. A trader's goal is to pick a profitable trading strategy based on the anticipated direction of the market. In order to place a trade, traders will make a trading assumption based on market evidence by collecting information from market internals, support and resistance, and their trading plans in order to determine whether the market is going up, sideways, or down. Based on a trader's determination about the market's direction and momentum, she will implement her own trading strategy. The markets are an auction where each participant has a different belief about the value of the product being traded, these differences of opinions make the markets move and provide opportunities for traders to build their trading assumptions.

Trading is really about gathering information, making decisions, and executing a plan. As a trader, you will make a decision about placing a trade by buying or selling a trading instrument. If you believe that the instrument you are trading is going to increase in value, then you would buy at a low price and sell at a higher price. What may be counterintuitive at first is that a trader can also make money by selling first and buying back at a lower price. Depending on the trading strategy and instrument you are using, you can either buy at one price and sell at another or sell at one price and then buy it back at a different price. Even sophisticated trading strategies are just combinations of buying and selling.

> ### Sarah's Trading Tip
>
> *When I began to learn to trade, I needed a way to filter the new information I was getting. I usually had lots of questions and often felt overwhelmed, especially when it came to remembering what all the trading terms meant. In order to help get the most out of every learning opportunity, I found it very helpful to create a notes page that was divided into two columns. I encourage you to create such a page and to write down key points in one column and any definitions that you are still learning in the other column. Sorting the information in this way will help you when you need to review your notes at a later date. Your notes pages should have brief pieces of information that help jog your memory. You might even find it helpful to rewrite your notes from time to time to help you remember the information. Also, when you are in front of your computer trading, keep these notes close to you so that you can refer to them if you need them. Regardless of whether you trade futures or options, you will need to understand at least the basics of trading language so that you can formulate your own trading plan.*

YOUR PERSONALITY, BEYOND GOOGLE STOCK

Everybody wants to trade APPL or GOOG because they hear about the big moves of Apple or Google in the news. Even though there are some people who make their living trading only these stocks every day, many more traders can lose the shirts off their backs if they invest too heavily in these stocks without considering an appropriate investment size relative to their account size. These stocks are flashy and get lots of media attention, which can make them seem appealing, but these stocks can be quite costly to trade. Many of these stocks can have big price swings that make them less than ideal for the average trader, and especially the beginner trader. Just remember that if a stock has a big move one day to the upside, it can also have a big retracement (a move back to the average price) the next day. Don't get caught chasing a big move in the hope that it will have another big move the next day if you aren't prepared to take some heat (this is trading slang for holding a position or trade while it's losing you money) until it rebounds again.

The top news desks almost do a disservice to the general public when they talk only about trendy stocks because there are *many* more stocks to trade. There are also many more ways to trade than just buying stocks. Each trading instrument has its own personality, so let's explore this in a little more detail so that you can begin to evaluate whether a stock is a good choice for you to consider adding to your trading plan.

Sarah's Story

Facebook is a perfect example of why traders shouldn't put all their faith into the projections they hear in the media. Prior to the public release of Facebook stock (FB), the news outlets were projecting FB stocks to rise when it went public. But when it was released, the stock declined. The people who made money on this stock were those who were in the initial public offering (IPO) before it went public or those who shorted it. The Facebook lesson is a great reminder to watch a stock, analyze the internals, and act according to what is actually happening in the market, not what the media think will happen. Trading is about evaluating what you see in front of you, being decisive, and following through—not guessing where you think the market will go. Be advised that "hope-and-pray" trades rarely work.

STOCKS, EXCHANGE-TRADED FUNDS, OPTIONS, AND FUTURES, OH MY!

There are many markets and many trading instruments, providing many choices for a trader. Each instrument and market will have its own personality and subtle nuances that a trader will become familiar with over time. Even though many traders will often use the word *stock* when they refer to the markets, they may not be referring to the actual trading instrument. The word *stock* is used interchangeably to define a trading instrument like Apple (AAPL) but also used as a term to describe a broad range of investments. When I discuss stocks in this book, I am referring to the stock as an individual trading instrument like AAPL.

Stocks can be either bought and sold directly, or bought and sold through the use of options. This book will discuss investing in stocks and ETFs with the use of options.

Many Ways to Invest in a Market

There are many ways to invest in a market. For example if you want to participate in the performance of the Standard and Poor's 500 (S&P 500) index, you can choose to trade the E-mini S&P 500 Futures contract (ES), the SPDR S&P 500 ETF (SPY), or options on the S&P 500 Index (SPX), and don't forget about options on the ES and SPY contracts. In each of these markets representing the S&P Index, the trading instrument is different but the underlying market direction assumptions and trading strategy are similar. No matter whether you trade stocks, ETF's, futures, or options, the strategies in this book will be applicable to all of these trading instruments. Having the ability to trade multiple instruments gives you an advantage when one type of instrument is not performing as well as the others.

Stocks

Stocks are the traditional investment—what most people think about when they hear the word *investing*. There are specific advantages and disadvantages to choosing stocks as your trading instrument (see Table 2.1).

ETFs

An ETF is traded in the same way as a stock is traded. With an ETF rather than owning a percentage of a company (as you would when you trade stocks), you purchase shares in an investment fund that tracks an underlying investment like a stock index or a commodity. ETFs are used mainly to replicate the performance of an index, or underlying investment. ETFs

TABLE 2.1 Stocks as your trading instrument

Pros to Trading Stocks as Your Trading Instrument	Cons to Trading Stocks as Your Trading Instrument
• A stock is an ownership of a company, e.g., AAPL. • Stocks don't expire. • You can hold stock in a portfolio for an indefinite amount of time.	• It can require a lot of money to build a portfolio of stocks. • This can use up a lot of margin in a small or typical account for the average person. • It can take time to realize a profit.

trade just like stocks. Any strategies you use with stocks can also be used with ETFs. The pros and cons are similar to those of stock investing (see Table 2.2). Think of ETFs as a pool of money that fluctuates based on an underlying investment such as an index.

TABLE 2.2 ETFs as your trading instrument

Pros to Trading ETFs as Your Trading Instrument	Cons to Trading ETFs as Your Trading Instrument
• You have the ability to purchase ownership of a company, group companies, or product for less than buying the underlying investment on its own. • They are liquid. • They are available to trade on most brokerage platforms. • Some ETFs provide added leverage.	• They may not track the returns of the underlying investment exactly. • You may be forced to invest in companies you don't like when buying on index tracking ETFs.

The terms *stocks* and *ETFs* produce some confusion because they are used as both an umbrella term for "trading in the stock market," but they also refer to trading instruments within other markets such as options on stock and ETFs. Some investors will use the purchase and sale of ETFs as a means to diversify a portfolio or a longer-term investment strategy.

Futures Market

Futures were used traditionally to lock in commodity prices for producers such as farmers. However, lately, the futures market has become a popular market for day trading. It is important to note, however, that the futures market continues to be the way that actual commodities are bought and sold in agricultural industries. Technically, if you buy a lot of contracts in the corn market, if you don't sell them before the contract deadline, then you could own a lot of bushels of corn.

Futures provide a way to trade directionally. A futures trader will sell a futures contract if he thinks that the market is going down, and then he will buy back the contract at a cheaper price. If he thinks that the market is going up, he will buy a contract at a cheaper price, and then he will sell it back at a higher price. A trader collects the difference in price between what he sells and what he buys as his profit. The more the market moves in his favor, the more money he will make on the trade, provided that he trades in the correct direction. Chapter 6 will discuss actual trade setups in the futures market.

Sarah's Story

When I began trading, I started trading futures. In order to trade futures, you make a trading assumption based on your market analysis to place a trade because you think the market is going to go up or down, and you place a trade accordingly. One might say that it is easier to trade futures because all the trader needs to worry about is whether the market is moving up or down. It is a great way to apply your market analysis for relatively shorter trades throughout the day. When I began trading, my account was small, so I wasn't able to hold futures trades over night. I was often in and out of a trade for no longer than one hour approximately. Most often the trade would either work or stop me out right away. Most of my time trading futures involved watching the markets. Watching and observing the markets served me well when I began to apply my market analysis to options. So my advice is to remember that even if you aren't placing a trade at the moment, watching the markets will offer lots of insights to help you refine your entries and exits in futures or to place trades in options.

Options Market

Just as the name suggests, trading options provides many ways to place trades. You can trade an option on a stock or an ETF, as well as options on futures (this is a more advanced trading strategy). Options give traders the right to buy or sell a trading instrument using many strategies. This book will review some of the ways to trade options, including credit spreads, directionals, iron condors, strangles, straddles, calendars, and butterflies. There are many more ways to trade options, and each of these strategies can be traded using basic setups or more sophisticated setups. Most often I trade using basic trade setups—either credit spreads or directionals. Three of my favorite setups will be discussed in detail later in Chapter 5. Remember that it doesn't matter how many strategies you know or how sophisticated they are. If they aren't allowing you to reach your trading potential, it doesn't matter. Basic strategies can be just as profitable as more sophisticated ones. One trading setup in options is not any better than an another as long as it aligns with your risk parameters and your trading personality.

The multiple trading strategies in options are why many people are reluctant to try trading them. It's easy to get overwhelmed with the trading language or strategies if you try to learn them all at once. But just as the name suggests, having more than one way to trade also can provide many opportunities to trade.

Off to the Market to Market

Once you have made the decision about which market you want to trade, choosing the right trading software for your needs should not be overlooked. Don't just sign up with the first company you find. Do some research first. The market for trading software is similar to your local farmer's market—there are lots of choices. Some vendors sell platforms for many markets, whereas others specialize in one area. Some companies offer both a charting package and a trading platform, whereas others specialize in one or the other. There are many choices to make, including which type of account to open and what broker to use, so take some time to do your research and find a company that works for you. Just as at a farmer's market, you often can sample a piece of fruit before you buy it. Most reputable trading platforms will allow you to try out the platform in a simulated account before you transfer funds to that company. You will also notice that all the charting examples throughout this book are from MultiCharts because I believe that it offers a great value and product. I have found the platform easy to use and fast, and the software links up to multiple data feeds and multiple broker platforms. It is a flexible tool that provides many ways to personalize your trading screens, and it comes with many built-in indicators.

Decoding "Tradespeak"

The language of trading is where many new traders feel overwhelmed. There are many terms and much lingo to learn, but you shouldn't let this be a limiter to trading. Watching an episode of your favorite medical television drama can be a good reminder that even though the doctor or medical examiner is speaking in English, he is using a sophisticated language that the average person will not understand completely. We all watch the shows and enjoy them but can acknowledge that we don't know the definitions of all the terms used. The same is true in trading. There are many terms that can make trading seem complicated, but in fact it is actually the trading language that is sophisticated. Once you get a handle on some of these definitions, you are well on your way to trading. Also, knowing all the trading lingo does not necessarily mean that you know how to trade.

It's important that you can speak and understand the language, sure, but most important, you need to know how to place good trades.

I would suggest that you begin to learn the trading language by keeping track of any terms that are new to you. You might want to make yourself a chart such as the one in Table 2.3. As you are learning new terminology throughout this book, write down the term, the meaning, and how it might be relevant to your trading style. If you stumble onto terms that you don't understand, a quick search online can provide a definition, also write down how the term is relevant so that you are aware of its application.

Trading language can sound complicated, but focusing on some terms and slowly adding them to your trading repertoire over time will help you more than trying to memorize the meaning of every term. Be familiar with the trading terminology that is relevant to you for your trading setups and markets, and be willing to add more terminology to your repertoire over time. To illustrate this point for you, let me describe a trade setup using trading language and then again in everyday language. If you are new to any of the trading language, take time to make the connections to interpret what some of the words mean.

Sarah's Story

Trading language was a huge obstacle for me when I began trading. It actually took more than a year before I started having conversations with other traders. Often I would be intimidated by others who were able to articulate trades in what felt like a foreign language to me. Even though I was trading consistently, I felt like I didn't know enough because I couldn't explain the definitions behind some of the terms with the sophisticated trading language I heard others use. I realized, however, that there is a difference between understanding the terms and being able to apply them in an actual trading strategy. When I began trading, I knew that each of the colors and lines on my charts meant different levels of resistance. These levels of resistance are what I used to enter and exit trades. If someone asked me, I could have explained that the blue line was a stronger level of resistance than the red one. Even though the blue line represented the 21 Exponential Moving Average EMA, I referred to it as the blue line. This didn't make me sound like I had sophisticated trading language, but I was still able to place good trades because I knew that each of the colors of the lines had more weight in terms of support/resistance.

I would encourage all of you not to be to be intimidated by others who might have more sophisticated trading language. If you choose to refer to support and resistance lines on your charts by referring to their color on your screen rather than the time frame of the moving average (for example), that is fine. If you understand why you are trading based on the colors of the charts, then I think it is the same as using language such as, "I wait for a retracement to the 21 EMA." Don't let other traders intimidate you with sophisticated language. Speaking about trading and actually trading consistently are two different things. My hope is that this book will break down any barriers to trading language so that everyone feels empowered to speak the trading language fluently.

Here's an example of an options trade using "tradespeak":

An options trade I use often is an at-the-money credit spread. I begin by looking at the broad market and specifically look to see if it's a bull or bear market. I look at the market internals to see what levels the Ticks are holding at. Once I have decided whether the market is moving long or short, I will look at specific stocks and their corresponding options chain for the credit I can collect. If my market assumption is bullish, I will take a position with a weekly expiration in an at-the-money put spread.

Here's the exact same explanation in common language:

When I am looking for options trades, I will begin by looking at the bigger picture by examining a large index. For example, if I'm looking through my list of favorite stocks to trade and think that Google (GOOG) looks good, I will start by looking at the broad index that GOOG is part of—the S&P 500 Index—to get a feeling for whether I think this market is moving up or down. Then I will look at the actual Google stock. I use some market internal charts to help me make my overall trading assumption. As I look at a few charts of different time frames, I find areas of support and resistance to see if GOOG can move in a direction without breaking through levels of support and resistance. Then I will calculate the credit I can receive to figure out how much money I can make on that trade. If the amount matches my risk/reward parameters, I will place the trade.

Both ways to explain this trade will end in the same result; the only difference is that one uses more sophisticated trading language. You can choose to refer to your trades in whichever language you feel most comfortable. Most important, I don't want you to feel intimidated by trading because of the trading language. This book will switch between sophisticated and common language in order to help you to be on an equal playing field of knowledge. After all, every trader's goal is to be a profitable trader, not to sound like a trading encyclopedia. Don't let trading terminology stress you out; instead, focus on the most important decisions—placing and managing good trades.

TABLE 2.3. Key terms

Term	Meaning	Relevancy for You
Market	This term can be used interchangeably for the overall direction for everything that is traded, e.g., "looking at the broad market," as well as a specific area of the market, e.g., "futures market."	You need to know that this word is used in multiple ways.

(continued)

TABLE 2.3. Key terms (*continued*)

Term	Meaning	Relevancy for You
Trading instrument	This is what you are trading, e.g., stocks or ETFs, futures, bonds, etc.	There are many types of stocks and ETFs to trade; the instrument is what you are trading.
Stock	A percentage of ownership in a company.	Used as a trading instrument; can be bought and sold.
ETF	A fund that is traded on a stock exchange; can contain many different assets.	Used as a trading instrument; can be bought and sold.
Option	Contract to buy or sell a specified financial product at a certain price.	Commonly used as, "I trade options." Options provide many ways to trade; most people know these as puts and calls.
Contract	An agreement that a trader enters into at a specific price; also used to refer to the smallest amount you can purchase of a stock, ETF, or future.	You can trade one or multiple contracts at one time in any market.

Sarah's Story

Once you begin to trade, or if you trade already, you will quickly realize that your trading knowledge will shift your perspective when you speak to your friends or listen to market analysis in the media. As you move from wondering about what the many lines on charts represent to understanding that these are levels of support and resistance and market internals, your ability to analyze the markets will open up a new perspective for you. What you trade and analyze may be different from and more accurate than what you may be hearing from others as you develop your trading skills.

Most notably are days when reporters share such information as, "It's been a bad day in the Dow." Even though the media will often report that the market is good or bad based on whether the market closed with a gain or a loss on that day, a good or bad day in the markets is irrelevant to the price action moving positively or negatively. The reality is, from the perspective of a trader, that the relationship between the market being down so it's a bad day for the market or up so it's a good day isn't relevant. Traders can make money regardless of whether the market goes up or down. They just want to be trading in the direction that the market is moving. Some of my best trading days are when the market is down. As the old saying goes, "The market takes the stairs up and the elevator down." Days when the market is down provide a lot of opportunity to make money quickly (provided that you are shorting the market at the time, of course).

If you are trading the Dow Jones Industrial Index (Dow) short and the Dow moves down that day, this would mean that you made money. It might be bad for some people if the Dow is down, but it might be good for others. As you interpret the markets using your own tools on your own charts, you will make better trading decisions. I've realized that my own analysis of the markets is more important to me when I trade than listening to news reports.

STILL DECIDING WHAT TO TRADE?

Although some readers may already have a clear idea about what they would like to trade, others may still be wanting to learn more about the futures and options markets to help them decide what market to trade. Most traders will be more successful if they find a market that matches their personalities, strengths, and available times to trade. If you are considering what market to trade, take the following "Trading Personality Quiz." This quiz will highlight some of the "personalities" of markets that might help you to find one that suits you.

Trading Personality Quiz

These questions are meant to help you consider your trading personality. Think through these questions as you begin to set up a trading plan. The answers may help you to decide whether to trade futures, options, or both. This quiz is meant to be a starting point only—to help you reflect on your own personality so that you might trade in a way that best suits you. Circle the letter for the answer that best reflects your point of view.

1. Do you have time during the trading day to sit in front of a computer and watch the markets?
   a. I have all day to watch the markets.
   b. I plan to trade on my lunch break or for an hour or two during the day.
   c. My time varies from day to day.

In order to trade, you will need to allocate time to watch the markets. Depending on the trading strategy that you are implementing, this will require more or less time in front of a computer screen. As a general rule, when you are trading futures without an automatic trading system, you will need to be in front of your computer screen while you are waiting for, entering, and exiting a trade. Options will provide a little more flexibility if you are setting up trades that are designed to be held for a day or longer.

2. Do you panic when a trade becomes a loss before it becomes profitable?
   a. I can handle watching my trade move close to my stops and my targets without panic.
   b. I'm more comfortable with smaller moves, and I understand that this means smaller gains.
   c. I haven't figured it out yet, so I might try both.

The swings from highs and lows are different in each market. It's important to find a market, whether futures or options, that reflects your comfort level with big moves. Remember that big swings in one direction will be great if they are in the direction you favor, but the market also can swing in the opposite direction.

This question will also help you to think about how to set up your stop losses. This is your exit strategy out of a trade if it is losing money. At a specific level or dollar loss, the trade should be closed. A stop is a means to control your losses so that your loss in one trade doesn't get too large too quickly. I always trade with a stop. Sometimes the stop is actually placed on the trading screen, whereas other times my stops are decisions I have made before entering the trade. However, I recommend for people who are just starting out in the markets to always set an actual stop when they trade. This is good practice to help you to stay in control of your emotions and, most important, control your losses.

3. Would you prefer to make small gains with multiple trades, or is your style to spend a longer time looking for a perfect setup with larger gains and higher risk?
   a. I want to get into the market and out during the same day.
   b. I can narrow my focus and won't get overwhelmed with many choices.
   c. I don't worry about missed opportunities. I focus on what is to come.

The trade parameters that you set for yourself will define what types of trades you will set up in both futures and options markets using any of the trading instruments you choose. Your risk/reward ratio will guide your entries and exits for your trades. Think about your personality in other areas of your life. If are you generally more comfortable with slow and steady growth, then take more small trades more often. If you prefer making larger trades, you also need to consider that you will deal with larger consequences if things don't work out. Interestingly, I have observed that many beginning traders start trading thinking that bigger is better and put on too many contracts in one trade, only to have their account take a big hit when the trade doesn't work for them. Most traders I know have made a career or a strong trading reputation by making many different trades using mostly smaller sizes in each trade more often rather than one or two bigger trades. As their account sizes grow, many successful independent traders add contract size—but always relative to the size of their account.

This question will also help you to reflect on the size of your trading account. If you are trading with a small account, you don't ever want to set up a trade that will take your account to $0 if the trade doesn't work for you. Trade within your trading parameters. A common rule of thumb is to never risk more than 3 to 5 percent of your account in one trade. This is not a hard and fast rule. It needs to be a personal decision that you will make based on what you are comfortable with.

4. Do you get overwhelmed with terminology or learning a new language, or do you rise to the challenge?
   a. Yes, and I'm not willing to spend the time learning too much language.
   b. I am interested in learning new terminology, but this doesn't deter me from trading.
   c. I might learn a little more, but I can get overwhelmed easily.

I believe that options trading has a more complex trading language to learn than futures trading. Although you can trade both without knowing absolutely every term, there will be more terms to learn when trading options. Futures trading has fewer terms to learn.

5. Are you hoping to place trades and watch them over a week/
   month, or you are more comfortable with a shorter time frame?
   a. I prefer shorter time frames, ideally in and out of a trade
      on the same day.
   b. I am comfortable holding trades over a few days.
   c. I like the idea of either one.

Generally, futures trades have shorter time frames. These trades can be as quick as a minute. Most people cannot hold futures trades overnight (you need a large account to do this), so futures trades are generally day trades. Options trading provides an opportunity to set up a trade that can occur during the day or over a week or month. The longer time frames may be more beneficial for someone who doesn't have the time to be in front of a computer screen while in a trade.

If you are new to both futures and options trading, I would encourage you to read the chapters about these markets (Chapters 5 and 6) and make your decision about which market you relate to at the end of those two chapters.

These questions are designed to spur your thinking. The answers will support your planning for deciding whether to trade either futures or options.

What Do Your Answers Mean?

This quiz is based solely on my observations of people I know who trade and those whom I have coached. It is meant to spur your thinking. If you have your heart set on trading one market versus another or have some expertise in one or the other, by all means, choose the one in which you would like to trade. After all, the most successful traders are those who personalize a trading strategy that works just for them.

If you are still trying to figure out which market to trade, go back and look at the answers you circled. If you chose mostly answer a, then you might want to begin learning to trade futures before options. Based on my experience with helping traders, many people who trade futures like to become familiar with a market and trade the movements up and down. If you chose mostly answer b, then you might want to begin learning options. Based on my experience with helping traders in options, typical personalities are those who like putting on many trades at once over different time frames. These are also people who may choose to be in front of their computer screen all day but don't necessarily have to be. They are placing trade setups that offer a little more flexibility during the day.

If you chose mostly answer c, you might still be figuring things out or might benefit from trying both.

Sarah's Trading Tip

Everyone can learn to trade; it's all about understanding the markets and applying that knowledge. Knowing how to consistently grow your account size is what makes a long-term trader. When you are learning the markets, you will need to understand the various ways to trade, but you should always learn through the lens of your account size, your comfort with risk, and your own solid trading plan.

Your Trading Goal

A trader's expectations need to match the way she places trades. An experienced trader will have a very good idea of her probabilities and profit ratios for each of the trading setups she uses. An experienced trader will trade in a manner that is size appropriate for her trading account. The trading profits that such a trader can expect are in line with a trading goal she has set for herself. Every trader will trade responsibly when she trades in a manner that is mindful of what her trading losses can be while also being aware of profit targets to match her trading goal.

A Trading Plan

Regardless of what market you choose to trade, every trader needs a trading plan. The trading plan is an anchor and guide to navigate trades. A trading plan will contain the information a trader will gather to formulate a trading assumption, steps for entering and exiting a trade, ways to manage trades, and risk/reward ratios that are aligned with the trader's account size. It will

Sarah's Trading Tip

Each of you has picked up this book for a different reason and will approach the markets from a different perspective. Regardless of the reason, you should be aware of your trading goal, which will help you to determine your trading action plan. The amount of money you would like to make in the market must match your trading account size, your risk parameters, and the types of trades you place. A trader who hopes to make $1,000 every week by trading a $5,000 account is not setting himself up for success or to trade responsibly. A trader's goal must be relative to the trades he is placing.

take time to refine a plan that is well thought out for each individual trader. What works for one trader will not necessarily work for another. This plan will also help a trader to stay accountable so as to make rational decisions while in trades. (Later in this book I will provide a template I designed that will guide you step by step in writing your own MY TRADE plan.)

When you trade, you make the decision to enter and exit a market based on certain market variables. Your trading plan will outline the market internals that you will analyze to help you make your decision about when and what to trade. Without a detailed trading plan, your emotions will get the best of you, and you may not end up making good trading decisions. The challenge lies not only in creating a specific actionable trading plan but also in following through on the plan. This may sound simple, but many traders have lost their shirts because they did not follow through on their plans.

A trading plan should detail the conditions in the market that you look for in order to enter and exit a trade. As you create your own trading plan, you will identify specific key pieces of information that you will analyze to make your decisions. The trading plan helps you to create an objective plan that is separate from your emotions. It will also outline your plan of action when a move goes against you. A trading plan will not guarantee that you will always make money, but it will help you to decide on your next steps. Remember that your plan is always created *before* you enter a trade.

Your Uniqueness Will Be Highlighted in Your Trading

Every trader has his or her own unique spin, individual risk parameters, and trading plan. Even though it might be tempting to trade exactly like Warren Buffett, you probably are not working with the same capital as he is. Traders will have the most success when they personalize a trading strategy that meets their specific strengths and needs. Trading based on your own trading assumptions rather than copying someone else is what will lead to a long-term career as a trader. When you manage your own trades, you are able to benefit from timing your trades successfully, managing risk based on your own risk ratios, and feeling empowered because you are capable of making good trading decisions.

Your trading mindset should be rooted in your motivation to trade, but you will also need to have a realistic timeline to meet your goals. Setting yourself up with realistic goals will keep your trading decisions grounded. Realistically, you will have some losing trades. The difference between a successful full-time long-term trader and one who loses her shirt in the market is how each manages her winning and losing trades. In fact, many experienced traders probably would agree that it is more important to understand how to manage your trading loses than your winning trades. As we delve more deeply into trading in the coming chapters, and as you begin to create your own MY TRADE plan, keep in mind the important information that you read here. Trading doesn't have to be complicated. Don't be intimidated by others who may sound like they know what they are talking about (but who may only know how to speak "traderspeak" as opposed to actually knowing how to trade profitably). Always be aware of your trading goals and motivation as you make your trading decisions. Believe in your ability to develop the skill of trading because it is a learnable skill like any other. And know that you too can trade if you choose to.

Key Take-Aways

- We have only scratched the surface in this chapter in order to help you to begin to think about what you want to trade, the account size with which you will trade, and how you will trade.
- This chapter reviewed different trading instruments, including stocks, exchange-traded funds, futures, and options.
- Trading terminology can be complicated at first, but it doesn't have to be.
- Decisions about what and when to trade should be made based on each trader's personality—you have choices to make.
- Good trading is rooted in a solid trading plan.
- Experienced traders are aware of their trading performance, risk/reward ratio, and trading goals.

3

ANALYSIS WITHOUT PARALYSIS

Illustrated by Noble Rains

Chapter Key Concepts

- *The basic differences between technical and fundamental analysis are covered.*
- *The trend is your friend.*
- *It doesn't matter what you think; it matters what you see.*
- *One bar does not a trend make.*
- *Stay calm and trade on.*

Once a trader understands the basics of the markets, the next step is to understand how to collect evidence in order to develop a trading assumption. This collection of evidence ultimately will support the trader's trading decision. The more evidence that a trader has to support a move in one direction, the stronger the assumption will be.

Analysis can get complicated very quickly. The key is to ensure that you are able to interpret enough information to make a trading assumption about which you have confidence without feeling overwhelmed. This chapter focuses on a basic way to read charts to determine a trend. The basics of reading charts in this chapter will lay the groundwork necessary to discuss more detailed technical analysis in the next chapter.

TECHNICAL VERSUS FUNDAMENTAL ANALYSIS

There are two broad categories of analysis: fundamental and technical. Both types of analysis are hotly debated as the best way to form an opinion about the markets. Fundamental analysis focuses on the health of a company, as judged by various financial ratios. Trading assumptions are made based on whether or not the trader feels that the company is over- or undervalued when a theoretical price is calculated based on accounting ratios and compared with the price in the markets. Fundamental analysts believe that there is a relationship between stock price and the financial health of the company and will base their trading assumptions on this relationship.

Sarah's Trading Tip

My personal opinion is that technical analysis provides real, current evidence to support my trading assumptions. There are other traders who probably feel just as passionate about other forms of analysis. What's important is that you find a style that matches your personality. Just as I believe that a trader will be at his best when he trades a market in which he feels confident, I also believe that you need to find ways to collect evidence from the markets that make the most sense to you and give you confidence.

I choose to interpret the markets based on what I see happening through various time-frame charts and market internals. I keep it fairly simple, and this works for me. My opinion is that the fancier or more complicated analysis may sound sophisticated and cool, but it does not necessarily mean better analysis. There are many types of analysis and just as many opinions as to which analysis techniques work best. The best suggestion I have is not to get overwhelmed and to narrow down your analysis techniques to a few that you understand and are comfortable using. I feel that the best way to analyze a stock is to use technical analysis. This type of analysis is a skill that I have developed over time. There have been many volumes written about this topic, but I feel that for a new trader, a few key concepts are all that are needed to start trading.

This type of analysis gathers evidence from company reports to ascertain how the company fits within its own financial sector and the broad economy to determine how these factors will affect the future price of the company's stock. For example, if the economy is in a recession and people are losing jobs, a fundamental analyst might think that more people will need to buy cheaper foods because they have less money to spend. A fundamental analyst might think that the stock price for Kraft will go up because of increased sales of macaroni and cheese as a result of consumers trying to save money.

In contrast to fundamental analysis is technical analysis. Put most simply, technical analysis is the study of stock price. A technical analyst will look at charts to determine her trading assumption based on what she sees the trading instrument doing at the time. Technical analysts use the movement of the stock on a chart, especially patterns, to determine the direction of the market. Using information from a price trend and support and resistance on charts is the foundation of technical analysis. These two key concepts are the foundation of my technical analysis on which I base my trading assumptions. Without getting too technical, I believe that the foundation of any good market analysis is understanding how to determine a trend, as well as how to determine levels of support and resistance in multiple time frames.

BEGINNING TO READ CHARTS

Charts are the source of information for a trader using technical analysis. Charts are a way to visually display price. They can be set up in many ways with many different indicators. I believe that it is helpful to pick a trading instrument and analyze it in a simple straightforward way. Even though there are many indicators that can be added to a chart to help you determine whether the price of a stock is moving up or down, adding too many indicators to a chart can create conflicting indications of the direction in which the price is moving. Every trader will tailor indicators that work best for him. I believe that the two most important pieces of information on your charts is the representation of price and levels of support and resistance shown by moving averages.

There are many different ways to visually represent price on a chart. Most commonly used are line charts and candlestick charts. Line charts plot the closing value of price at a specific interval. Candlestick charts give the trader more information such as open, high, low and closing values of price for a given interval of time. It is up to the individual trader to pick the best chart type for him.

A trader can add moving averages to a chart to help visualize price movement. Moving averages can show the average price over a short time or long time frame. Traders may want to add a few moving averages of different time frames to their charts to visualize how price is behaving over different time frames. For example, on my charts I use the 13, 21, 50, 100, and 200 Exponential Moving Averages (EMA). I use these lines on my chart to help determine levels of support and resistance. The lines or moving averages are referred to as *levels of support and resistance* because they act like magnets, either attracting or resisting the price of the trading instrument. When two magnets of the same charge are held together, they push each other away. Price is repelled from levels of support and resistance, just like the two magnets are repelled from each other. The more moving average lines that are parallel to each other, the stronger your trading assumption will be about the direction of price. Ultimately traders should be looking for the cleanest looking chart to place a trade, when price and moving averages are all moving in the same direction. The cleaner the chart, the more likely the trade will work if you trade in the same direction as the trend.

Take a look at the following charts and take the following steps to learn how to begin to analyze them. Each chart provides a different perspective.

How to read a chart:

1. Begin by reading the chart from left to right.
2. On each chart, look for the overall direction of price. Is it up or down?
3. Are the levels of support and resistance all moving in the same direction?

In Figure 3.1*a*, begin by reading the chart from left to right. In Step 2, notice that the candlesticks are moving up. In Step 3, notice that the moving averages are acting as support, and are all moving in the same direction. None of the moving averages have crossed.

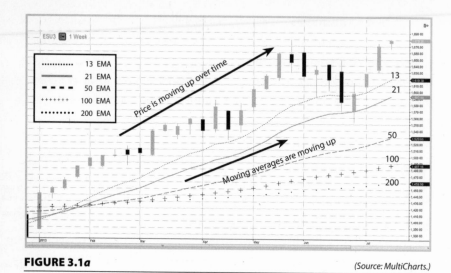

FIGURE 3.1a

(Source: MultiCharts.)

Figure 3.1*b* provides another example and a different perspective. Following the steps from above, begin by reading the chart from left to right. In Step 2, notice that the candlesticks have broken through some of the moving averages. Price has moved through the 13, 21, 50, and 100 period moving averages. In Step 3, notice that the moving averages have crossed twice.

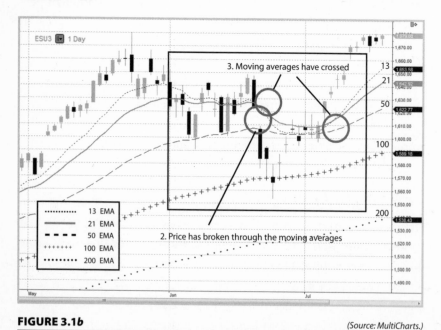

FIGURE 3.1b

(Source: MultiCharts.)

Figure 3.1*c* provides a different perspective. Notice that the candlesticks are moving sideways. Also note that price has moved through the 13, 21, 50, and 100 period moving averages. When price moves through support it is referred to as breaking support. Notice that the moving averages are not all moving in the same direction, and they have crossed in some places. The overall direction of price on this chart is sideways.

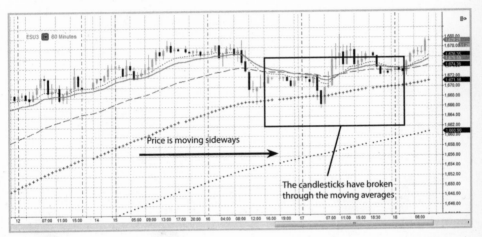

FIGURE 3.1c   (Source: MultiCharts.)

The basics of chart analysis include looking at price to determine its direction and whether the moving averages are acting as support or as resistance. Regardless of the market you are trading, the information that you can gather from your charts will support your trading assumptions. Over time as you begin to try different length moving averages, you may find that you prefer one length to another, and have your favorite moving averages of various lengths to represent support and resistance.

THE TREND IS YOUR FRIEND

Trend is a common pattern used by traders to inform their opinions as to the direction of the market. A trend is created by price moving in one direction over a period of time. A trader determines the direction of a trend based on the direction that price is moving on the chart. Even though a trend can be determined on any chart a trader uses, a trend on a longer-time-frame chart is generally a stronger trend than one on a shorter-time-frame chart. Ideally, a trader would like to see a trend appear in the same direction across multiple time frames. Generally, an *uptrend* is defined as a series of candlesticks that shows higher highs and higher lows. A *downtrend* is defined as a series of lower highs and lower lows.

Traders will refer to the trend of a market by using such terms as *bull*, or *long, market* (trending up) and *bear*, or *short, market* (trending down). Determining a trend is a matter of personal opinion. What one trader considers a trend might not be considered a trend by another trader. Let's move to some examples to determine whether these charts have trend and, if so, its direction.

Figure 3.2*a* is a daily E-mini S&P 500 Futures Contract (ES) chart that shows a trend that is long, bull, or trending up. Price is making higher highs and higher lows.

FIGURE 3.2a   *(Source: MultiCharts.)*

Figure 3.2*b* is a 60-minute ES chart without a trend. Price isn't continuing to move in either direction, instead it appears to be moving sideways. When a chart doesn't look like it's continuing to move in one direction, it means that a trend has not been established.

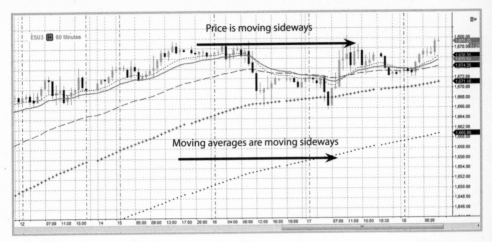

FIGURE 3.2*b* (Source: MultiCharts.)

Generally, the more time frames that show the same trend, the stronger the trend is, and the longer it should persist. Using charts with different time frames provides a glimpse of price action from different perspectives to help inform your trend assumption. It is like seeing a forest from an airplane, from the top of your house, and from the forest floor. Each time frame will give you a different view of the price action.

As you can see in Figure 3.3, the longer- and shorter-term trends offer different perspectives on the market. The weekly chart (Figure 3.3*a*) continues to show a long trend, but the daily chart (Figure 3.3*b*) shows that the trend has been broken. The longer the time frame, usually the stronger the trend, and the better price will follow the trend.

Traders will generally use trend to trade in two ways, trading with the trend or counter-trend. They will be considered a trend trader if they place trades in the same direction as the prevailing trend, or they will be considered a counter-trend trader if they place trades in the opposite direction of the trend because they think the trend will change directions. Most traders will find that trading with the trend is more profitable for them than counter-trend trading or trading against the prevailing trend. The basics of trend trading involve trading when there is a strong uptrend or downtrend and not trading when there is an absence of trend.

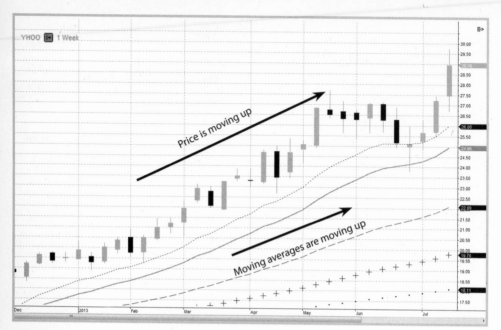

FIGURE 3.3a

(Source: MultiCharts.)

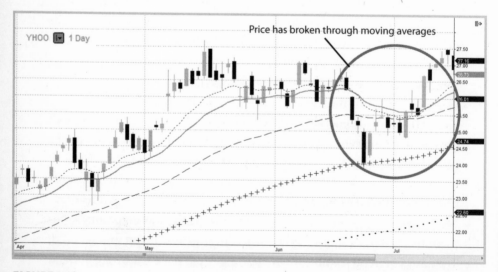

FIGURE 3.3b

(Source: MultiCharts.)

Sarah's Trading Tip

I believe that the key to trading is being on the correct side of the trend. Trend trading, in my opinion, has a greater level of success than counter-trend trading. Each trader should create his own system to identify a longer-term trend to judge whether the stock has an uptrend, a down-trend, or no trend at all and as a means to identify an entry or exit point in a trade.

It Doesn't Matter What You Think; It Matters What You See

Traders will scan many stocks throughout the day to look for trades. More often than not, they will scan and realize that there is no trend and then move on to the next stock. Trend traders look for charts that have trends and then choose between the best of those charts to place their trades. When you stop basing your trading assumptions on what you think is going to happen and begin making your trading decisions on what the price action is telling you, you will begin to feel more empowered by your trading decisions. Technical analysis will help you to trade using the information you see in front of you. You will begin to believe in yourself and your analysis because you are making trading decisions as you see them in front of you, not based on what you think might happen.

I also want to caution you against creating market assumptions because of what might make logical sense. There are times when bad news comes out and the markets continue to rally (move higher). It's important to always base your trading assumption on what the price action is telling you at the time. If you hear yourself saying, "I think things will move," stop yourself and switch your language to, "I see this happening in the weekly charts, and this correlates with. . . ."

One Bar Does Not Make a Trend

Waiting for a trend to become apparent to inform your trading will ensure that there is more validity to your analysis. It will take time for a trend to emerge, so don't expect to find a trade as soon as the market opens. There are some traders who trade the open; in fact, some trade *only* the open.

Sarah's Trading Tip

An important tip is to question what is being reported in the news when you are trading. If you spend some time watching a chart of the market such as the S&P 500 at the same time that CNBC is talking about the markets, you will quickly learn that the market does not respond to the news in the way that might be reported. It often amazes me what I hear coming from large media outlets about the markets when I am looking at the markets at the same time. I often do not see what they are reporting, or the information is no longer relevant because even a delay of a few minutes means that the markets have already moved based on the news. It really helps every trader to stop and reflect on what is hype and what is actually happening in the markets at the time. Everyone loves a good story, and I appreciate that media outlets are trying to report the news in a way that is entertaining for their audience, but as you become more secure with your own market analysis, you will soon rely on your own trading assumptions rather than listening to what is reported.

The open offers large moves, but large moves also can mean that price may change direction a few times before a meaningful trend is established. Generally, I do not trade the market open because I prefer to wait for trends to appear and the market to settle in a particular direction for the day.

Because a trend consists of more than one bar on a chart, a trader who uses the trend to trade will have to wait to see a few bars move in one particular direction. With every shift in the direction of the market, a trader will generally look for a series of bars to align in one direction. One bar does not a trend make. Let's look at some examples in order to determine if there is a trend appearing on the following charts. We will begin looking for a trend on a longer time frame then move to a shorter time frame of the same trading investment. Moving from longer to shorter term charts is a good way to determine the strength of a trend and whether to place a trade in the direction of the trend. It will be discussed in more detail in the next chapter.

In the Visa (V) weekly chart in Figure 3.4*a*, a long trend is apparent. The chart shows that V has been consistently making higher highs and higher lows, and the general direction of price is upward.

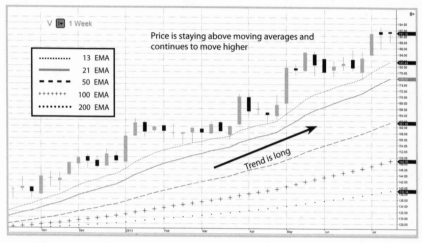

FIGURE 3.4*a* *(Source: MultiCharts.)*

Figure 3.4*b* shows a daily chart of V, where the trend continues long but is not as clean as on the weekly chart. From left to right on the chart the price is still moving up, but price has broken some moving averages.

FIGURE 3.4*b* *(Source: MultiCharts.)*

The shortest time frame in this example is a 60-minute chart. Figure 3.4c shows a 60-minute chart of V, which does not indicate a strong trend. The candlesticks have begun to break some key support levels.

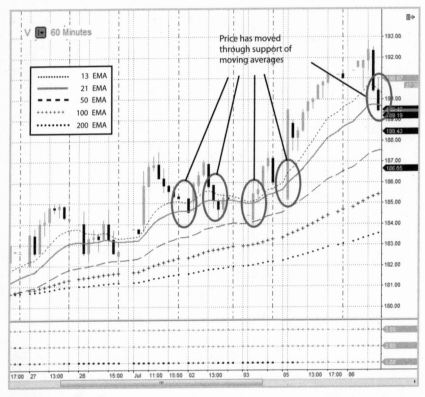

FIGURE 3.4c   *(Source: MultiCharts.)*

Sarah's Trading Tip

Because I use a 60-minute chart when I am deciding to trade V, I would not place a trade in V based on the charts in Figure 3.4. I would probably wait another hour or two to see what happens on the 60-minute chart and then place a trade based on the long trend shown on the weekly and daily charts, with an entry off of support from the 60-minute chart.

Now let's look at an example with a strong trend.

Figure 3.5*a* is a weekly chart for United States Natural Gas Fund (UNG) in which we are seeing the beginning of a downtrend. The bars are making lower lows and lower highs. The support and resistance levels have crossed, so there isn't a strong trend on this chart but it is worth looking at shorter time frames to confirm a trend.

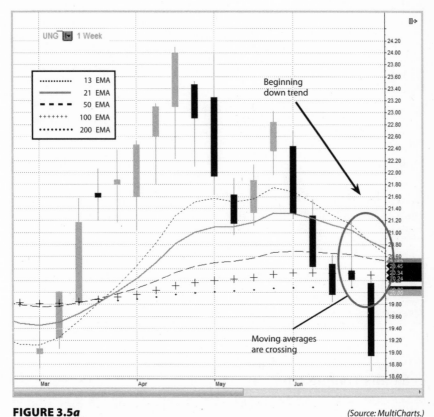

FIGURE 3.5*a*   *(Source: MultiCharts.)*

As we continue to look at the UNG daily chart (Figure 3.5*b*), it appears that the downtrend is continuing. A trader may begin to formulate her trading assumption that this stock is trending lower.

FIGURE 3.5b   *(Source: MultiCharts.)*

Figure 3.5c is a 60-minute chart for UNG that confirms that this stock is in a downtrend. Trend traders like me would place a short trade in UNG.

FIGURE 3.5c   *(Source: MultiCharts.)*

The same approach to identifying a trend is true in futures. The weekly Gold futures contract (GC) chart in Figure 3.6a shows that price is moving lower.

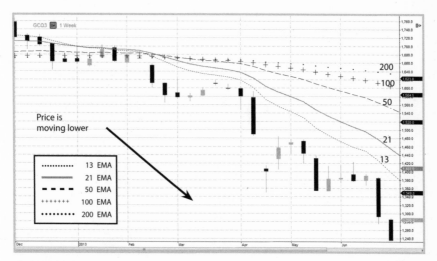

FIGURE 3.6a   *(Source: MultiCharts.)*

The daily chart in Figure 3.6b confirms the weekly downtrend price is also moving lower. Traders looking at this contract might begin to think that it is worth trading. But as we move on to the shorter time frames, the trend does not paint the same picture.

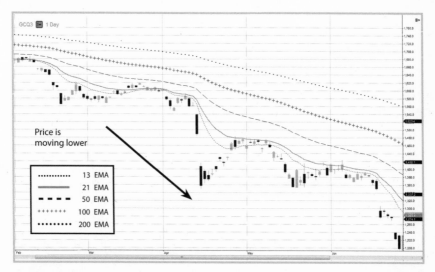

FIGURE 3.6b   *(Source: MultiCharts.)*

The 60-minute GC chart in Figure 3.6c shows an uptrend. The bars are making higher highs. This chart is in opposition to the two preceding charts.

FIGURE 3.6c   *(Source: MultiCharts.)*

The five-minute GC chart in Figure 3.6d is currently sideways. There isn't a clear trend in either direction. Based on the GC chart in Figure 3.6a, I wouldn't place a trade. I would move on to look for other trading possibilities elsewhere. I might come back to GC later to see if a trend has emerged.

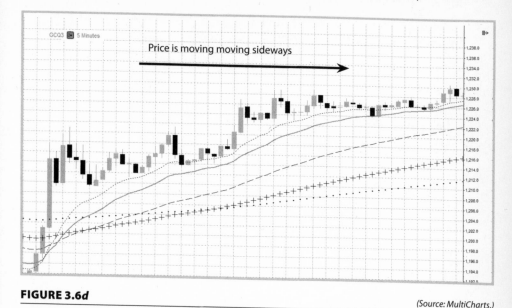

FIGURE 3.6d

(Source: MultiCharts.)

It is important to note that one trader may think that these charts show a trend, whereas another trader might not. Chart analysis is always a matter of personal opinion. We will continue to build on this chart analysis in Chapter 4.

STAY CALM AND TRADE ON

By keeping your analysis simple and easy to follow, you will be able to apply the same analysis to any instrument you trade. Refining your chart analysis over time will ensure that your skills are always improving. By having confidence in your analysis methods, you will be able to execute trades quickly without hesitation and not second-guess your stops and targets. Many new traders fall victim to placing trades based on hunches that they have heard from some analysts in the media or from some analysis provided by large financial institutions. It is your decision as to whether you want to use this information to help formulate your trading assumptions. What is important is that, either way, you have created your assumption based on the way you have interpreted this information. Believe in yourself and your analysis.

Sarah's Trading Tip

You are probably reading this book because you wanted to empower yourself to either refine your trading or begin trading. It amazes me how so many people will say that they want to trade on their own but rely on someone else's market analysis. A little support is perfectly fine, but you should always be personalizing the information you are analyzing to work for you. Don't be afraid of technical analysis—it is a powerful tool.

KEY TAKE-AWAYS

- Market analysis doesn't have to be overly complicated. In fact, by keeping things simple and having key items that you identify in your charts, you will make chart analysis meaningful to your trading.
- There are many types of analysis. One is not better than another, but one will most likely relate to you and your trading personality. Some traders believe that the analysis they use is the only correct method. Instead of getting caught up in the debate, find elements of analysis that make the most sense to you, and use them on a consistent basis.
- Determining a trend in a market can help you to create a strong trading assumption. The more time frames that align with the trend, the stronger the trend, and the stronger your trading assumption will be. Use of both long and short time frames will help you to determine a trend.
- Don't waste time worrying about why things are happening; it often doesn't matter. A trader will react to the market based on what she is seeing. Trading can create opportunities where you need to act fast. Don't waste energy on a long debate about why something is happening. This can be great dinner conversation, but it doesn't always equate with timely decisions during the trading day. The *what* and *how* are more important than the *why*.

4

INTERPRETING CHARTS: TRANSLATION 101

Illustrated by Noble Rains

Chapter Key Concepts

- *Identify ways that charts are useful.*
- *Understand how to collect market evidence using market internals, support and resistance, different time-frame charts, instrument characteristics, and the foundations indicator.*
- *Understand how to interpret market trends.*
- *Recognize when to follow the leader.*
- *Identify with a trader's point of view.*
- *Become familiar with Sarah's simple steps to develop a trading assumption.*

Now that we have reviewed some basic information about how to determine market direction from a chart, let's get into more detail to bring more precision to our analysis. In order to glean the most information from our charts, we must pay attention to the direction of price, market internals, and the range in which price is moving, so that we can begin to understand when to enter, manage, and exit trades. There are five characteristics that are essential to analyzing charts effectively. This chapter will break down these five characteristics using simple technical analysis to allow you how to develop a market assumption. Together we will review charts in a practical manner so that you can apply your analysis to any market you choose to trade.

WAYS THAT CHARTS ARE USEFUL

Charts can be interpreted based on five characteristics:

- Long- and short-term time frame charts
- Support and resistance based on moving averages
- Market internals
- Trading instrument characteristics
- The Foundations indicator

These five characteristics will help you to develop a clear picture of the behavior of the trading instrument you would like to trade. The more often a trader sees these five characteristics aligned, the higher the probability is that she will be on the right side of the trade. The information you gather from your charts is directly connected to your trading assumptions. This information can be thought of as collecting evidence to support an entry or exit for each trade. The evidence from market internals, levels of support and resistance, different time frames characteristics of the trading instrument and the Foundations indicator should be combined together to form the basis of your chart analysis. Let's review each one.

Short-, Medium-, and Long-Term Time Frame

Charts are visual representations of price. As traders review charts from different time periods, they are able both to achieve an overview of the market and to gather specific details about a particular time frame.

Charts of different time frames provide information from different points of view. Traders use charts of multiple time frames in the same market to look for the direction of price action, trend, and congruence of patterns from multiple perspectives to form a trading opinion. Savvy traders will have some charts with longer time frames, such as yearly, monthly, and weekly charts; medium-term time frames, such as daily charts; and shorter-term time frames such as 60-, 15-, 5-, and 1-minute charts. Longer- and shorter-terms charts are used for different reasons. Longer-term charts are used to help a trader determine a trend, while shorter-term time frames help a trader decide appropriate levels for trade entries and exits.

Think of a forest. The farther away you are, the less detail you see. This is like a monthly or weekly chart—you see the overall trends but do not see the important details. A trader needs to look at all perspectives to form an accurate perspective.

Long-Term Chart

A daily chart shows information about market action over the last few months. Each candlestick represents the price movement for that day. Figure 4.1 is an example of a longer-term time frame in a futures market. It provides a trader with historical data in bars that represent one day of trading. A long-term chart allows the trader to see information that dates back a few months to gain a longer-term perspective.

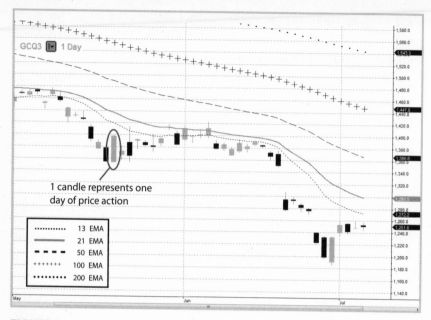

FIGURE 4.1

(Source: MultiCharts.)

Longer time-frame charts allow more information to be displayed on the screen. Picture trying to chart two years of five-minute data. The chart would be much wider than your monitor would be able to display. With a daily chart, information is displayed in a manner that is much more manageable, allowing the trader to see a longer-term trend on one screen.

Figure 4.1 represents a long-term perspective but limits the trader's ability to see finer details. Using the forest analogy, the longer-term time frames provide a view of a forest from a distance. As you walk closer to the forest, you start to see individual trees, and even closer yet you can see saplings just starting to grow on the forest floor. The same is true in trading. A trader needs to include evidence from longer-term perspectives to get the big picture and then combine that information with details from the shorter term. As traders narrow their focus with shorter time frames, the details become more prominent. Using different time frames provides the benefit of being able to see the big picture *and* smaller details.

Figure 4.2 provides a shorter, more detailed perspective on the market. Traders can see very small moves in the stock appear quickly. Small changes in a trend can be seen easily. This chart provides information on a shorter-term time frame that typically will help traders to decide on their entries and exits.

FIGURE 4.2 (Source: MultiCharts.)

The following charts are examples of how differently the same futures contract can look to a trader depending on what time frame the trader is using. Both Figure 4.3a and Figure 4.3b are considered longer-term time frames; they are the weekly and daily time frames. The longer time frame in Figure 4.3a shows a correlated but slightly different picture from that in Figure 4.3b. Figure 4.3b shows that the daily E-mini S&P 500 Futures contract (ES) price action has broken many of the levels of support, including the 21-period exponential moving average (EMA) in the last several days. However, Figure 4.3a shows that the weekly ES price action has held the 21-period EMA. These two perspectives will inform a trader about how strongly the long trend is holding. If we combine the analysis from both of these long-term charts, we can see that both charts of the ES are moving up in the long term.

As the trader moves to shorter time frames, a clearer picture begins to appear. In Figure 4.3c, the ES 60-minute and in Figure 4.3d, the ES 5-minute chart shows many places where price has broken support. In fact at times it looks like price is moving sideways. This example shows a "bullish" trend in

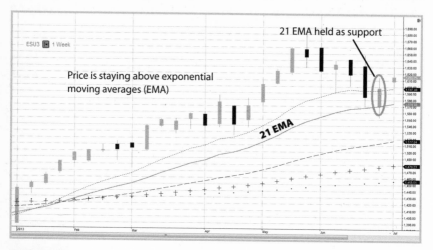

FIGURE 4.3a

(Source: MultiCharts.)

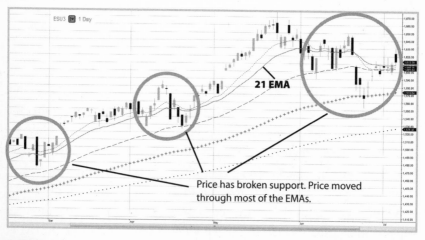

FIGURE 4.3b

(Source: MultiCharts.)

the long term, but the shorter-term time frame could be indicating that the long trend is about to reverse. A trader will need to look at the other four chart characteristics to gather more evidence to support a trade in the ES.

When traders understand how to incorporate analysis from the forest *and* the trees, they can interpret the market action more accurately in order to determine solid trades. A long-term perspective helps traders to determine the trend, and an overall market direction, whereas shorter-term time frames help to pinpoint entries and exits. By zooming in and seeing more detail, traders are better able to view the levels they are targeting to enter a trade, whereas a longer-term time frame offers a global picture.

FIGURE 4.3c   (Source: MultiCharts.)

FIGURE 4.3d   (Source: MultiCharts.)

Sarah's Trading Tip

Many traders will have specific time frames that they believe give them an advantage. Time frames of almost any period can be chosen from your charting software. Find some time frames that you like that allow you a long- and short-term view of the trading instrument you are trading, and see if this adds clarity to your trading. I like the weekly, daily, 60-minute, and 5-minute time frames.

Looking Inward and Understanding Internals

Along with charts from various time frames, traders use market internals to add support to their trading assumption. Just as there are many time frames available to traders, there are many market internals to consider. Market internals help traders to understand whether the market is moving up or moving down and going from strength to weakness or weakness to strength. Some internals trend with the broad markets, and some are counter to the broad markets.

Market internals simply show what is going on within the stocks or trading instruments that make up the market. It is a visual way to consolidate and analyze the large volume of data on a trader's charts. Internals also help to provide context for what is happening in the market. They help traders to understand whether just a few stocks are moving in one direction or whether there is strength across the entire market. Market internals provide a more detailed view of a trading instrument to help create strong support of the market direction. Market internals should not be used in isolation to determine a trade; they should always be used with charts or other information to build your market assumption.

There are many market internals that can be added to your charts. Each trader should have some market internals that he will use to help guide his assumption about market direction. I believe the Standard and Poor's 500 Index (S&P 500), the Chicago Board Options Exchange Market Volatility Index (VIX), Average True Range (ATR), and NYSE Tick Index (TICK) are very important market internals to use to support my trading assumption. Let's look at each of these market internals in more detail to help understand why they are such valuable tools.

Sarah's Trading Tip

Just as with any market indicator, the more internals you have that confirm a trend, the stronger your trading assumption can be. There are times, however, when the internals can become disconnected, making them less relevant. Traders are always looking for confirmation of their market assumptions from more than one market indicator.

S&P 500 as a Broad Market

The S&P 500 also can be referred to as the *broad US market*. This index is made up of the top 500 U.S. stocks. It is a good sample of the movement in many stocks and, as such, informs traders about the overall direction of the market. The S&P 500 can be traded as a trading instrument and/or used as a proxy for the overall US market.

How I Use This Information

I like to chart the S&P 500 E-mini futures contract (ES) to inform my overall opinion about market direction. I use the ES as an internal for both futures and options trading. Throughout the day, and especially in the morning, I will have the ES on my screen to keep an eye on the strength or weakness of the broad market. I use the ES to look for strengthening or weakening in the current price trend or whether the market is choppy and sideways.

I also use the ES to visualize the relative strength of the stocks I might be interested in trading. I like to know whether the stocks I am looking to trade are acting weaker or stronger than the market. For example, in Figure 4.4 Google (GOOG) is up 2 percent on the day and the ES (Figure 4.5) is up only 0.5 percent. GOOG is showing relative strength compared to the market.

Figure 4.4 is a chart of GOOG on a five-minute time frame. This price is moving up. A trader like me will look at a stock like this and compare it with a broad market such as the ES in Figure 4.5. I'm looking for strength in the broad market, which will then support my decision for individual correlated markets.

FIGURE 4.4

(Source: MultiCharts.)

This information will help me as I collect more evidence from other market internals such as the TICKs and specific support and resistance in short- and long-term time frames to determine whether GOOG is worth trading that day.

Sarah's Trading Tip

Some other broad markets I watch include Gold Futures (GC), Crude Oil (CL), US Treasury Bond Futures (ZB), and E-mini Nasdaq 500 (NQ) markets. I chart all these contracts on one chart. I look for consistency in the correlation between the markets and carefully watch for indications of one or more markets becoming out of sync. These markets will change from time to time as the relationships between the markets change. I will occasionally change the markets I look at and continuously look for new correlated markets to chart.

FIGURE 4.5

(Source: MultiCharts.)

New York Stock Exchange TICK Index

One of the more popular market internals is the NYSE TICK Index, commonly referred to as TICKs. The TICKs represents the number of stocks that are increasing in price versus the number of stocks that are decreasing in price based on the last tick of price change. On average during the day, the TICKs will move back and forth. Anytime there is a clear direction in the movement of a stock, the TICKs will begin to show significant values either positive or negative. If the TICKs reading is +800, this means that there are net 800 more stocks increasing in price than are decreasing in price. A positive number is bullish, meaning that the market is moving up, and a negative value is bearish, meaning that the market is heading down. In the same way, if the TICKs is hovering around 0, this indicates indecision or a sideways market.

How I Use This Information

The TICKs is very helpful, especially when I trade futures. The TICKs helps me with trend directions, conviction in the market, and trade entries and exits. I pay particular attention to what number the TICKs is reading and whether it is positive, negative, or hovering around zero.

When I see that the TICKs is more negative than positive, this will support an assumption that the market is short or that the trend is changing to short. When the TICKs is mostly positive, this information supports my trading assumption that the market is moving long. Anytime a TICK reading is showing a significant value (either plus or minus 800), I believe that there is some real conviction in the direction of the market. I will enter trades in the direction that the TICK is moving when it is close to plus or minus 800. This is especially true when I see the TICK moving in the same direction as the trend.

Not only does the TICKs help me with market direction, but I also use it to indicate a pullback to enter a futures trade. Because I don't want to overpay for a trade or trade at the top of a move, I will use the TICKs as an indication to wait for a small pullback in the market and then enter the trade.

Figure 4.6 is an example of the TICKs. The line across the chart helps you to see whether the TICKs is positive or negative. The more positive the TICKs, the stronger the momentum is for a long market. The more negative the TICKs reading, the more momentum is to the downside. The TICKs is especially important when it is reading around 0. TICKs that are hovering around 0 usually mean that the market is moving sideways or is choppy. Traders looking for big moves when the TICKs is hovering around 0 probably won't find them.

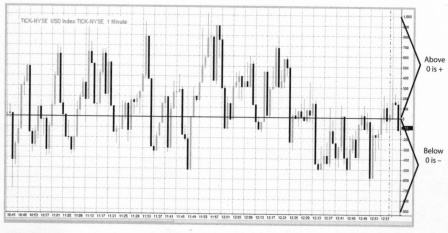

FIGURE 4.6

(Source: MultiCharts.)

volatility ↑ $ price ↓

↓   —   ↑

VIX

Another great internal to monitor is the VIX. The VIX is a measure of market volatility. It helps traders with their market assumptions about the direction of the overall market by measuring increases and decreases in market volatility. Typically and most important for traders to understand is that the VIX moves in opposition to the equity markets. Traders watch to see volatility increase, which is a signal that the market generally should move lower. As volatility decreases, traders will anticipate the markets are generally moving higher and thus place trades in that direction. The VIX can be used as part of a trader's tools to measure market internals, but the VIX also can be traded using options or futures.

How I Use This Information

I will look at the VIX for trends and changes in a trend. Because the VIX moves inversely to the overall market, it can be helpful in differentiating between a change in market direction and a pullback in the market (thus providing a good entry to trade in the direction of the trend). The VIX is a helpful tool when it is compared with the behavior of the overall markets. For example, if the market opens in an uptrend and the VIX is also moving up, there is a strong probability that any early-morning countertrend move is actually a change in trend. A trader should be aware of this correlation so as to avoid entering a long trade assuming that it is a pullback and end up being stopped out of the trade.

However, if the VIX and the broad markets are moving in opposite directions, then any moves in the broad market that are against the prevailing trend are most likely a retracement that can be traded. For example, if the market opens up and then pulls back, a trader can treat this move as a retracement and an opportunity to enter a trade in the direction of the prevailing trend. This example is an opportunity to buy because the markets should continue to move up as the VIX moves down. The VIX can prevent a trader from shorting, thinking that the market is heading down when the movement is actually an opportunity to trade in the direction of the trend.

The VIX also has another role in the options market—it influences premium. Specifically in options, when the VIX is spiking up, there is more premium in options that are available to sell. Because I like to collect premium when I trade options (selling spreads either at or out of the money), the VIX also helps me to confirm whether I will place a trade as a spread to collect premium or buy directionally (more on this in Chapter 5). Typically, I will sell more spreads when the VIX is pushing up because there is more premium to collect.

As a more advanced technique, I will also pay attention to previous support and resistance on the VIX in anticipation of reversals at those levels. Just like the support and resistance levels found on charts from moving averages, the VIX can be used in a similar fashion.

Figure 4.7 shows the VIX in a one-minute time frame. This snapshot of the VIX shows a steady decrease over one day. I will use this information and compare it with the overall broad market, expecting the market to move higher if the VIX is moving lower.

FIGURE 4.7

(Source: MultiCharts.)

Average True Range

Average true range (ATR) is a measure of how many dollars or ticks an instrument has moved over the last few periods. ATR is available on most charting platforms as a free indicator. I like to use the standard 14-period indicator from MultiCharts. ATR shows the total move per period for the specified number of periods.

The ATR will help traders to pick stops and targets for their trades. It shows traders how much the market is moving within the time frame being traded. Understanding how far the market is moving will help to ensure that a trader sets a stop outside the average range of the instrument being traded at the time (provided that the stop levels also align with your risk/reward ratios) or might avoid the trade altogether if the range is too large.

Because the ATR shows a range of price action, it helps traders to avoid getting stopped out because their stops were set too tightly for the volatility of current price movement. For example, if the market is moving an average of 2 points every five minutes, a trader might consider placing his stop outside a 2-point range. If the trader chooses a 1-point stop when the market is moving an average of 2 points, he is probably going to be stopped out of the trade.

The ATR also can be used in reverse to set targets to exit a profitable trade. If the ATR is averaging less than 1 point, then a trader should only expect less than a 1-point move. If the trader is looking for a 3-point target but the ATR is at 1 point, then it is more probable that the trade is not going to hit the target. By having stops outside the ATR and targets within the ATR, traders improve the chances that their trades will achieve their trading goals.

How I Use This Information

I like to use the ATR to gauge stops and targets for my trading. I have the ATR on the chart I use for my entries, the five-minute chart for futures. The ATR also works nicely with the Foundations indicator.

I watch the ATR to decide where to place stops as well as to decide whether the market is too choppy for me to enter. The ATR will help me to decide how much movement I can expect.

The ATR is at the bottom of the five-minute chart in Figure 4.8. Notice the #1 on the average true range indicating price action is moving close to 2 ES points. The corresponding #1 on the chart confirms this. Whereas the #2 on the ATR indicating price action is moving less than 1 ES point at that time. So If I wanted to place a trade while the ATR is indicating 2 points, I would set my target less than 2 points. I'm not going to expect to set a higher profit target than what is showing on the ATR.

FIGURE 4.8

(Source: MultiCharts.)

Sarah's Trading Tip

Typically, each of the market internals I mentioned are displayed on my trading screens at all times. In the preceding examples, I have separated each indicator and internal and shown them individually on a chart, for added clarity. I typically have more than one indicator on a chart at any time.

All these market internals should be used in conjunction with each other and with information from the charts. The more the market internals are aligning, the more strength a trader has for her trading assumption. Review market internals as a means of collecting evidence to support your assumption about market direction, but none should be used in isolation to inform a trading decision.

SUPPORT AND RESISTANCE FROM THE TIME FRAMES AND MOVING AVERAGES

Levels of support and resistance are lines that a trader will place on each of the time frame charts. Even though I have mentioned them throughout this book, I have yet to define them for you. I am referring to levels of support and resistance as moving averages, specifically *exponential moving averages* (EMAs).

When the market is long and the price action is moving above these lines, this is referred to as *support*. Any lines that price action needs to move through to continue in the direction of the trend are considered to be *resistance*. Even though traders put a lot of weight on the levels of support and resistance, they aren't magical lines. These levels are actually an average price for a specific amount of time displayed on a chart. Traders use this information because typically market behavior will be affected by these support and resistance levels, especially for the 21-period EMA.

Moving Averages

Moving averages are simply an indicator of historical prices for a trading instrument. They can average prices for whatever period a trader wants. The price average can be calculated using many different mathematical formulas, but the two most popular are the simple moving (arithmetic) average and the exponential moving average. The *simple moving average* is simply the total of all prices for the period of analysis divided by the time frame. The *exponential moving average* is calculated by taking the simple moving average and multiplying it by a smoothing constant.

An exponential moving average (EMA) will track price closer than a simple moving average (SMA) will. Because it reacts faster, there are traders who prefer using the EMA over the SMA. The 21-period EMA is a popular level that many traders use to define their entries and exits. It is probably the most popular line of support and resistance. Decisions about price direction and entries and exits can be made very easily with the aid of the 21-period EMA on a trader's charts.

If you watch the markets, you will notice that price will either reverse at key levels of support or need real momentum in order to move through levels of resistance. Historical levels of support and resistance are important; they show traders at what price levels in the past market participants stepped in and purchased or sold a stock or the broad market. Typically, traders will pick a few different periods of moving averages and have these on all their charts.

How I Use This Information

Many traders, including myself, use levels of support and resistance to help determine entries and exits for trades. The longer the time frame of the chart, the stronger are the levels of support and resistance. I use the 13-, 21-, 50-, 100-, and 200-period moving averages on all my charts. I pay most attention to the 21-period moving average as a strong level of support and resistance. To determine my entry points, I use the moving averages in combination with the foundations indicator on my shortest time frame chart (5-minute chart for futures and 60-minute chart for options).

Figure 4.9 is a 60-minute chart of GMCR with five moving averages. The 13-period moving average is the small dashed line, the 21-period moving average is the solid line, the 50-period moving average is the big dashed line, the 100-period moving average is the plus sign line, and the 200-period moving average is the dotted line. This chart shows that there isn't a clear trend at this point. The moving averages have crossed, and the candlesticks have broken through some of the moving averages, including the 21-period moving average.

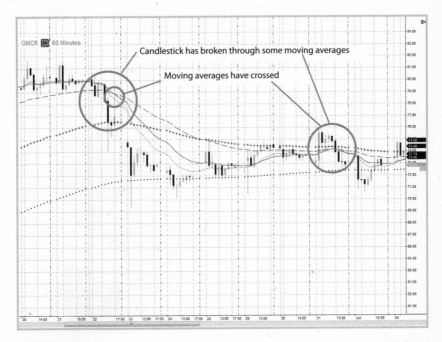

FIGURE 4.9   *(Source: MultiCharts.)*

Now that we have discussed ways to gather evidence from charts, we need to address how to search for individual stocks and ETFs to place trades. After all, just knowing how to read a chart will not produce a trade. Each trader needs to have some parameters to find opportunities to trade in specific markets.

CHARACTERISTICS OF A TRADING INSTRUMENT

A trading instrument refers to a stock, ETF, or futured contract. With thousands of stocks and new ETFs coming on the market all the time, searching the market for instruments to trade can become overwhelming. Traders need to establish the parameters they will use to decide which trading instruments they will trade. Professional traders won't just place trades randomly; they will have specific instruments on their watch list that meet key criteria. Some traders will place trades in startups, whereas others (like me) look for stocks that have good liquidity, volume, and volatility.

Sarah's Trading Tip

I will only place trades in instruments that have good liquidity and volume (meaning that many other people also trade them) and good price movement (volatility). I have found that by sticking to trading instruments with good liquidity, volume, and volatility, I can narrow my focus and stick to bigger, better-known instruments to trade. In my opinion, finding trades with these three characteristics makes for better trades. Generally liquid instruments give an options trader the advantage of having a narrow bid/ask spread (this helps reduce trading cost) and ease of trade entry and exit.

Liquidity

Liquidity refers to the number of shares or contracts of a particular instrument that are being traded. Liquidity is a relative term: low, medium, and high liquidity will mean different things to different traders. Thinking back to our auction example from Chapter 1, liquidity can be measured by looking at the price at which people are willing to sell the instrument and the price at which someone else is willing to buy the instrument. This price auction is referred to as the *bid/ask spread*. Low liquidity affects the bid/ask spread of the instrument by increasing the difference between the price you must pay to buy the instrument and the price at which you can sell the instrument. The lower the liquidity, the wider is the bid/ask spread. Instruments with low liquidity are more difficult to trade because there are less supply and demand for them.

How I Use This Information

The futures contracts discussed in this book—ES-mini DOW (YM), Russell 2000 Mini Index Futures (TF), E-mini S&P 500 Futures (ES) and EUR/

USD Futures (6E)—are all liquid and have bid/ask spreads that are only one tick wide. I am concerned primarily with liquidity when I am placing options trades. I mainly trade the larger names on the NYSE because these are liquid, so liquidity is not something that I always need to focus on every time I trade. Stocks and ETFs such as QQQ, XOM, V, GS, and so on always have good liquidity. I would rather place a trade in an instrument with a small bid/ask spread so that it's more likely that I can get a better price for my trade. For example, an exchange-traded fund (ETF) such as the PowerShares QQQ Trust (the QQQs) is liquid. It generally has a bid/ask spread of $0.01. This means that it takes only $0.01 of movement for a trader to break even on a trade.

Sometimes I trade lesser-known stocks, but only if they are liquid. Before I place a trade in a lesser known instrument, I make sure that there is sufficient volume in the options to make it worthwhile trading. I look to see if the underlying stock trades a few million shares per day and has open interest in the options of a few hundred to a few thousand contracts. If there is no open interest or the volume is low, then I will not trade the stock.

Volume

Volume is tied to liquidity, but volume is generally considered for a specific time frame, whereas liquidity is more of an overall view of an instrument. *Volume* is most simply the number of shares or contracts that have been traded over a specific time frame. Volume lets a trader visualize the number of shares of the stock that are being traded. Unfortunately, a trader cannot tell whether volume is on the buy side or sell side and whether traders are closing positions or initiating new positions.

How I Use This Information

I look for the stocks and options that I trade to have enough trading volume so that there is a narrow bid/ask spread and so the instrument is easier to trade. When I trade futures, I make sure that enough people are trading at the time I want to place the trade. I use volume to measure how much activity is happening at the time of placing the trade.

Figure 4.10 shows a chart with volume indicated at the bottom of the chart. The bars on this indicator will be taller when there are more people trading in the contract at that time. When the bars are shorter, there are fewer people trading at that time. Generally, I want to be placing trades when volume is high because this means many other traders are in the market.

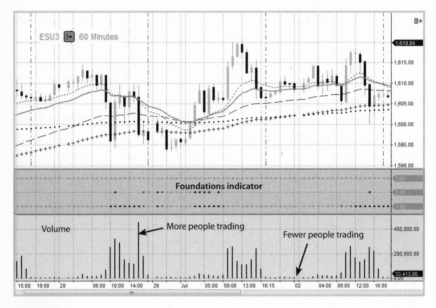

FIGURE 4.10   (Source: MultiCharts.)

Volatility

Volatility is a measure of how much the price of a trading instrument moves; the more volatile an instrument, the larger are the price swings it will have. Volatility is usually measured by standard deviation. Volatility also can be referred to as *beta*. Beta is a standardized measure of volatility that compares the stock with a benchmark, such as an index, and rates the volatility accordingly:

- A beta of 1 means that the stock moves as much as the index.
- A beta of 2 means that the stock moves around twice as much as the index.
- A beta of 0.5 means that the stock moves half as much as the index.

- Beta can be negative, meaning that the stock will move in the opposite direction of the market.

How I Use This Information

The more volatile an instrument, the more that instrument will move both to the upside and to the downside. I like to trade instruments that have some volatility, but this is really a personal preference. Your decision to trade a market that is more or less volatile should be tied to your trading personality.

Volatility also will spike in advance of earnings and news events. It is important to monitor and understand volatility if you are in a market where volatility is rising or declining because this becomes very important for most options strategies.

The Google (GOOG) chart in Figure 4.11 shows the volatility at the bottom. Notice that volatility has moved up and down throughout the day. Volatility will always change; it is never a constant. In options trading, as volatility increases so will the premium in the price of the option.

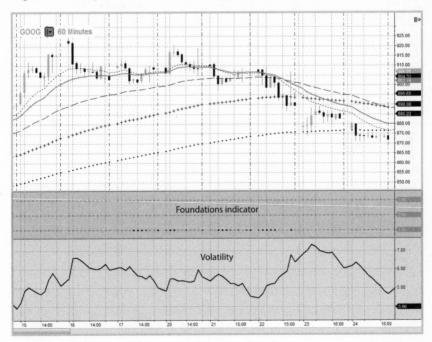

FIGURE 4.11   *(Source: MultiCharts.)*

Sarah's Trading Tip

Volatility is important for both futures and options trading. One example would be the S&P 500 (ES) versus the Russell 2000 Index (TF). The TF contract is more volatile: for every 4 ticks that the ES moves, the TF may move up to 10 ticks. The more volatility, the more profit and loss potential there is for the trade.

In options, implied volatility is important because it affects the price of the option. When implied volatility is high, there is more premium built into the price of the option (which means that the option will cost a trader more to buy or provide more credit to sell). This means that volatility will work in a trader's favor when selling options and against a trader when buying options.

FOUNDATIONS INDICATOR

The *Foundations indicator* compiles information about what the market has done in the past, and it monitors the current trend. You will notice that it is on the chart that I use to determine entries and exits for my trades (Figure 4.12). This indicator helps me to decide where I will enter a trade. You can trade without this indicator, but I have found it very effective at saving me time and helping me to find good trades. For more information about this indicator, visit www.shecantrade.com.

Benefits of the Foundations Indicator

- It compiles information from various time frames onto one screen, removing the need to have many screens open in order to trade.
- It makes it faster to look through charts to find trades.
- It is more efficient at finding trends.
- It keeps my trading screens clean and clutter-free.
- It allows me to trade from a laptop without needing to have many screens open.

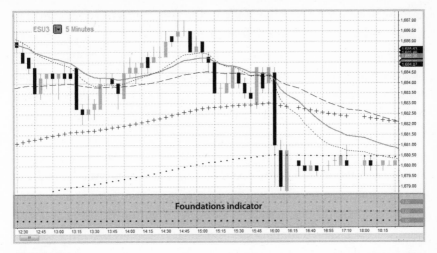

FIGURE 4.12   *(Source: MultiCharts.)*

Information from charts for a technical trader is essential regardless of what instrument or market is being traded. Collecting evidence from charts will help traders to look for key information that will lead to a trading decision. Combining the evidence that can be gathered from various time frames, moving averages, instrument characteristics, and the Foundations indicator will support a clear picture for a strong trading assumption.

INTERPRETING MARKET TRENDS

Understanding the trend and then trading in its direction are much easier than trying to guess when the market will change directions and jumping in front of that move. Trading with the trend allows a trader to place trades in the same direction as current market movement. In order to set up trades with the trend, a trader will need to understand how to read charts to determine whether there is currently a trend and its direction.

A trader will use charts to visualize the trend by examining support and resistance levels from moving averages that have occurred in the past. The terms *support* and *resistance* designate the levels where moving to averages might hold either to support a level or to act as a barrier (resistance) to movement in price. Support is the level of price where traders have been willing to buy the stock in the past; conversely, resistance is where traders would have sold in the past.

Support and resistance decisions also can be made based on prior inflection points in the market, such as highs and lows, as well as areas of consolidation where the market has paused before. Levels that held in the past will tend to hold in the future. This is why traders will look at data from varying time frames to determine levels of support and resistance. Support and resistance levels on charts will help to determine the trend. When the support and resistance levels are parallel, a trader would say that the instrument is *trending*.

The strength of a trend also can be determined by reading the charts. If the levels of support and resistance are trending with a steeper trend, then the trend is generally stronger and will persist longer. A strong trend provides more opportunity for trades to be successful and increases potential profit, "The stronger the trend, the stronger a trade."

The Apple (AAPL) chart in Figure 4.13*a* is an example of a trading instrument that is in a trend based on comparing the price movement over various time frames. This chart shows a clear downtrend on a weekly time frame. All the moving averages are parallel, and each bar is staying below the 21-period moving average. Based on this chart, I would begin to create my trading assumption to place a trade short once I have confirmed the trend on shorter time frames.

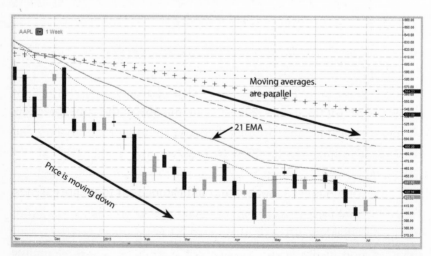

FIGURE 4.13*a*

(Source: MultiCharts.)

Figure 4.13*b* is the daily AAPL chart. I can see that the trend continues short. The 13- and 21-period moving averages have crossed; this means that the trend may not be as strong as I had originally hoped but still could be continuing. I will move to a shorter term frame to make my final decision about entering this trade.

FIGURE 4.13*b*   *(Source: MultiCharts.)*

Figure 4.13*c* is a 60-minute AAPL chart that also continues to show a downtrend. All the moving averages are moving in the same direction. Using this chart, along with the other AAPL charts from the daily and weekly time frames, supports my trading assumption that AAPL is in a downtrend.

There are many techniques and indicators used to identify trends. Keep your trading decision simple, and do not try to be too precise about the angle of the line. There is no need to break out a protractor—a simple evaluation of flat, moderate, or steep is sufficient to determine the strength of a trend.

FIGURE 4.13c

(Source: MultiCharts.)

Sarah's Trading Tip

Once you have determined support and resistance levels and the price trend, you have built the initial framework for your trading assumption. This information gives you an idea of the direction the trading instrument will move and where the move should slow down with the highest probability. This is the basic framework of technical analysis and reading charts. As you develop your skills, you can add more variables and fine-tune your filters. Be cautious of adding so many things to your analysis that you end up feeling unable to make a decision. I have found simple strategies that work for me without needing to get too complicated.

When to Trade and When to Stand on the Sidelines

Charts can also help you to understand when you shouldn't be placing a trade. Professional traders don't have to be trading every minute of every day. When their indicators are not signaling a trade, they will wait until their indicators once again signal a trade before they will commit capital to the markets. There are times when the markets will move sideways or whip back and forth. On these days, the evidence from chart analysis will not align either; this indicates to a trend trader that it's best to wait before placing any new trades. For example, if the market is rallying but the TICKs show a sell-off, this indicates a divergence. The more divergences there are between the instrument you want to trade and the market internals, the less likely it is that a trend trader will place a trade at that time.

Sarah's Trading Tip

As I'm looking at my charts and trying to find one that indicates to me that I might want to place a trade, I follow these three steps:

- *I look for a stock or an index that is trending well.*
- *I look at the internals to see if there is any reason not to take the trade.*
- *If there is conflict within the internals or if the internals do not confirm the direction of the trend, then I do not take the trade.*

When to Follow the Leader

Charts are useful for visualizing the market as a whole and how the instrument you are trading aligns with the broad market. A market will not move in one direction in isolation but will often follow the trend of a correlated or broad market. Some markets lead, and some markets follow. Knowing this piece of information can help a trader better evaluate trades by having more pieces of information they can use in creating their trading assumptions.

TABLE 4.1

Stock	Correlated with
GOOG	S&P 500
AAP	Nasdaq

If the stock is a large component of the index, then it can have an influence on the direction of the index. Watching moves in the correlated stock can help to indicate moves in the index. For example, if AAPL has a strong up move at 2:30 p.m. EST, then expect that the Nasdaq will have a pop as well. This is especially helpful for futures traders who are looking for smaller, more frequent trades. Watching index components is one way to help predict broad market moves and gives you a better glimpse into the inner workings of the market.

Another way to follow the leader is to see what stocks and sectors are outperforming or underperforming and look to invest in the leaders that are showing strength or weakness both in their individual sectors and in the overall market. Watching for key areas of strength or weakness will help you to narrow your short list of trades and give you a starting point for your analysis.

The market generally will show indications of what it is going to do. As a trader, you need to look for those signs—look at the various indexes, not just the S&P 500; look at the Dow, the Russell 2000, currency pairs, gold, bonds, and crude oil to see how they correlate with what you are trading and to see what information you can get from watching those markets along with your favorite list of stocks. You will be surprised at the patterns you can observe to help improve your trading.

The final concept for follow the leader is the number of stocks contributing to a rally or sell-off. If there is broad participation, then this is a follow-the-leader type of scenario, and the indexes are most likely going to show a trend in that direction. However, if the move in the indexes is being caused by one or two stocks, then this is a market that is more likely to reverse because it is not moving based on broad participation.

Figure 4.14*a* is a Goldman Sachs (GS) chart that shows a big move at 10 a.m. GS was up strong in the morning. This move had an influence on the index and was a contributing factor to why the index was up that morning. If you see that there are many individual stocks that are showing strength in the morning, then it is common for the broad market to have follow-through and push higher as well. However, if the index was up based on a spike-up in one or two stocks, then there is a good probability that the trend will not persist.

FIGURE 4.14a   *(Source: MultiCharts.)*

Figure 4.14*b* is a chart of a correlated index to GS the ES. The chart also shows the resulting up move in the markets that was initiated by the underlying components of the index, such as Goldman Sachs (GS) having a strong move to the upside. On that day, there was broad participation by stocks, and the up move persisted throughout the day.

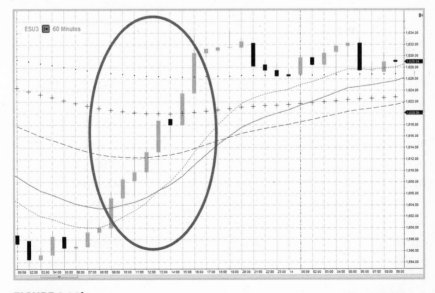

FIGURE 4.14b   *(Source: MultiCharts.)*

If the stock you trade is very market correlated and moves tick for tick with the broad market, then charting the two and watching for any divergences can help your trading. As you can see in Figure 4.15a, Priceline.com (PCLN) is in an up move and slowly grinds higher throughout the day.

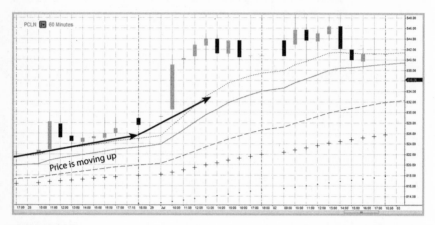

FIGURE 4.15a   *(Source: MultiCharts.)*

Now contrast that with the ES chart in Figure 4.15b, which shows the market being neutral to lower on the day. Generally, a stock such as PCLN will move with the broad markets.

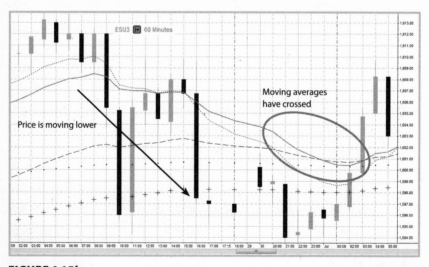

FIGURE 4.15b   *(Source: MultiCharts.)*

Because you can see the divergence between the market and PCLN, this could be a warning sign if you are trading PCLN on that day. In this case, PCLN has a long-term trend that is up, so the strength in PCLN is something that can be continued to be traded to the upside. But this also indicates that there is a bit of a disconnect that day between PCLN and the market, so you might want to be more cautious or use other indicators to confirm your trading decision.

> **Sarah's Trading Tip**
>
> *Markets have behaviors that can sometimes be relatively predictable. As you get to know the ins and outs of a specific market, you will begin to notice times when the market is not acting as it usually does. A difference in behavior doesn't necessarily indicate that a big move is going to happen; rather, it signals that something might happen. During these times, I will step back and wait until the market regains its trend before I place a trade in that market.*

A Trader's Point of View

We have just reviewed how to collect information from charts. Now we need to also address how to organize all the information you have gathered. We have all seen images of traders with many computer screens in front of them. They have numerous charts, trading instruments, and indicators displayed. This can look impressive to some people, but the reality is that each individual person can look at only so many things at once and process that information. Even though it might be nice to have a lot of information displayed on the screens, our brains can process only so much information at once. The number of screens a trader requires comes down to personal preference. At a minimum, two screens are best. Typically, one screen would be for charts, and the other screen would be used for the actual trading platform, e-mail, Internet, and so on. Basically, the ideal setup allows you to view your key charts and place trades without having to move or minimize windows. Especially if a trader has multiple positions on at once, she needs the room on her screens to be able to monitor trades and continue to search for others.

The number of computer screens you use will also be determined by how you like to review your charts and how many market internals you monitor at one time. I like to set up my trading desktop with charts that show a short-, medium-, and longer-term time frame based on how I am trading, which requires one computer screen dedicated to those charts and some market internals. For example, if I am taking futures trades off a 5-minute chart, I will also have a 60-minute and a daily chart on my desktop all on one screen so that I can visualize the overall trend of the market.

Experiment with your charts to find a combination that works for your trading. I keep my charts clutter-free and limit the number of indicators that I use. Two screens allow me to have a screen devoted to executing trades and a screen to monitor the broad market at the same time. A trading screen is full of information that must be processed by the trader. Limiting data overload is key to keeping trading setups clean and easily executable.

Sarah's Trading Tip

You will find that over time you will add and remove charts from your trading screens. Screens should show only information that you actually use on a regular basis. Try to make a habit of removing charts, internals, and indicators that you don't use consistently. Keep your screens clean and current so that you can have confidence in your trading assumptions.

Create a Trading Routine to Review the Charts Before You Place a Trade

Solid market analysis and trading require good trading habits and follow-through. All the information that was reviewed earlier should be reviewed on a regular basis before you place a trade. It's important to develop a routine to follow in order to review the information from your trading screens efficiently and effectively so as to make good trading decisions. Developing a routine to review charts also removes any emotional connection to trading decisions and grounds your trading assumption in evidence collected from your screens. Trading routines should include steps that you will follow premarket, and during the day, and all should be connected back to your MY TRADE plan. Every day it is important to

- Review your watch list to look for trading instruments and overall markets in a trend
- Determine your own market assumption based on the information you gather from the charts, market internals, and Foundations indicator with an unbiased view each time
- Look at specific charts using multiple time frames to gain a long- and short-term outlook to determine entries and exits
- Reflect on what you did well and what you can improve

Sarah's 10 Simple Steps to Review Your Charts

We have worked through charts 101 in a manner that provides a foundation for your market analysis. We have reviewed what market internals to pay attention to, how to read and set up moving averages on your charts, and the importance of both long- and short-term views of the markets. Now let's apply this information to some trades.

These simple steps will help you to understand the what, when, and how to collect information from charts to form a trading assumption.

1. Determine the trend of the overall/correlated market. Are the markets behaving similarly? Is there a trend moving up or down?
2. Choose a few market internals to look at. Are they indicating that the markets are moving up or down?
3. Determine a direction for your overall market assumption.
4. Pull up charts for long- and short-term time frames for the instrument you want to trade.
5. Where are the levels of support and resistance on the long-term time frame charts? Have they crossed?
6. Where are the levels of support and resistance on the short-term time frame charts? Have they crossed?
7. Where is the 21-period EMA on each of the time frame charts? This is a level of major support/resistance that I will use often to place or exit trades.
8. What is the Foundations indicator showing on the shortest-term time frame chart?

9. Determine your market assumption based on the evidence you have gathered.

10. Using a 60-minute (options) and/or 5-minute (futures) chart, determine the entries and exits of your trades and which trade setup to use.

Chart Analysis Walk-Through Examples

The following examples help to illustrate how a technical trader will review the charts and then make a decision about his market assumption. The market assumption is then applied to specific trading setups and specific trading instruments. Even though the trading instrument might be different, the steps used to review charts to determine a market assumption about the direction of the market are the same. The following examples will apply Sarah's Simple 10 Steps. Details about specific trade setups are listed in the related futures and options chapters.

Figures 4.16*a* through 4.16*d* display the various long- and short-term time frames for setting up a futures trade in E-mini DOW (YM). Using Sarah's 10 simple steps, let's work through this example together:

Example 1

1. Review a correlated and a broad market to determine whether it is trending in the same direction as the market you wish to trade.
   The YM is correlated with the ES. I will compare what is happening in a long-term ES chart with a long-term chart of the correlated.

2. What are the market internals showing?
   I will look at the TICKs to see if action is closer to +800, 0, or −800 and the ATR for the range in which the market is moving.

3. Determine a direction for your overall market assumption.
   I have determined that currently the overall market direction is up.

4. Pull up charts for long- and short-term time frames for a specific trading instrument.
   Because I'm going to consider trading the YM futures contract in this example, I will pull up long- and short-term charts for the YM.

5. Where are the levels of support and resistance on the long-term time frame charts? Are they crossed?

The moving averages are all moving upward but not sharply on the long-term charts.

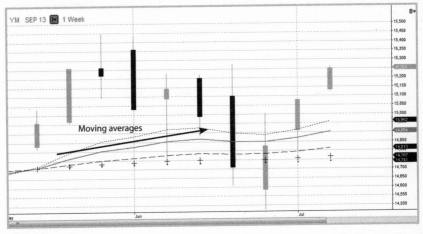

FIGURE 4.16*a*

(Source: MultiCharts.)

The moving-average levels on the weekly chart appear to be moving upward.

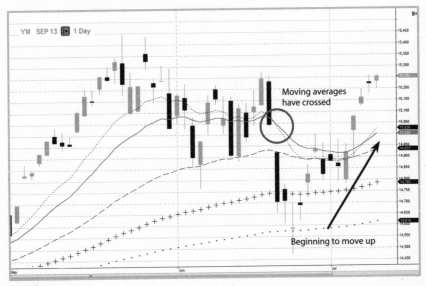

FIGURE 4.16*b*

(Source: MultiCharts.)

The moving-average levels have crossed on the daily but look like they may be beginning to move upward again.

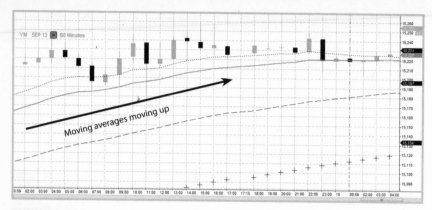

FIGURE 4.16c

(Source: MultiCharts.)

6. Where are the levels of support and resistance on the short-term time frame charts?

The 60-minute chart indicates that the upward trend is established, but the trend is not very steep.

The five-minute chart shows that the moving averages have broken but appear to have reestablished. The trend is long.

7. Where is the 21-period EMA?

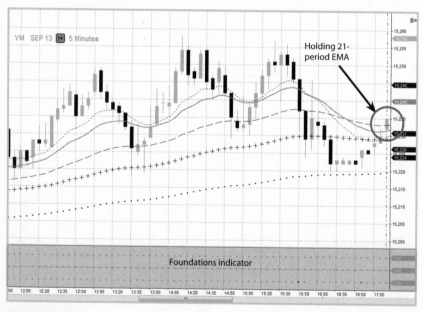

FIGURE 4.16d

(Source: MultiCharts.)

Figure 4.16d shows the 21-period EMA as the solid line on the chart. The last five-minute bar held the 21-period EMA. I would like to see more five-minute bars holding the 21-period EMA before I place this trade.

8. What is the Foundations indicator showing on the shortest-term time frame?

   Figure 4.16d shows that the foundations indicator is signaling white dots on all three levels. At this time, the indicator is firing long.

9. Determine your market assumption based on the evidence gathered.

   Based on all the information I have gathered, my market assumption is that the market is long or going up. I would place a long trade.

10. Determine the entries and exits of your trade and which trade setup to use.

    Because this is a futures trade, using the five-minute chart, I will begin to think of what trading setup to use and where to enter. (Next, steps to place this trade are discussed in the upcoming chapters.)

Example 2

1. Review a correlated or broad market to determine whether it is trending in the same direction as the market you wish to trade.

   The ES is a broad market.

2. What are the market internals showing?

   I will look at the TICKs to see if action is closer to +800, 0, or −800 and to see whether the ATR in the market is moving.

3. Determine a direction for your overall market assumption.

   The overall market direction is long because the ES is moving up.

4. Pull up charts for long- and short-term time frames for a specific trading instrument.

   Because I'm going to consider trading the ES futures contract in this example, I will pull up long- and short-term charts for the ES.

5. Where are the levels of support and resistance on the long-term time frame charts? Are they crossed?

   The moving averages are all moving upward nicely on the long-term charts.

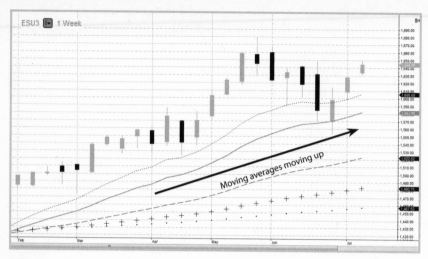

FIGURE 4.17a   *(Source: MultiCharts.)*

6. The moving average levels on the weekly chart are moving upward.

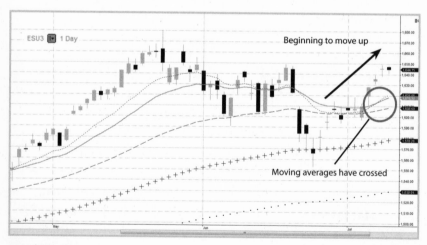

FIGURE 4.17b   *(Source: MultiCharts.)*

The moving-average levels have crossed on the daily chart but look like they may be beginning to move upward again.

7. Where are the levels of support and resistance on the short-term time frame charts?

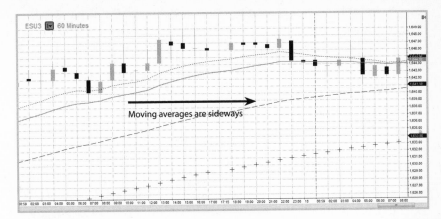

FIGURE 4.17c   *(Source: MultiCharts.)*

The 60-minute chart looks like the trend is moving sideways. The moving averages are all bunched together and look almost flat.

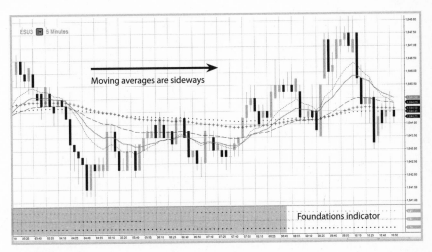

FIGURE 4.17d   *(Source: MultiCharts.)*

The five-minute chart shows that the moving averages are below prices. The trend is flat or sideways.

8. Where is the 21-period EMA?

Figure 4.17d shows the 21-period EMA as the solid line on the chart. The last five-minute bar is below the 21-period EMA.

9. What is the foundation indicator showing on the shortest-term time frame?

   Figure 4.17d shows that the indicator is signaling white dots on only two levels. At this time, the indicator is firing long but with caution. I wouldn't place a futures trade at this time. I would wait for a stronger trend to appear.

10. Determine your market assumption based on the evidence gathered.

    Based on all the information I have gathered, my market assumption is that the market is sideways and that I will not place a trade.

11. Determine the entries and exits of your trade and which trade setup to use.

    (I will move on to look at another instrument to trade at this time based on the market information I have gathered.)

Example 3

1. Review a correlated or broad market to determine whether it is trending in the same direction as the market you wish to trade.

   The ES is a broad market correlated with Staples (SPLS). I use the ES as the broad market for most of my options trades.

2. What are the market internals showing?

   I look at the TICKs to see if action is closer to +800, 0, or –800 and to see which way the VIX is moving.

3. Determine a direction for your overall market assumption.

   The overall market direction is long because the ES is moving up.

4. Pull up charts for long- and short-term time frames for a specific trading instrument.

   Because I'm going to consider trading SPLS options in this example, I will pull up long- and short-term charts—weekly and daily charts as long term and 60-minute charts as short term.

5. Where are the levels of support and resistance on the long-term time frame charts? Have they crossed?

   The moving averages are all moving upward nicely on the long-term charts.

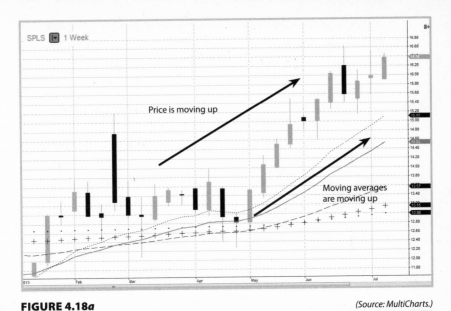

FIGURE 4.18a   (Source: MultiCharts.)

The moving-average levels on the weekly chart are moving upward.

FIGURE 4.18b   (Source: MultiCharts.)

The moving-average levels on the daily chart are all moving upward.

6. Where are the levels of support and resistance on the short-term time frame chart?

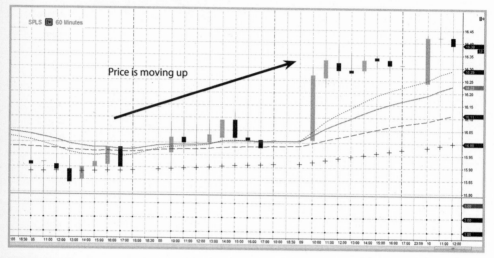

FIGURE 4.18c

(Source: MultiCharts.)

The 60-minute chart looks like the trend is long.

7. Where is the 21-period EMA?

Figure 4.18c shows the 21-period EMA as the solid line on the chart. The 60-minute bars have stayed above the 21 EMA since 11 a.m. The bars broke the 21 EMA earlier in the day and days previous.

8. What is the foundation indicator showing on the shortest-term time frame?

Figure 4.18c At this time, the indicator is firing long but with caution. I would move my attention to the options chain at this point to decide what trade setup to use.

9. Determine your market assumption based on the evidence gathered.

Based on all the information I have gathered, my market assumption is that this instrument does have a trend.

10. Determine the entries and exits of your trade and which trade setup to use.

(Next, steps to place this trade are discussed in the upcoming chapters.)

Example 4

1. Review a correlated or broad market to determine whether it is trending in the same direction as the market you wish to trade.
   The ES is a broad market correlated with Deere & Company (DE). I will use the ES as the broad market for most of my options trades.
2. What are the market internals showing?
   I will look at the TICKs to see if action is closer to +800, 0, or −800 and which way the VIX is moving.
3. Determine a direction for your overall market assumption.
   The overall market direction is up.
4. Pull up charts for long- and short-term time frames for a specific trading instrument.
   Because I'm going to consider trading DE options in this example, I will pull up long- and short-term charts—weekly and daily as long term and 60-minute charts as short term.
5. Where are the levels of support and resistance on the long-term time frame charts? Are they crossed?
   The moving averages are moving down on the long-term charts.

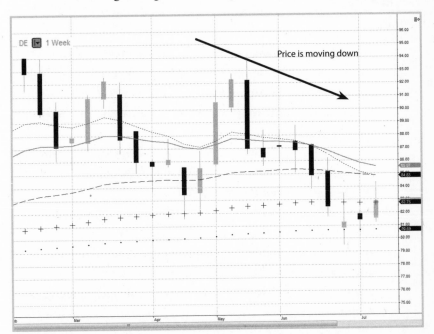

FIGURE 4.19a   *(Source: MultiCharts.)*

The moving-average levels on the weekly chart appear to be moving down slightly. The movement down does not have a strong conviction, which makes me think that the trend is not very strong.

Price is moving down

FIGURE 4.19*b*

(Source: MultiCharts.)

The moving-average levels on the daily chart are all moving upward, except for the last two days. This also confirms my feeling that the market trend could be down, but it isn't clear at this time.

6. Where are the levels of support and resistance on the short-term time frame chart?

   The 60-minute chart looks like the direction is short. The moving averages have not crossed today but did yesterday.

7. Where is the 21-period EMA?

   Figure 4.19c shows the 21-period EMA as a solid line. The 60-minute bars have broken the 21-period EMA today.

8. What is the foundations indicator showing on the shortest-term time frame?

   Figure 4.19c shows that the indicator is signaling all black dots. At this time, the indicator is not supporting a trend, nor is it signaling to trade this instrument at this time.

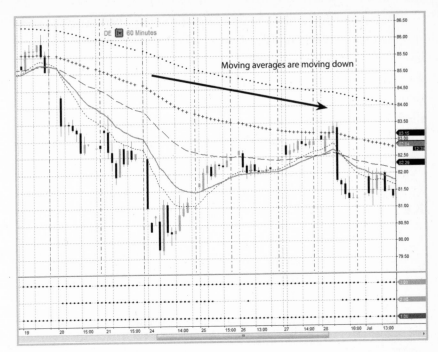

Moving averages are moving down

FIGURE 4.19c *(Source: MultiCharts.)*

9. Determine your market assumption based on the evidence gathered.
   Based on all the information I have gathered, my market assumption is that this instrument does not have a trend that I would trade. I will look for another trade.

10. Determine the entries and exits of your trade and which trade setup to use.
    I will move on to look at another instrument to trade at this time based on the market information I have gathered.

Sarah's Trading Tip

To apply your knowledge, you might want to come back to these examples after you have read about the trading setups to decide which trading setup you would use with each of these examples.

Whatever you choose to use as part of your chart analysis, make sure that you understand why it is there and how to use it. This chapter has remained focused on exploring charts in a meaningful and practical way. The process of reviewing charts is directly connected to the trade setups that follow for options and futures. This chapter has only scratched the surface of chart analysis but gives you a solid starting place, to create your trading assumptions for the trade setups in the futures and options chapters ahead.

KEY TAKE-AWAYS

- Interpret the market trend in both long- and short-term markets. Every trader will find that a specific time frame is most helpful. I recommend that you start with the basics—weekly, daily, and 60-minute charts—and add the 5-minute chart for futures. Experiment with other time frames as well because you might find that you like a different one.
- Market internals will help to guide your entries and exits. They can help to show you the strength in the market, especially how much power a specific trend has. Use this information to inform your trading.
- Markets are correlated. Traders use information from underlying stocks or the relationships between correlated markets to help with their trading assumption. Always be on the lookout for the best deal. If an index or ETF will cost you less to trade than individual stocks and both are behaving in the same way, you might consider trading the instrument that will cost you less and/or be most profitable depending on your risk/reward parameters. Be aware of these correlations as a powerful tool for any trader's toolbox.
- Every trader needs to create rules or steps to follow to create good trading routines to determine a trading assumption. Use my steps as a place to get started, or develop your own; either way, you need a process that you routinely follow so that you do not let the power of your emotions interfere with good trading decisions. Look for evidence in the markets to determine your trading assumption.

- We are all busy people and can appreciate the support of an indicator to help focus the information gathered from a longer-term time frame into a shorter-term time frame. The foundation indicator will help to determine an entry into a market and only requires a shorter-term time frame chart to be open, thus saving you time and screen space. More information about this indicator is available at www.shecantrade.com.

5

SARAH'S OPTIONS STRATEGIES

SOMETIMES TRADING OPTIONS SOUNDS LIKE A SECRET LANGUAGE. REMEMBER A SPREAD IS *NOT* WHAT YOU WILL FIND ON AN HORS D'OEUVRES TABLE.

Illustrated by Noble Rains

Key Chapter Concepts

- *Learn what an option is.*
- *Review the advantages/disadvantages of options.*
- *Understand Trader Terminology Part I: puts and calls, buying and selling, expiry, weeklies and monthlies, premium, strike price, spreads, and options chains.*
- *Understand Options Trader Terminology Part II: Greeks, value of an option, standard deviation, calculating premium, and premium decay.*
- *Discuss the many options with options: What are put spreads, call spreads, iron condors, calendars, butterflies, straddles, and strangles?*
- *Distinguish trading directionally and trading spreads.*
- *Discuss considerations for your trading entries and exits.*
- *Understand Sarah's top three options trading strategies.*
- *Provide examples of trading scenarios.*

Options provide many opportunities to trade but are often deemed to be appropriate for experienced traders only. I believe that trading options does have some complexity, but it should be viewed as a skill that can be developed by anyone. Options provide more ways to trade beyond just buying or selling a stock, which I believe provides many advantages to traders.

Just as with the other chapters in this book, the information presented herein is meant to remain practical and straightforward. This chapter will not review everything there is to know about options; instead it focuses on information that I believe is essential. Options can seem to be complex, so in order to keep things straightforward, this chapter is divided into three foundational sections reviewing (1) trading terminology specific to options, (2) ways to trade options, and (3) detailing how to place trades using three specific options strategies that I use regularly. It is reasonable to assume that once a trader understands these three foundational areas, she can use options to open up a variety of trading possibilities to match her trading personality and risk parameters.

WHAT IS AN OPTION?

An *option* is an agreement that gives a trader the right but not the obligation to either buy or sell stocks, exchange-traded funds (ETFs), and/or futures within a specific time frame. Rather than buying or selling a specific stock, you buy or sell an option on that stock. The stock that is linked to the option is referred to as the "underlying instrument" or simply "underlying." For example instead of buying Ford (F), you can buy an option on Ford. The underlying in this example is the Ford stock.

Just as the name suggests, trading options provides many opportunities to trade within varying time frames and varying risk/reward parameters. Options trades can be held for a matter of minutes, days, or longer. There are a number of strategies that can be used when trading options, but these strategies can get complicated quickly. By sticking to a basic options strategy, a trader can develop a solid trading plan that suits his individual trading style.

Sarah's Trading Tip

As an example, you might think of an option as a coupon or voucher. A coupon is valuable only if it will save a consumer some money on a product she wants, and it hasn't expired. A buyer can use the coupon if she thinks that the coupon has value or give it to someone else who will value it. The coupon provides an opportunity at any time before it expires to buy the product at a reduced price and get a good deal. However, once the coupon expires, it is worthless. You can think of an option in the same way. The option is like a coupon or voucher to be used at or before a specific date and only if the trader believes that the option is a good deal (perceived value). A trader can either use the coupon by buying an option or sell an option by giving the right to use the coupon to someone else.

When a trader enters into an agreement to trade options (when he trades it), he will choose to buy or sell a call or put at a specific price or a combination thereof. Basically, traders can trade options using a number of strategies. At the root of every trade is linking an appropriate options strategy to the direction a market within a specific time frame.

How to Trade Options

There are many ways to trade options and many stock options and ETF options to choose from. The number of choices can seem overwhelming to traders, but what many of these traders do not realize is that even professional traders do not trade every options strategy. Instead, many professional traders use a few strategies that they like and have specific trading rules to help them decide which strategy to use depending on market conditions. Some options traders will trade using only directional strategies or only spreads, whereas others will trade a combination of strategies. Complicated strategies do not necessarily mean better trades or more profit. Basic options strategies can be just as profitable as some of the more complex ones. This chapter will cover some basic strategies. These are the strategies that I use most, and they are also used by many other traders.

Sarah's Trading Tip

I refer to basic strategies as straightforward trade setups such as buying directionals and selling credit spreads. These setups have a clearly defined set of rules for entries and exits, and adjustments are not made mid-trade. I believe that some traders get too involved in rolling contracts, adding too many legs, and overcomplicating trades. When traders get caught up using too many strategies with options, they lose sight of their actual goal of being profitable. Adding more complexity to a trade only makes things more difficult and more time-consuming to monitor. Sometimes these complicated trade setups focus too much attention on avoiding a loss rather than making a profit.

Complex strategies can be added to any trader's toolbox once she is comfortable with basic spread and directional trade setups, but they are not necessary to trade profitably in options.

Advantages and Disadvantages of Options

Options, just like any other trading instrument, have advantages and disadvantages that should be understood by all traders before they begin trading. The advantages and disadvantages should be weighed and prioritized by all traders to help them decide whether options is a trading instrument that they believe suits their trading personality (Table 5.1).

TABLE 5.1. Options

Advantages	Disadvantages
• Don't need to be in front of the computer all day. • Can have a defined risk/ reward using spreads. • Multiple ways to trade a market move. • Profit even if the market doesn't move. • Provide an ability to hedge trades. • Ability to defend losing trades.	• Terminology can be confusing. • Many terms to learn. • You must be correct on timing and direction: the market may do what you assumed but after the option has expired. • Risk/reward ratio may be out of alignment, e.g., 10:1.

I believe that options are a great way to trade and provide many advantages, especially if you do not have all day to devote to watching the markets. Selling spreads out of the money is one strategy that is particularly beneficial for new or part-time traders. This trade involves selling a spread outside of where you believe the price of the stock will be at expiry. For this options strategy, you place a trade outside of where you believe the stock price will actually move. As a result, you may make less money per trade, but you do not have to worry about monitoring the trade as closely as a more aggressive trade setup. (This trade setup is detailed at the end of this chapter)

Another advantage is time. Time is on your side when you trade options. Options also provide you with the ability to trade based on different options expirations. An options trader has the flexibility to choose between options traded using a contract that will expire in different time frames by trading monthly or weekly contracts. This flexibility in time also may mean that if the trader has more time to spend at the computer during one week, he may place more weekly trades that need more monitoring while also placing some longer time frame trades that need less monitoring. The profits from each of these trades will be different, but they may balance out some of the risk in a trading plan.

The many choices available can become overwhelming for someone who is new to trading and might seem like a disadvantage. Many setups also require an understanding of specific terminology and vocabulary that will need to be learned. This is where many people learning to trade options become overwhelmed and lost without clear explanations. However, once traders become familiar with basic terminology, the variety of trade setups provides opportunities to find trades based on predefined risk/reward parameters. Strategies such as spreads provide an opportunity to calculate maximum loss and maximum gain prior to entering the trade. The predefined risk/reward ratio provides a huge advantage to options trades versus other types of trades because the unknown of loss and gain is removed. Newer traders appreciate having smaller profits in exchange for knowing their maximum profits and losses in a trade before they place it.

TRADING LANGUAGE IN OPTIONS

Options provide many ways to trade, but many ways to trade can also mean that new traders get lost in the language of trading options. Even though it is written in English, options terminology can at first feel like a different language altogether. Once a trader understands the definitions of these terms, she will be able to apply this knowledge to specific options strategies. Together we will review some fundamental terms and then apply them to examples to consolidate your understanding. These terms are separated into two parts based on their level of complexity. Trader terminology part I describes essential terms that you will need to understand in order to read an options chain. Options Terminology Part II describes essential terms that you will need in order to understand the price of an option. At the end of each part, I will walk you through a trade example so that you can understand how the terms are used in context. All of these terms will be important as they will be used to detail three options trade set ups at the end of this chapter. I want to make sure you know the *what* and then the *how*.

> **Sarah's Trading Tip**
>
> *As you read through the next section, write down the terms and their definitions. I recommend that you keep this list of terms close to you or post it in your trading office so that you can refer to it often as we go through the trading strategies and setups. When I first began to trade, I made a list of definitions and terms and kept it close to me until I understood what all the terms meant.*

Trader Terminology Part I

Each of the terms in this section will be defined first, and then an example of how to use it in a trade will be provided (see Table 5.2).

TABLE 5.2. Trader Terminology Part I

Puts	Expiry	Options Chain
Calls	Premium	Strike price
Weekly	Buy	Spreads
Monthly	Sell	Assigned the underlying

Trading Terms: *Puts* and *Calls*

For every option traded, there are two sides—a put and a call. Both the put and the call can be bought or sold. A trader entering into an option trade holds the right to buy or sell 100 shares of the underlying at the exercise price when the contract expires. Buying or selling a put or call is what most people think of when they hear of options trading.

- A *call option* gives a trader the right to buy 100 shares of the underlying at a specific price (the *strike price*) at expiry.
- A *put option* gives a trader the right to sell 100 shares of the underlying at a specific price at expiry.

TABLE 5.3. Buying and selling an option

Option	Buy	Sell
Put	Assumption is that the stock is going down.	Assumption is that the stock is going up or sideways.
Call	Assumption is that the stock is going up.	Assumption is that the stock is going down or sideways.

Trading Terms: *Buying* or *Selling* an Option

Puts and calls can be bought or sold. The action of buying or selling is the same as when you go to an online auction site like eBay; you can either purchase an item or list an item for sale. When you trade options, you have the choice of a trading strategy that allows you to buy the option, meaning that you own that option until it expires, or you can sell the option to someone else. The action of selling an option allows a trader to collect the credit or the cost that someone else needs to pay. Buying and selling both have their advantages and disadvantages.

When a trader buys an option, her risk is defined by what she paid for the option. A trader cannot lose more than she paid for the option. When a trader buys a call, he believes that the market will continue to move up. This trade technically has unlimited profit. When a trader buys a put, she believes that the market is going down. This trade can technically profit until the stock reaches $0 (because stocks can't drop below $0).

Options traders also can sell an option. This type of trading can seem complicated, but it is really quite simple. When a trader sells an option, she collects a credit (money placed in the trading account). Selling an option is like getting the profit from the trade at the beginning of the trade. This means that your profit is limited to the credit you take in.

Your losses, however, can be unlimited for calls and very high for puts (again, because a stock can't go below $0). Buying or selling an option is called *trading directionally*.

In options trading there is also another way to trade. These strategies are called spreads. When an options trader buys and sells a put or call at the same time, this is referred to as a *spread*.

Sarah's Trading Tip

I buy options only when I trade directionally, and I sell options when I trade at-the-money spreads or out-of-the-money spreads. Even though it is possible to trade many more ways, these strategies have been worthwhile for me. These strategies and the steps to actually trade in this way are described at the end of this chapter.

Trading Term: *Spreads*

Spreads provide an opportunity for traders to define their risk/reward parameters when entering a trade. A *spread* is a trade in the direction of your market assumption while also ensuring that there is some protection if your trading assumption is wrong. It is buying and selling a put or call at different strike prices, basically picking a level where the trader believes that the market will not move past and also picking a different level as backup in case the trader is wrong.

Spreads provide an opportunity for traders to understand their maximum gain and maximum loss for each trade before they place it. Spreads may seem complex, but when a spread is broken down to its basic components, it is a combination of puts or calls at different strike prices that are combined to make up a trade. There are many types of spreads, and each one has an advantage based on the direction a trader feels the market is moving.

Some examples of spreads include

- Put credit spreads
- Put debit spreads
- Call credit spreads
- Call debit spreads
- Straddles
- Strangles
- Iron condors

Figure 5.1 is a graphic organizer that gives you an idea of the many types of spreads that an options trader might choose from.

Sarah's Trading Tip

Even though there are many types of spreads, I typically trade using put and call credit spreads that are traded at levels that are either at or out of the money. These trading setups will be outlined at the end of this chapter.

Trading Term: *Options Chain*

An *options chain* is like a dashboard. It is a screen that displays a lot of information that a trader needs in order to choose what trades to place. The options chain includes such information as the price of a stock, the premium, the strike price, and the Greeks. Just as with an auction, the options chain is the board that has all the information for the auctioneers and the auction participants.

There is a column for the prices traders are willing to pay to buy the options and a column for the traders who are interested in selling the option. These are called the *bid* and the *ask*. The options chain will be updated constantly as each trade moves through the exchange.

A trader will focus his attention between the multiple time frame charts of the trading instrument he is considering and the related options chain. By combining the information contained on both of these screens, the trader can determine all the information he will need to place a trade.

Figure 5.2 provides an example of an options chain bid and ask that are circled on the options chain and represent what other traders are willing to pay to buy or receive to sell an option at each strike price.

Trading Term: *Expiration*

Options expire at regular intervals; they will expire either weekly or monthly. After the date on which the option expires, the option is no longer traded. An options trader is very concerned about when an option will expire because the time left until expiry will affect the price of the option. Depending on the strategy of the trade, a trader will keep the option until it expires or sell it before it expires.

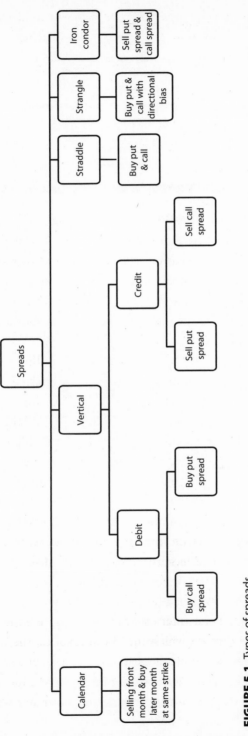

FIGURE 5.1 Types of spreads

119

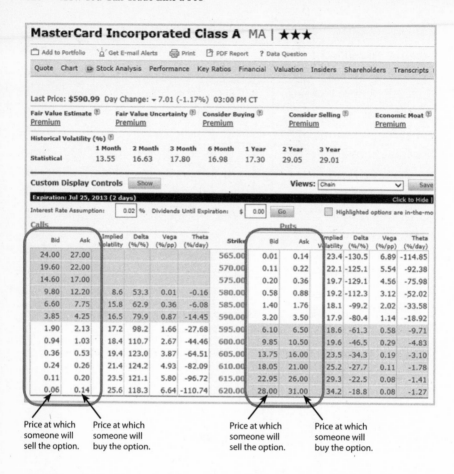

FIGURE 5.2

(Source: Morningstar.)

If a trader holds a long options contract to expiry, two things can happen; the contract can expire with value or without value. When a contract expires worthless, it is because the price of the underlying closed at a different price from the strike price you traded. This would be considered *expired out of the money*. If it expires out of the money, when you log into your brokerage platform on Monday morning, you will notice that the contracts have been removed from your trading screen. If the option expires in the money, it still has value. In this scenario, when you log into your brokerage platform on Monday morning, you will see that you are either long or short the underlying product (you may now own the stock) you were trading.

Trading Terms: *Weekly* and *Monthly Contracts*

Options have different times to *expiry;* some options expire every Friday, some expire on the third Friday of the month, and some expire a year or two in the future. When a trader selects an options trade, she will need to consider how long she thinks her assumption is going to be correct and choose a contract with an expiry that matches her assumption. For example, if a trader feels that a trading instrument is going to have a quick move, she may choose to place a trade using a contract that will expire in a few days to a week. If the trader feels that the trading instrument will have a long, grinding move, she may choose to trade using a contract that expires further out in the future.

Some options traders choose to trade weekly, monthly, or a combination of both types of options. There are various trading strategies for each of these time frames.

Figure 5.3*a* shows screen captures of an options chain. A trader will choose an expiry, and then look at the corresponding strike prices that are influenced by that expiry. Figure 5.3*a* shows a weekly expiry. Notice that these contracts will expire on July 25, 2013.

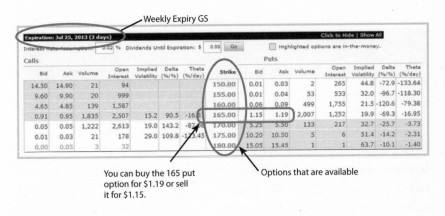

You can buy the 165 put option for $1.19 or sell it for $1.15.

Options that are available

FIGURE 5.3*a* *(Source: Morningstar.)*

Figure 5.3*b* is an example of a monthly contract. Notice that these contracts will expire on the third Friday of the month. The corresponding strike prices are different for the weekly and monthly expiries.

Monthly Expiry GS

Expiration: Aug 16, 2013 (23 days) — Click to Hide | Show All

Interest Rate Assumption: % Dividends Until Expiration: $ 0.00 Go — Highlighted options are in-the-money.

Calls							Puts						
Bid	Ask	Volume	Open Interest	Implied Volatility (%/%)	Delta (%/%)	Theta (%/day)	Strike	Bid	Ask	Volume	Open Interest	Implied Volatility (%/%)	Delta (%/%)	Theta (%/day)
15.00	15.25	62	1,452	19.4	10.6	-0.07	150.00	0.31	0.35	173	2,259	25.5	-33.9	-8.93
10.35	10.65	37	2,025	20.3	14.0	-0.32	155.00	0.71	0.72	308	2,771	23.2	-32.2	-6.35
6.25	6.35	248	2,731	19.0	19.5	-0.86	160.00	1.54	1.57	362	3,263	21.2	-29.2	-4.00
3.05	3.15	931	3,557	18.2	27.2	-2.0	165.00	3.30	3.35	804	1,784	19.8	-24.2	-2.09
1.15	1.17	707	2,747	17.6	37.4	-4.3	170.00	6.35	6.50	245	264	19.8	-18.3	-0.93
0.34	0.36	175	1,064	17.6	47.6	-7.7	175.00	10.55	10.80	4	109	21.8	-13.1	-0.42
0.09	0.13	29	500	18.5	53.9	-1.73	180.00	15.30	15.60	3	10	25.6	-9.6	-0.25

You can buy the 165 put option for $3.35, and sell it for $3.30. The prices for the same strike is different from that in Figure 5.3a, the weekly GS contract.

FIGURE 5.3b *(Source: Morningstar.)*

Trading Term: *Assigned the Underlying*

All traders must make sure that they are aware of the expiration dates of their trades and make sure to close out any trades that still have value (this is considered *in the money)* prior to expiry if they do not want to be assigned the underlying stock. *Assignment* means that the option that expired with value (in the money) will be exchanged for a position in the underlying stock automatically at expiry.

Sarah's Trading Tip

Make sure that you understand your broker's assignment policy so that you do not get assigned or have your trades automatically liquidated if you do not want that to happen. Watching a position get liquidated because you didn't realize that it still had value (it was in the money) can be a helpless experience. Different brokers will liquidate positions at different times prior to expiry; their assignment policy will clearly detail this, so make a point of knowing the policy so that it doesn't affect your trades.

Trading Term: *Premium*

In its simplest form, *premium* is an extra amount of cost that is built into the price of an option. The amount of premium will change over the life of the option, but eventually, it will be reduced to zero at expiration. Most simply, premium is based on time to expiry and volatility of the underlying asset. An option with a lot of premium built into the price will be an advantage for a trader who is selling (increasing the credit that the trader collects for selling the option) versus a trader who is buying an option and who will need to pay the extra premium to own the option (premium will increase the cost to buy it).

Trading Term: *Strike Price*

The *strike price* is actually the price at which the owner of an option can buy or sell the underlying at expiration. An options chain will list many different strike prices that a trader may choose from. A trader will use the strike price as a marker to determine a level at which she wishes to trade. The trader will need to negotiate with the market to buy or sell an option at that level.

Option strike prices vary by trading instrument. Most options are available at $5 or $1 intervals, but other intervals can be seen. The difference between the strike prices is referred to as the *width* of the strike price. For example, MasterCard (MA) has a $5 wide strike. This means that you can only buy or sell options every $5. Each line on the options chain will be $5 apart. Some products, such as the SPDR S&P 500 (SPY), will have options that trade every $1.

A Walk Through the Markets Part I

Now that we have defined some of the terms needed to trade options, let's apply them to an example so that you can understand how these terms are used in context by taking a walk through the markets. It is an example to help you understand how a trader uses these terms as she looks at the markets. I will continue to build on this example after Options Trader Terminology Part II.

The time is 10 a.m. on Tuesday. After reviewing the S&P 500 Index (S&P 500) to establish my assumption about overall direction, I move to look at some of my favorite stocks to trade. I pull up the charts for MasterCard (MA) and take a look across the multiple time frames. I determine my directional assumption based on the weekly (Figure 5.4*a*), daily (Figure 5.4*b*), and 60-minute (Figure 5.4*c*) charts. All three are showing a trend long.

Because these charts indicate that the trend of MA is long (up), I determine where I think there is a level of support on the charts. I then move my attention to the *options chain* Figure 5.5. I look at the *strike price* that corresponds to the support level on the chart. Since there is support at the 580 level on the daily MA chart (Figure 5.4*b*), I will begin by looking at the 580 strike on the options chain (Figure 5.5). I look to see the amount of credit that is available if I were to sell a put credit spread out of the money. The options chain with a *weekly expiry* shows that the bid is .58 and the ask is .88.

I need to decide now what type of trade to place, either a directional trade or a spread. I will need to calculate which option is the best deal to trade. (This walk-through will continue once we review Part II of Options Trader Terminology.)

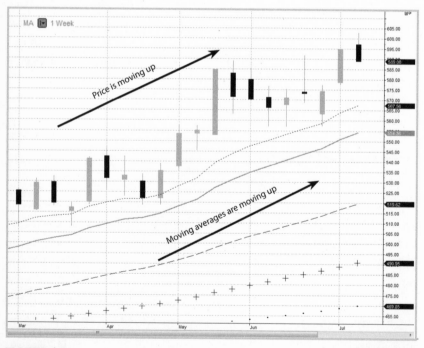

FIGURE 5.4*a*

(Source: MultiCharts.)

FIGURE 5.4b *(Source: MultiCharts.)*

FIGURE 5.4c *(Source: MultiCharts.)*

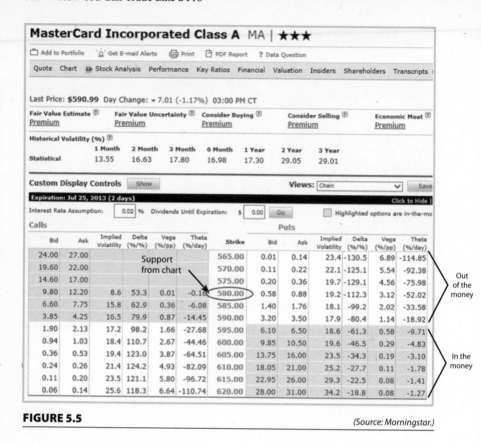

FIGURE 5.5

(Source: Morningstar.)

OPTIONS TRADER TERMINOLOGY PART II

Now let's add some more complex terms to your options vocabulary and then look back at the same trading example so that you can see how the terms are applied. These terms include the Greeks; understanding the difference between in the money, at the money, and out of the money; premium decay; and standard deviation (Table 5.4). These terms are important because they are what will help you determine the value of an option and expected movement of price. Just like the previous walk through, this is an example only. I will detail specific step-by-step instructions to review the market later in this chapter. This example is to provide context to the terms that we reviewed.

TABLE 5.4. Options Trader Terminology Part II

Greeks	In the money
Standard deviation	At the money
	Out of the money

Trader Terminology: *Value of an Option*

The terms *in the money, at the money,* and *out of the money* are thrown around in many conversations about options and can sometimes confuse new traders. The term *money* refers to whether the option has value. An option that is in, at, or out of the money refers to the option's strike price compared to the price of the underlying.

Out-of-the-money options are composed entirely of premium, whereas *in-the-money* options are made up of intrinsic value *and* premium. Since in-the-money options have intrinsic value, they will cost a trader more than options that are out of the money. This has important consequences for options traders. Different trade setups and expectations should be used for options that are in, at, and out of the money as each has a different risk and reward. Figure 5.6 illustrates the value of out of, at, and in the money.

To determine the *value of an option*, it's always easiest to begin by determining what strike is *at the money*. Simply put, at the money is the current price of the stock. This is where stock price is equal to the strike price of the option. In the money and out of the money are the strikes above and below the strike that is at the money. Calls are in the money if the strike price is less than the stock price, and puts are in the money when the strike price is above the stock price. Notice in Figure 5.6 that in the money and out of the money for a put option will be opposite to the call options that are in the money and out of the money. As shown in Figure 5.6, Goldman Sachs (GS) is trading at $165, so a $165 strike is at the money. Any call option with a strike less than $165 is in the money. Any call with a strike above $165 is out of the money. It is simply the reverse for puts.

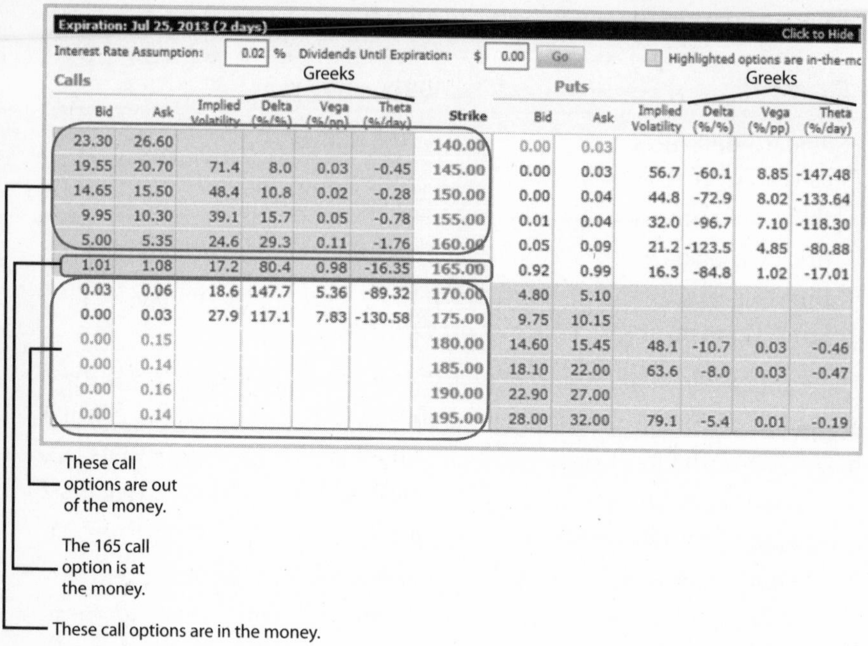

Expiration: Jul 25, 2013 (2 days)												Click to Hide
Interest Rate Assumption: 0.02 % Dividends Until Expiration: $ 0.00 Go										Highlighted options are in-the-mc		
Calls			Greeks				Puts			Greeks		
Bid	Ask	Implied Volatility	Delta (%/%)	Vega (%/pp)	Theta (%/day)	Strike	Bid	Ask	Implied Volatility	Delta (%/%)	Vega (%/pp)	Theta (%/day)
23.30	26.60					140.00	0.00	0.03				
19.55	20.70	71.4	8.0	0.03	-0.45	145.00	0.00	0.03	56.7	-60.1	8.85	-147.48
14.65	15.50	48.4	10.8	0.02	-0.28	150.00	0.00	0.04	44.8	-72.9	8.02	-133.64
9.95	10.30	39.1	15.7	0.05	-0.78	155.00	0.01	0.04	32.0	-96.7	7.10	-118.30
5.00	5.35	24.6	29.3	0.11	-1.76	160.00	0.05	0.09	21.2	-123.5	4.85	-80.88
1.01	1.08	17.2	80.4	0.98	-16.35	165.00	0.92	0.99	16.3	-84.8	1.02	-17.01
0.03	0.06	18.6	147.7	5.36	-89.32	170.00	4.80	5.10				
0.00	0.03	27.9	117.1	7.83	-130.58	175.00	9.75	10.15				
0.00	0.15					180.00	14.60	15.45	48.1	-10.7	0.03	-0.46
0.00	0.14					185.00	18.10	22.00	63.6	-8.0	0.03	-0.47
0.00	0.16					190.00	22.90	27.00				
0.00	0.14					195.00	28.00	32.00	79.1	-5.4	0.01	-0.19

These call options are out of the money.

The 165 call option is at the money.

These call options are in the money.

FIGURE 5.6

(Source: Morningstar.)

Trader Terminology: *The Greeks*

Some traders pay attention to the Greeks on the options chain, while others do not. You may choose to refer to the Greeks when you place options trades, or if you are new to trading options, you may choose to add this information to your trading plan as you become more familiar with options trading.

The Greeks represent how the price of an option is determined. The Greeks can help a trader choose an appropriate strike to place a trade. You can spend a lot of time learning to trade based on the Greeks, but basically I think it's important that you understand that time (theta), volatility (vega), and price of the underlying (delta) will affect the price of an option. Paying attention to delta, theta, and vega will help you decide which strike price is the best deal, especially for directional trades. There are other Greeks that can be used to form a trading opinion but, I concentrate on these three:

- *Delta* measures the option's reaction to changes in the price of the underlying. It is an estimation of how much the price of the option will move. A trader needs to know what strike has the highest delta and what strike has the lowest delta. As a general rule, delta increases as you select strikes that are deeper in the money. A delta of 1 means that every time the price of the underlying moves by $1, the option price will also change by $1. A delta of 0.70 would mean that every time the price of the underlying moves by $1, the option price will move by $0.70.

  An option that has a strike that is far out of the money will not have much reaction to any price moves of the underlying, and as such the delta will be low. Conversely, if you have a deep in-the-money option, the option price can almost move dollar for dollar with the price of the underlying. Delta is especially important to pay attention to if you want to place a trade where the option is currently being traded. (I will discuss using delta when we get to trading setups later in this chapter).

- *Theta* is an option's sensitivity to time. The further the option is away from expiry, the greater is the amount of theta in the price of the option. Theta is a component of an option's premium. Theta will decay or disappear as the option nears expiry. Theta decay works in favor of short puts and calls and against long puts and calls. Theta is a larger component of an option's price the further out from expiry the option is.

- *Vega* is a measure of the volatility of the underlying stock. The higher the volatility, the more vega premium the option will have. Vega changes constantly and can increase or decrease over an option's life. Increasing vega benefits long puts and calls, and decreasing vega benefits short puts and calls

Trader Terminology: *Standard Deviation*

Standard deviation is a mathematical calculation that shows the typical range of movement of the price of a stock or ETF option. Put most simply, it is the amount of movement expected in the price of the product you are trading over a specific time frame. The higher the standard deviation or volatility, the more you can expect price to move. Standard deviation measures the historical movement of stocks. Often traders will refer to 1 or 2 standard deviations as an expected move of a stock or ETF. Each standard-deviation move has a percentage of probability that it will be expected to move. Traders use this information to trade by assuming the stock's likelihood of moving a certain amount.

Mathematically speaking, a 1-standard-deviation move is expected to have a 32 percent probability of occurring, whereas a 2-standard-deviation move has a 6 percent probability of occurring. Naturally, it is easy to understand why many traders begin selling out-of-the-money options 2 standard deviations away. If they place this trade, mathematically, the odds are in their favor because they have a 94 percent chance that the trade will work for them. Most options trading platforms will calculate this information for you. A handy calculator is available at www.shecantrade.com.

The downside to trading 2 standard deviations away is that the premium you can collect is low. Sometimes the practicality of trading 2 standard deviations away doesn't provide enough premium to make the trade worthwhile; trading commissions sometimes take away the profits from a winning 2-standard-deviation trade. The other consideration for 2-standard-deviation trading is that it's not a 100 percent guarantee that the trade will work. Remember that 6 percent of the time the trade might not work out. If you are placing all your trades at 2 standard deviations away, but one trade (the 6 percent of the time) wipes out all your profits from the first nine trades, then all you are left with is commissions to pay to your broker and nothing in your pocket. When looking at targets for trades, take a look at the percentage chance that your stock will get there. Most options platforms provide this information, so you don't need to calculate it.

Sarah's Trading Tip

As I have traded options over time, I have stopped focusing solely on placing trades at either 1 or 2 standard deviations. I prefer to look at the charts and place my trades based on support and resistance levels instead. Trading at levels 2 standard deviations away just doesn't provide enough premium to collect versus the risk of maximum loss.

Trader Terminology: *Premium Decay*

To generalize, *premium decay* refers to how an option loses value over time. There are many ways to calculate premium and further details to learn about why premium decay occurs. Premium decay influences the price of the option. The change in premium becomes more pronounced as the option nears expiry.

Premium decay is good if you are the seller of an option, and it works against you if you are the buyer of an option.

Premium decay is what surprises most new traders who buy directionals out of the money. They place a directional trade by buying a call, the stock slowly moves up, and at the end of the month, their option loses value even though the stock went up—and they wonder why. To make money by buying out-of-the-money directional options, price movement must overcome premium decay. Premium decay is why I would never trade a directional that is out of the money. Instead I believe directionals should be placed in the money.

A Walk Through the Markets Part II

This walk-through is a continuation of the MasterCard (MA) example from Part I of Options Trader Terminology. The example below is to help you understand how trading terms are used to set up a trade. You will notice that I use two trading terms that haven't been defined yet. Spreads and directionals are ways to trade options. I will discuss the details of spreads and directionals in the next section of this chapter. Now that I have determined that MA is in a long trend, next I need to decide if I'm going to place a spread or a directional trade. To help me decide what type of trade to place, I will combine the information I see on the charts with the information from the options chain. Using the options chain (Figure 5.7), I determine the amount of credit that is available at different strike prices. I will confirm where the *1-standard-deviation* move has been calculated for MA this week to help me decide where I will sell the spread. Notice in Figure 5.7 that an out-of-the-money strike like the $580 put shows a bid of $0.58, and the ask is $0.88 with the weekly expiry. The $575 strike shows a bid of $0.20, and the ask is $0.36. To calculate my credit roughly, I subtract the $575 strike bid ($0.36) from the $580 strike ask ($0.58). If I decided to sell a $580/$575 put spread, I would be able to receive about a $0.22 credit (most trading platforms will do this calculation for you).

If I decided to buy a directional, I would look on the call side of the options chain and look for a strike that was deep in the money with a high delta. Looking at the delta column, I look for a strike that is usually between 60 and 80. In Figure 5.7 a strike that is in the money is $585.

Combining all of this information I will decide what is the best trade setup to use. If you are still learning these terms, you may want to review them regularly or learn more about them over time. Now that you've had some experience with the terms, let's focus our attention on trade strategies and setups.

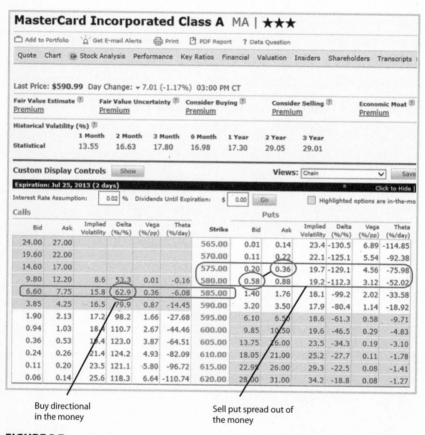

FIGURE 5.7

(Source: Morningstar.)

Sarah's Trading Tip

Even though I have been trading options for some time, I often come back to three basic trading setups. I usually trade options by selling credit spreads at levels that are considered at or out of the money and buying directionals. These are the trade setups that I will detail step by step later in this chapter. Even though other strategies can be added, in my experience, the simpler I keep the trades, the cleaner they are, and the easier they are to enter, manage, and exit. You can trade more complicated strategies. Trust me, there are a ton of them out there, but complicated doesn't mean better. With so many choices to trade within options, unlike many other things in life, you have options in options.

OPTIONS STRATEGIES

Now that you are aware of the key terminology in options, let's apply this information to understanding some ways to trade options. The option strategy that most people are familiar with is to place a trade by buying a call because they believe the market is going up, or buying a put because they believe the market is going down. This is referred to as trading directionally. There are many advantages to trading this way; it can yield higher profits and is flashy. But trading directionally isn't the only way to trade options. Different strategies are more appropriate for different market conditions, and each carries different risk/reward ratios. This should be a main consideration when choosing which strategy to use. Options traders make decisions about which trading strategy to use based on their assumption about market direction and momentum. One trader might place a trade by selling a call credit spread, another trader might choose to trade directionally. There is always more than one way to place a trade in options, even if multiple traders have the same assumption about market direction.

Ways to Trade Options: Credit Spreads

Credit spreads are a good place to get your feet wet in options. They provide the luxury of knowing your maximum loss and maximum gain and are a strategy that can be used by everyone, including those with small accounts. Credit spreads are also sometimes called *vertical spreads*. The basic premise behind a *credit spread* is to sell an option at one strike price and buy back another option at the next strike price to be used as insurance. The act of selling one strike and buying back another will produce a credit for a trader. This credit is the profit that the trader hopes to keep when the option expires.

Spreads allow you to benefit from differences in price between the credit you receive for the option you sell and the cost of the option you buy. The cost of the option you buy for insurance is less than the credit you receive for the option you have sold, leaving you with a net credit for the trade. This is the reason they are called *credit spreads*. The idea is to collect the credit that you sold the spread for and to let it expire worthless. Spreads provide the luxury of understanding the maximum profit and maximum loss of the trade before you enter it. Also, this means that you don't have to know exactly where the market will move; you are trading based on an assumption on which you can be slightly wrong and still make money. You can choose your strike prices for a spread by adjusting the width of the strike, the level of the strike, and the time until expiry.

Strategies that I have found to be profitable in trading spreads include selling four types of spreads (Table 5.5):

1. Selling out-of-the-money call spreads
2. Selling out-of-the-money put spreads
3. Selling at-the-money call spreads
4. Selling at-the-money put spreads

TABLE 5.5 How to choose which spread to use

Options to Trade the Option	Put Spread	Call Spread
At the money	Reduces risk compared with buying a call; you believe the stock price will increase with good momentum.	Reduces risk compared with buying a put; you believe the stock price will decrease with good momentum.

Options to Trade the Option	Put Spread	Call Spread
Out of the money	Selling a spread to collect a credit; you believe the stock will trade sideways or up.	Selling a spread to collect a credit; you believe the stock will trade sideways or down.

Call Credit Spreads

This strategy is used when your trading assumption is that you believe the price of the trading instrument will move sideways to down before the option expires. The trader will sell a call with a strike at one price and buy back a higher strike. The trader makes an assumption that the stock will not go higher than the option she sold at expiry.

Since call spreads can be sold at different levels, a trader will decide between selling a call spread either *at* or *out* of the money. Depending on the risk that the trader wants to assume, she can choose to stay well away from the price at which the stock is being traded by placing a trade that is out of the money, or she can sell an at-the-money call spread that is trading near the current price of the stock.

Call credit spreads at the money will generate more credit for the trader, but there is also a higher probability that the spread will not be profitable. The trader assumes that when he sells an at-the-money call spread, the stock will have a strong move lower.

Out-of-the-money call credit spreads primarily take advantage of premium decay. A trader places a call spread that is out of the money because she wants to stay away from the current price of the underlying. She is placing a trade where she thinks the price of the stock will NOT go before it expires. As long as the stock does not have a large move against your position, your spread will expire and you will be at maximum profit on that trade.

Call credit spreads offer the ability for traders to know their maximum risk when they initiate the trade.

Steps to Trade a Call Spread

1. Trading assumption is that the stock is going down.
2. Look at charts—weekly and daily—for levels of support and resistance.
3. Pull up the options chain.
4. Determine a strike price that is above the resistance levels identified in step 2.
5. Sell a call at the strike price you have identified, and buy a call one strike higher than the call you sold.

Let's take a look at TLT as a candidate for a call credit spread both at the money and out of the money. Figure 5.8a shows the options chain for iShares' 20+ Year Treasury Bond ETF (TLT). Figure 5.8b is the corresponding chart of TLT. As you can see, TLT is in a downtrend and is a candidate for a call credit spread. It could be traded at the money and out of the money depending on how much lower you think it will move.

Notice in Figure 5.8a that by selling the $105/$106 call credit spread at the money, you are able to take in approximately $0.36 in credit per contract. If you wanted to increase your credit, you could trade a $5 wide spread. If you sold the $105/$110 spread, you could take in a $1.08 credit, but your risk also would be higher. You must have a strong belief that the stock is going to continue to decrease in price before expiry if you place a trade as an at-the-money spread.

Using the same chart in Figure 5.8b, a trader could also place a credit spread out of the money. If you think that the stock is going to continue its downtrend but you are not sure whether the momentum will remain as strong, you can consider placing an out-of-the money call credit spread. You will take in less credit, but an out-of-the-money spread has a higher rate of success. In this case, you could use the 50-period exponential moving average (EMA) off the 60-minute chart as support, and you can sell a $5 wide spread such as the $108/$113 and take in $0.31. You take in less credit, but the probability that you have a successful trade is higher than if you trade at the money.

Put Credit Spreads

This strategy is used when your trading assumption is that you believe that the price of the stock will move sideways to up before the option expires. To place a trade as a put credit spread, a trader will sell a put option at one level and buy back a put option at a lower level with the same expiry. The trader buys back an option at a lower level as protection just in case the stock moves past that strike. Depending on the risk that the trader wants to assume, he can choose to stay well away from the price at which the stock

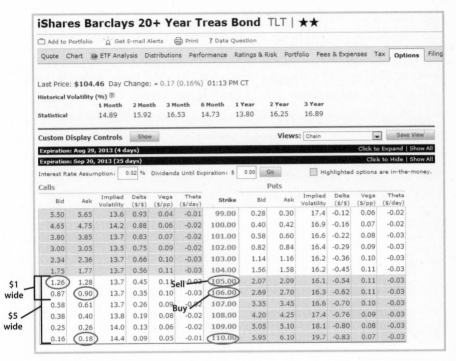

At the money credit spread 1.26 – .90 = 0. 36

FIGURE 5.8a (Source: Morningstar.)

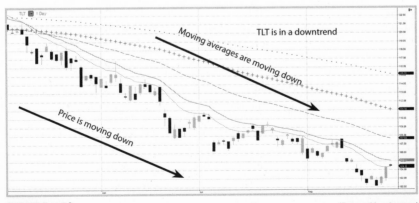

FIGURE 5.8b (Source: Morningstar.)

is being traded by placing a trade that is out of the money, or he can sell an at-the-money put spread that is trading near the current price of the stock. Put credit spreads at the money will generate more credit for the trader, but there is also a higher probability that the spread will not be profitable. Selling a put spread at the money means that you anticipate that the stock price will have a strong move up, but you want to limit your risk.

Out-of-the-money put credit spreads primarily take advantage of premium decay. As long as the stock does not have a large move against your position, your spread will expire at maximum profit. Both at-the-money and out-of-the-money spreads take advantage of the bought put limiting losses if the stock price decreases. Put credit spreads provide the ability for traders to know their maximum risk when they initiate the trade.

Steps to Trade a Put Spread

1. Trading assumption is that the stock is going up.
2. Look at charts—weekly and daily—for levels of support and resistance.
3. Pull up the options chain.
4. Determine a strike price that is below the support levels identified in step 2.
5. Sell a put at the strike price you have identified, and buy a put one strike lower than the put you sold.

Let's take a look at NFLX (Figure 5.9) as a candidate for a put credit spread both at the money and out of the money. Figure 5.9b shows that NFLX is in an uptrend. Based on this chart, a trader can choose to place a spread either at the money or out of the money depending on how much he thinks NFLX will move before the option expires. Figure 5.9a shows the options chain for Netflix (NFLX).

Since price seems to be really moving up, you could consider placing this trade at the money. By selling the $285/$280 put credit spread at the money, you are able to take in about $1.44 in credit per contract. You must have a strong belief that the stock is going to continue to increase in price before expiry if you choose to trade at the money.

If you think that the stock is going to continue its uptrend but you are not sure whether the momentum will remain as strong, you can con-

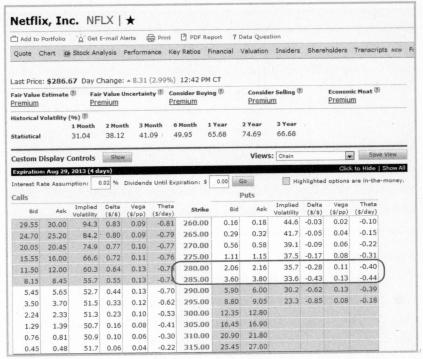

Calls							Puts					
Bid	Ask	Implied Volatility	Delta ($/$)	Vega ($/pp)	Theta ($/day)	Strike	Bid	Ask	Implied Volatility	Delta ($/$)	Vega ($/pp)	Theta ($/day)
29.55	30.00	94.3	0.83	0.09	-0.81	260.00	0.16	0.18	44.6	-0.03	0.02	-0.10
24.70	25.20	84.2	0.80	0.09	-0.79	265.00	0.29	0.32	41.7	-0.05	0.04	-0.15
20.05	20.45	74.9	0.77	0.10	-0.77	270.00	0.56	0.58	39.1	-0.09	0.06	-0.22
15.55	16.00	66.6	0.72	0.11	-0.76	275.00	1.11	1.15	37.5	-0.17	0.08	-0.31
11.50	12.00	60.3	0.64	0.13	-0.76	280.00	2.06	2.16	35.7	-0.28	0.11	-0.40
8.15	8.45	55.7	0.55	0.13	-0.76	285.00	3.60	3.80	33.6	-0.43	0.13	-0.44
5.45	5.65	52.7	0.44	0.13	-0.70	290.00	5.90	6.00	30.2	-0.62	0.13	-0.39
3.50	3.70	51.5	0.33	0.12	-0.62	295.00	8.80	9.05	23.3	-0.85	0.08	-0.18
2.24	2.33	51.3	0.23	0.10	-0.53	300.00	12.35	12.80				
1.29	1.39	50.7	0.16	0.08	-0.41	305.00	16.45	16.90				
0.76	0.81	50.9	0.10	0.06	-0.30	310.00	20.90	21.80				
0.45	0.48	51.7	0.06	0.04	-0.22	315.00	25.45	27.60				

FIGURE 5.9a   *(Source: Morningstar.)*

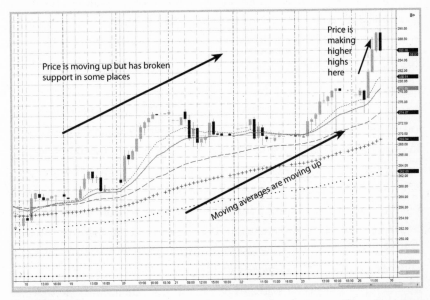

FIGURE 5.9b   *(Source: Morningstar.)*

sider placing an out-of-the-money put credit spread. You will take in less premium, but your chances of the spread expiring in the money are higher. In this case, you could use the 50-period EMA off the 60-minute chart as support and sell the $275/$270 put credit spread, taking in $0.53 cents of premium. You take in less credit, but the probability that you have a successful trade is higher than if you buy at the money.

Other Trading Strategies to Consider

Other trading strategies to consider include iron condors, calendars, butterflies, straddles, strangles, debit spreads, and naked puts. These strategies are ways that I will trade occasionally. I have included a brief definition of these strategies below.

Iron Condors

An *iron condor* is a put spread and a call spread both placed at the same time. This trading setup is applied when you think that the market is moving sideways. The goal is to sell out-of-the-money put and call spreads outside of where you think the price of the stock will be at expiry. It's like a sandwich. As long as the stock price stays in the middle of the put spread and call spread you sold, the iron condor will be successful.

This strategy can feel like a conservative trade setup because you take in a larger credit, but remember that it will remain conservative only in a sideways market. Trying to place iron condors in a market that is moving up or down will not be successful.

Calendars

A *calendar* is created when a trader sells an option at a front month and buys back at a later month; for example, selling a July call and buying back an August call with the same strike price. This trade setup takes advantage of time decay in the near expiry contract. The idea is that the July call will lose value faster than the August call. When the July call nears $0, you will buy back the both the July and August calls or let the July call expire worthless and buy back the August call. For example the July call might lose $0.20 of value and the August call will lose only $0.10 of value. You pocket the difference ($0.20 − 0.10 = $0.10). The idea is to take small amounts of profit, typically selling at the money. Because there is more time value in the later month, the risk is that the volatility will spike, which will result in premium going up in the long-term option more than the credit you took in on the short-dated option.

Straddles

A *straddle* is buying a put and a call at the same strike price. The strike price selected is the one closest to the current price of the stock. This strategy can be applied when a trader is expecting a big move in the stock or ETF but is unsure of the direction of the move. If the stock goes up, you will make money on your call, and your put will become worthless. If the stock goes down, the put will make you money, and the call will expire worthless. This play takes advantage of an increase in volatility. If the stock has a small or no move, then both your put and your call will lose money. Typically, the stock needs to have a change in price that is larger than the combined cost of the put and call in order for you to make money on the trade. For instance, if you pay a total of $6.50 for the straddle, then the stock must move up or down more than $6.50 for you to make money. It is difficult to make money trading straddles because most of the time volatility decreases after a large move and most large moves are preceded by an increase in premium. As the buyer of a straddle, you are also fighting time decay. If the large move does not happen soon enough, time value is working against you and decreasing the value of the straddle.

Strangles

A *strangle* is a straddle that is one or more strikes wide. Traders will choose a strangle over a straddle when they have a bias about the direction in which the stock will move. The stronger your bias, the more strikes wide you will place the trade. A strangle is placed by buying either the put or call at the money and the other side of the trade one or more strikes away from the current price of the stock.

Butterfly

A *butterfly* trade is set up when a trader feels that she knows the price at which the stock will close by the time it expires. In order to profit from a butterfly, the stock price must close exactly at the strike you traded the butterfly. A butterfly is selling two calls or two puts at the strike price where you think the stock will be at expiry and buying one contract of the same type and expiry on either side of the sold strike (one contract lower and one contract higher). The wider the width of the butterfly (the distance between the sold strike and the strike you buy), the more the trade will cost, and the more you can potentially lose if the trade goes against you—but the more you can profit if the trade works out in your favor. The most you can make is the difference between the middle and upper strike prices less what you paid for the butterfly. Your trade may be slightly profitable if the stock price is between the bought and sold strikes at expiry depending on what you paid for the butterfly, but in reality, you will not make much money unless you are very close to the sold strike at expiry. It does not really matter if you buy a put butterfly or a call butterfly; they will each lead to the same result at expiry. For example, if you wanted to buy a put butterfly on IBM in anticipation of IBM closing at $100 on expiry, you would sell two IBM $100 puts, buy one IBM $105 put and one IBM $95 put with the same expiry.

Naked Puts

I wanted to write about this strategy because it is a strategy that sounds very appealing, but just as the name suggests, traders need to ensure that they understand the risks. *Naked puts* are usually traded out of the money and far away from the current price of the stock. A put is sold if you think that the stock price will go up or sideways. The goal is that the trade expires worthless, and the trader keeps all the credit received when the put was sold. The warning with this type of trade is that it will take up a large margin in your account, and if the trade goes against you, it can go wrong very quickly. Losses can be very high; maximum loss would occur if the stock went to $0. Just as the Trading Tip comic on page 143 suggests, make sure that this trade looks good from all angles if you are going to use this trading strategy.

Debit Spreads

A *debit spread* is very similar to a credit spread, but it has some key differences. A debit spread is bought; you pay for the spread and make money by selling it for more than you paid for it. Debit spreads are traded in the

Illustrated by Noble Rains

same direction as a long option. If you think that the stock is going up, you would buy a call debit spread by buying the strike you are interested in and selling a strike lower for protection. A put debit spread would be bought if you believe that the stock price is going down. You would buy the put at a strike you are interested in and sell a strike lower for protection. Because you are buying the spread, if the stock price moves sideways, time decay works against you, and there is the potential for your spread to expire for less than you paid for it. The debit spread works well at the money and in the money. When trading at the money, carefully compare the risk and return to buying versus selling a spread. Pick the spread that offers the best risk/reward ratio.

Figure 5.10 illustrates the preceding trading strategies and indicates why you would follow them at different times.

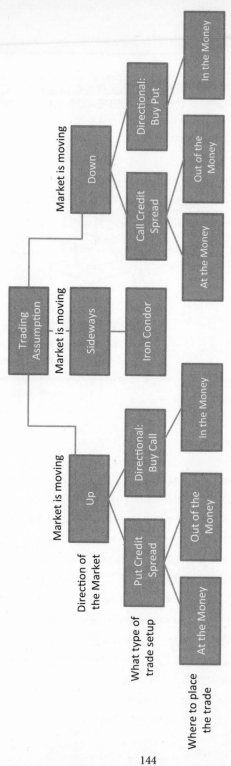

FIGURE 5.10

144

Sarah's Trading Tip

When you begin trading options, choose a few strategies to begin with, and then expand your trading strategies from there. Just because you know how to trade many options strategies doesn't mean that you will make any more money than sticking with a few options trading setups that you know how to trade well. I typically stick to selling out-of-the-money spreads, selling at the money spreads and directional trades. There are times when I will use some of the other trading strategies, but they are not my main go-to strategies.

If I think that the market is moving up, I will consider these three ways to trade most often:

1. *Buy a call for a directional trade in the money*
2. *Sell a put spread at the money*
3. *Sell a put spread out of the money*

If I think that the market is going down, I will consider these three ways to trade most often:

1. *Buy a put for a directional trade in the money*
2. *Sell a call spread at the money*
3. *Sell a call spread out of the money*

The Five Ws of Options Strategies

Table 5.6 has some key pieces of information about many of the strategies just described. It shows the *what, when, where, why,* and *who* of options strategies. It should help any trader differentiate between the various options strategies that can be traded.

TABLE 5.6 The 5Ws of options strategies

Strategy	What	When	Where	Why	Who
Selling an out-of-the-money put spread	You sell a put and buy another put one strike lower as protection with the same expiry. You make money from the credit you receive when you sell the spread.	When your trading assumption is that the stock or ETF is going up or sideways.	Out of the money, where you don't think the price of the trading instrument will close.	You want to know what your maximum gain and maximum loss will be.	Part-time trader Full-time trader Small account strategy
Selling an out-of-the-money call spread	You sell a call and buy another call one strike higher as protection with the same expiry. You make money from the credit you receive when you sell the spread.	When your trading assumption is that the stock or ETF is going down or sideways.	Out of the money	You want to know what your maximum loss and maximum gain will be before you enter the trade.	Part-time trader Full-time trader Small account strategy

Strategy	What	When	Where	Why	Who
Buying a put spread	You buy a put and sell a put one strike lower to offset the cost of the put.	Your trading assumption is that the stock or ETF is going lower.	At the money or slightly in the money.	You want to short the stock or ETF but want to limit your risk.	Part-time trader Full-time trader Small account strategy
Buying a call spread	You buy a call and sell a call one strike higher to offset the cost of the call.	Your trading assumption is that the stock or ETF is going higher.	At the money or slightly in the money.	You want to buy the stock or ETF but want to limit your risk.	Part-time trader Full-time trader Small account strategy
Selling an at-the-money put spread	You sell one put at a strike price and buy back at a lower price as protection; you make money by keeping the amount of credit you sold it for.	Your trading assumption is that the stock or ETF is going up.	At the money.	You want to know what your maximum gain and maximum loss will be.	Part-time trader (aggressive) Full-time trader Small account strategy

TABLE 5.6 The 5Ws of options strategies (*continued*)

Stategy	What	When	Where	Why	Who
Iron Condor	You place a trade on either side of where you think the stock will expire. As long as the stock stays within your range, you make money.	You think the market is going sideways; you make money by collecting a credit from the call spread and put spread that is outside of the range you think the stock will move.	Out of the money. You have defined risk and reward before you enter the trade.	Only one side can be a potential maximum loss; the credit from the other side will help offset the loss.	Part-time trader Full-time trader Small account strategy
Naked put	Selling a put without protection.	You choose a strike where price is statistically unlikely to expire below.	Far out of the money.	You want to collect premium based on time decay or take advantage of high implied volatility in the option.	Full-time trader Large account required

Strategy	What	When	Where	Why	Who
Selling an at-the-money call spread	You sell one call at a strike price and buy back at a higher price as protection; you make money by keeping the amount of credit you sold it for.	Your trading assumption is that the stock or ETF is going down.	At the money.	You want to know what your maximum loss and maximum gain will be before you enter the trade.	Part-time trader (aggressive) Full-time trader Small account strategy
Buying a put	You can buy a put in the money or out of the money.	Your trading assumption is that the stock price is going down.	In the money or out of the money; the further out of the money, the more risk, and the further in the money, the more the option will behave like the underlying stock.	You do not want to limit your gains, and you want to know the most you can lose on the trade.	Part-time trader Full-time trader Small account strategy Large account strategy

TABLE 5.6 The 5Ws of options strategies (*continued*)

Strategy	What	When	Where	Why	Who
Buying a call	You can buy a call in the money or out of the money.	Your trading assumption is that the stock price is going up.	In the money or out of the money; the further out of the money, the more risk, and the further in the money, the more the option will behave like the underlying stock.	You do not want to limit your gains, and you want to know the most you can lose on the trade.	Part-time trader Full-time trader Small account strategy Large account strategy
Buying a straddle	Buy a put and call at the same strike price.	You believe that the stock will make a big move, but you are unsure of the direction of the move.	At the money.	You want a limited-loss trade that will capitalize on a large move in the stock.	Part-time trader Full-time trader Small account strategy Large account strategy

Strategy	What	When	Where	Why	Who
Buying a strangle	Buy an at-the-money put or call and buy the opposite option a few strikes higher or lower.	You believe that the stock will make a big move, but you are unsure of the size of the move, but you have a bias in one direction over the other.	At the money.	You want a limited-loss trade that will capitalize on a large move in the stock, and you have a bias in one direction over the other.	Part-time trader Full-time trader Small account strategy Large account strategy
Calendar spread	Sell an at-the-money put or call for the current expiry month and buy the same option at the same strike price a month further out.	You think that the stock price will not move much, and you want to capitalize on the premium erosion of the front-month option.	At the money.	You want to trade premium erosion and a decrease in stock volatility.	Part-time trader Full-time trader Small account strategy Large account strategy

How to Select Trades

As you can tell from the Table 5.7, there are many options strategies available. Even though there are many ways to trade based on market conditions, the reality is that you shouldn't be trading just to place a trade; this is not how traders succeed. In order to be most profitable, each trader needs a process to determine when it is most beneficial to use a specific trading setup based on his market assumption.

Sarah's Trading Tip

I like to trade liquid stocks when I trade options. Some of my trading rules are listed below. I look for high volatility or beta and typically trade stocks and ETFs with weekly options. Sometimes, I might trade a week or two away, but I usually stick with the current week's expiration. I like to collect decent credit, especially when I'm selling spreads. So just because a chart might look good, if I can't collect enough credit, I won't place the trade. In fact, I probably have more trading rules on when not to trade than on when to trade.

Before you decide what options strategy you will trade, you will need to weigh the following:

- What is the assumption from my chart analysis?
- How much will it cost me to place the trade? How much credit can I collect?
- How much time is left before expiry?
- How much has the stock moved in the past? Is it a big mover, or does it usually move slowly in one direction or the other?
- What is my risk in the trade?
- What are my trading rules associated with each trade setup?

Options traders can choose from many strategies to trade options, I recommend using the preceding questions to determine the most appropriate options strategy to use.

Basically, at the root of all options trade setups is an assumption that the market is moving up, sideways, or down to varying degrees. Traders must consider what direction they believe the market is moving and also the momentum of the move in order to choose a strategy to trade. Once a trader makes the decision about the direction of the stock, the next decision is time. In options, traders must consider how long they believe it will take for that stock to make the move they have anticipated. Because options expire, traders need to have an assumption about how long it will take the market to go up, down, or remain sideways and buy or sell the option that will expire within that time frame. Once a trader has made a decision about direction and timing, the trader will consider appropriate trade setups to use based on defined risk as outlined in the trader's trading plan. Once all these factors have been evaluated, the trader will use this information to place a trade in options.

UNDERSTANDING THE LEVEL AT WHICH TO PLACE A TRADE

As shown in Figure 5.11, each strategy carries a different risk and reward.

FIGURE 5.11

Each level provides a different risk and reward. Generally, directionals are considered more risky, whereas selling out-of-the-money spreads can be considered less risky. This level of risk, however, is relative to the amount of money each trade can make or lose. Each trader needs to find a balance between placing trades that create enough profit over time while considering that some of the trades that don't work out shouldn't wipe out all the profits made previously. As traders gain more experience trading options, they will refine this balance of placing trades at different levels of risk/reward.

Sarah's Trading Tip

My strategy has always been to keep my trades diversified. I place different types of trades so that I have some trades placed with directionals and others with spreads. The behavior of the market at the time determines the strategy and level at which I place a trade. I believe that it is better to be diversified than place all my trades using the same strategy.

Some traders also determine the level at which they place trades based on standard deviations. Placing a trade at 1 or 2 standard deviations provides a mathematical probability that the trade will not move to that level. Standard deviations can be calculated manually, although most trading platforms calculate them for you. These levels of standard deviation can be used as a guide when you're deciding the level at which to place a trade, but in my opinion, they shouldn't be used as the sole piece of information to determine a level at which to place a trade.

There is a fallacy about conservative trading using standard deviation that exists in options trading to which, I believe, many new traders fall victim. Some traders will feel a false sense of security by placing a trade at 2 standard deviations away. Mathematically speaking, a trade that is placed out of the money at 2 standard deviations has more than a 90 percent chance of expiring worthless and thus making money. Traders believe that because of the mathematical odds that this level will work out, they can place this trade without worrying about the risk/reward ratio. However, this is a perfect example of how important it is to consider the amount of money a trade can make versus how much the trade can lose. Taking a 2-standard-deviation trade may be tempting, but if you are not taking in enough credit when you sell the option or spread, then your risk/reward ratio will prevent you from being profitable—it's simple math. All it takes is one trade (that small percent of the time) to wipe out all the profits from the previous winning trades.

Keep in mind that standard deviations in options are a rough guide and do not hold true all the time. There is risk in any trade. Remember that the risk/reward ratio is what should guide your trades. Don't stereotype all types of spreads at certain levels as riskier than others; this should only be a guide. Always be mindful of the cost and benefits of each trade strategy as it pertains to the markets that day. Risk is always relative.

Why Buy Directionally?

The purpose of buying directionally is to participate in a move made by the underlying trading instrument. Generally a trader will place a directional trade because she is expecting the trading instrument to really move. The trader expects that by the time the option expires, the price she paid will change in her favor so that she can sell it and make a profit. Directional trades are often considered more risky because they require a large move to be profitable.

Think of choosing between a spread and directional trades in the same way that concert tickets are sold. Some people are willing to pay a bit of a premium to be in a seat that is closer to the stage. They will have to pay a little more than someone who buys seats in the "nosebleed section." Anyone looking to buy a concert ticket needs to weigh how much she is willing to pay for the ticket versus how close she wants to be to the stage. Both ticket holders will hear the concert, but each can have a different experience. However, both ticket holders will look for what they believe is the best deal for them. Each trading strategy will have a different outcome, but each trader should always feel that whatever type of trade setup he used was the best deal for him.

Directional trades can be more lucrative than spreads, provided that the underlying moves far enough away from the strike price before expiry. When trading directionally, traders need to consider the impact the trade will have on their account size if the trade does not work out as anticipated. Even though it might seem enticing to always trade directionally because of the potential to make more money per trade, if the trade moves in an opposite direction to what was anticipated, the maximum loss also will be higher. Buying directionally can cost more and can take up more margin in your trading account. Because traders need room in their account to place several trades, allocating capital is a decision that is influenced by the type of trade you place.

The more a premium is affecting the price of the option, the more it also influences profitability because it will cost more to buy the option. Because of this expense, there will be times when traders may want to trade directionally in a specific stock but feel that it is too expensive. Such traders may then look at the correlated market or index to see if it will cost less to place a similar trade. For example, if Amazon (AMZN) looks like it is in a nice rally but is going to cost $5.25 to trade directionally, a trader might consider the SPY, which would cost $1.69 for a similar trade.

Sarah's Trading Tip

I will choose to trade directionally when there is a lot of momentum behind a move in a particular instrument. When I am considering directionals, I always consider whether it is best to place a directional trade in a stock or trade the index. I prefer to find the best deal, which means finding the cheapest instrument to buy that will still align with my risk/reward parameters.

Trading Directionally Versus Spreads

Making the decision to trade directionally versus spreads is based on several factors, as well as your preference. Depending on your risk/reward parameters, the momentum of the trading instrument and the amount of credit available will influence whether you choose to trade directionally or with a spread. It makes more sense to place a directional trade if a trader believes that there will be a big move in the trading instrument. If the trader feels that there will be a small, grinding move, then a spread will be more favorable. Because it typically costs more to buy a directional trade, a trader will need to weigh the risk and reward versus the risk and reward of a spread, given that a spread might cost less but have a smaller profit. When you are considering whether to place a directional trade or spread, you might consider the following:

1. What is the credit that can be collected at the money and out of the money?
2. Is it better to buy the option or sell a spread?
3. Is the momentum of the stock high or low?
4. What level offers the best risk/reward: in the money, at the money, or out of the money?

Let's look at some examples and then decide whether to trade using a spread or directional trade. Choose a spread if

- *Volatility is high.* Volatility will increase the credit that you can receive if you sell the spread.
- *The trading instrument is in a slow, grinding move.*
- *You like to sell out of the money.* You prefer to place trades away from the price action.
- *You like to get to know your maximum gain and maximum loss before you enter a trade.* Perhaps the benefits of knowing a maximum gain and maximum profit before the trade is entered is reason enough to stick with spreads.
- *You believe that a big move has already happened.* It will be beneficial to trade using a spread out of the money if the trader feels that a big move has already occurred and/or there is less time before the contract expires.

Choose a directional if

- *You believe that there is good momentum.* A big, fast move based on price action will benefit a directional trade.
- *A trading instrument is in a strong trend.* If the trading instrument is making higher highs or lower lows across different time frame charts.
- *In anticipation of a large move, you do not want to limit your profits, like with a spread.*
- *If you think that trading directionally will offer you the best deal.*

Sarah's Trading Tip

It's important to understand that even though many traders have the same trading assumption about market direction, they can each place different options trades. The variety of ways to trade options provides an advantage of choice based on risk parameters with which you are comfortable, unlike other trading instruments. I might look at the market and think that it is going long and place a spread, whereas another trader might agree that the market is moving long but place a directional trade. As with any other trading instrument, each decision in the markets is a personal one that should reflect your own trading parameters as outlined in your trading plan.

Examples of Choosing a Spread Versus a Directional

Together we will walk through examples of trades, and I will share why I would make the decision to trade a spread versus directionally. First, take a look at Figures 5.12a and 5.12b (one day and 60-minute chart for XOM).

I would choose to trade ExxonMobile (XOM) as a spread because the 60-minute chart shows a strong downtrend, but the daily trend is not as strong. Since the daily trend is a bit of a mixed trend, I would like to limit my risk and trade a spread. Thus, if XOM pulls back a little, I can still profit from time decay and am not entirely reliant on the strong 60-minute downtrend continuing.

Figure 5.13a shows one daily chart, and Figure 5.13b for Netflix (NFLX).

I would trade Netflix (NFLX) directionally because the daily chart is in an uptrend. The 60-minute chart shows that the 21 EMA held as support and price has resumed the trend to the upside. The last few bars on the 60-minute chart show price is making higher highs every bar. NFLX looks like it is about to make a new high. I believe this stock is showing good momentum to the upside. I would use a directional trade.

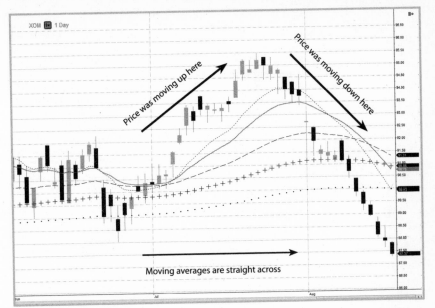

XOM 1 Day

Price was moving up here

Price was moving down here

Moving averages are straight across

FIGURE 5.12a

(Source: MultiCharts.)

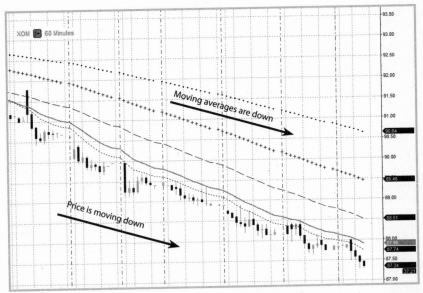

XOM 60 Minutes

Moving averages are down

Price is moving down

FIGURE 5.12b

(Source: MultiCharts.)

FIGURE 5.13a

(Source: MultiCharts.)

FIGURE 5.13b

(Source: MultiCharts.)

Figure 5.14*a* and Figure 5.14*b* are charts for Staples (SPLS).

Staples (SPLS) is in a nice uptrend on the daily chart, but the 60-minute chart is mixed. I believe that the trend will continue, but I do not neccessarly have the confidence that it will not have some pullbacks or consolidation. Because of this, I will sell a spread and take advantage of the ability to control my risk. I would trade SPLS to the upside using a put spread.

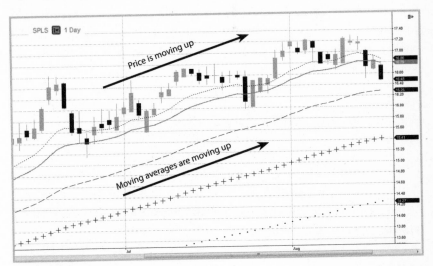

FIGURE 5.14a   *(Source: MultiCharts.)*

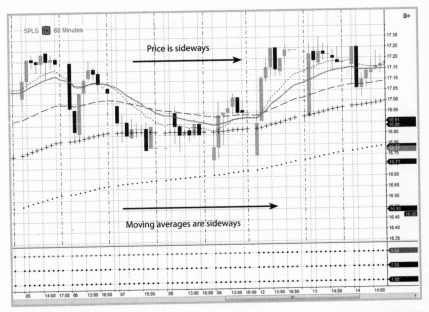

FIGURE 5.14b   *(Source: MultiCharts.)*

Entries and Exits

Once a trader has made the decision about the market direction, which strategy to use, and the level at which to place the trade, now she must set up her trade on her trading platform and make the decision as to when to actually enter the trade. Trades can be placed at any time; however, you always want to be mindful of getting the best deal and therefore the best entry.

Understanding when to wait for a pullback in the markets in order to enter at a good price and understanding when to get into a trade to catch momentum require a delicate balance. Most often traders will wait for a slight pullback before entering.

Sarah's Trading Tip

One good way to know if your trading assumption is right is if it takes a long time for your trade to get filled. Most often, if you are right, it will take longer to execute the trade. Don't be discouraged when you have placed your trade but you don't get filled. You are probably right and need to be patient to get in.

Entries and exits vary based on how aggressive a trader you are and the options strategy you are using. For example, if you are trading a weekly option directionally; for example, long a put or call, then your entries need to be more precise. If you are trading a monthly spread that is out of the money, then you do not need to be as precise on your entries.

Entries should be timed so that you are not buying the highs and selling the lows. If you are a trend trader, one way to help improve your entries is to wait for a pullback before you place a trade. This means that if the stock is in an uptrend, you will wait until there is a pullback to the downside before you place your buy order.

If you take a look at Figure 5.15, you can see that Apple (AAPL) is a candidate for a long trade, but where to enter? Let's look at the chart and see what it can tell us.

As you can see, AAPL is extended and has pulled away from the 13-period EMA. Over the last few days, AAPL has found support at the

13- and 21-period EMAs. If you think that AAPL is a buy, then wait until it retraces to the 13- or 21-period EMA, and look to enter your trade there. This will increase your odds of success. A good entry is to wait until the $506 or $508 level is reached and not to buy at the current price of $512.

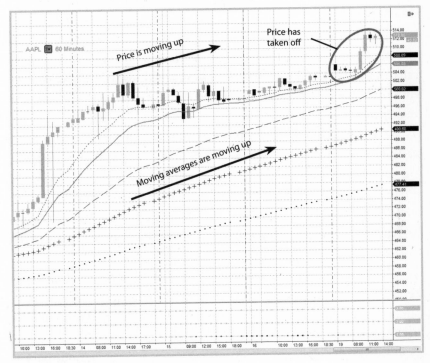

FIGURE 5.15   *(Source: MultiCharts.)*

Exits work in much the same way, except that strategies such as spreads do not always need to be exited. Ideally a credit spread expires worthless which means that the trader keeps the entire credit she received when she sold it. The goal of credit spreads is to have them expire worthless which means you keep the entire credit. There may be times it makes sense to close the spread out prior to expiry, if price is nearing your sold strike and you are worried that your trade might expire with a loss. To close or exit the spread, a trader has two choices. He can buy back the entire spread or save on commissions and buy back only the option he sold, removing all his risk from the trade. The remaining long option is a risk-free position. Closing spreads prior to expiry is a personal decision and is really up to the individual trader.

Now if a trader has a losing position, there are ways to roll the trade or add another leg to the trade. My personal feeling however is that if you have a losing trade, its best to get out of it and move on to find another trade.

When a trader places spreads, she needs to be concerned about a few different scenarios when the option expires. If the option on a credit spread expires worthless, a trader has reached her maximum gain. If the price of the option on a credit spread has moved well past the strikes she chose to trade the spread at, it will be at maximum loss. The long and short positions will offset themselves at expiry.

Now if the option has value or partial value at expiry, a trader will need to act accordingly if she doesn't want to be assigned the underlying. If at expiry you hold an option that has value, you will be assigned the underlying stock. If you do not have enough money in your account to cover the assignment or if you do not want to own the stock, then you need to make sure that you get out of any positions prior to the end of the day that it expires.

If you have a spread and the price of the underlying at expiry is between the strike of the option you sold and the strike of the option you purchased, you will also be assigned the underlying stock. Thus you need to close out the spread before expiry.

As you can tell, if you trade options, expiry days can be quite busy as you close out and manage trades.

Sarah's Trading Tip

There will be times when your timing is just right, and on entering a trade, your profit targets will be reached right away. Sometimes you will have a tendency to change your profit target to another level instead of exiting a trade with the profit. If you are in a trade and make more than what you had anticipated, get out of the trade and put the money in your pocket. Trust me. You will be very upset if all your profits turn right around and become a loss. Don't let a great profit turn into a missed opportunity. Pocket the profits, and move on to the next trade.

Ready, Set, Trade

Now that we have reviewed many important concepts about trading options, I want to share the ways that I trade most often. My top three trading strategies are outlined below step by step. I will place these three trades with some weekly and some monthly expiries depending on the market at the time. As I'm reviewing charts, I will always think about which of these three strategies is best to use to trade that particular trading instrument at that time.

Sarah's Trading Tip

I have noticed that I frequently have a number of these trades on at the same time. I try to manage the risk in my account by using all three types of trades at one time. I rarely have only directionals traded at once; instead, my account usually has some spreads and some directionals with a variety of expirations in different trading instruments at one time. This diversity allows me to better manage my risk.

All three of these trading setups begin with the market analysis described in Chapter 4. Once I have reviewed the market and determined a trend, I go to my next level of analysis to decide which strategy to use. Please read the following disclaimer and reflect on it; it is important that you consider your risk before you place any kind of trade.

Disclaimer

Trading options involves substantial risk of loss and is not suitable for all investors. You should carefully consider whether trading options is suitable for you in light of your circumstances, knowledge, and financial resources. You may lose all or more of your initial investment. Consult your registered financial representative before investing any of your money. No investing recommendations are being made in this book. Always trade following your own plan.

You need to modify these trade setups based on your trading plan and the markets you will be trading.

SARAH'S TOP THREE OPTIONS TRADING STRATEGIES

These three strategies are the ones I use most often:

1. Out-of-the-money call and put spreads
2. At-the-money call and put spreads
3. Directional trades (puts and calls)

Trading Tools for These Trading Strategies

I begin by looking to find a trading instrument that is trending. I use market internals as well as the ES to determine whether there is a well-established trend in the correlated market and the actual trading instrument I am considering.

The market internals I review include:

- TICKs index
- NYSE Advance Decline Line (ADD)
- Average True Range (ATR)
- Correlated broad market (typically the ES) and Foundations indicator

I look at all of these market internals together to determine whether I believe that there is a trend in the trading instrument I am analyzing and whether it will continue moving up or down. I look for solid signs of evidence about the market direction by determining:

- Whether the TICKs index is staying well below or above zero.
- Whether the ADD is positive or negative.
- What is the value of the ATR? What is happening in the ES or other correlated market? What is appearing on the Foundations indicator.

Once I have confirmation based on these steps, I move my attention to selecting the options strategy I want to use at that time. I use my trading rules for each type of strategy to determine which one will provide the best risk/reward ratio at that time.

The time-frame charts I use are:

- Weekly
- Daily
- 60-minute with the Foundations indicator

The moving averages on these charts include the:

- 200-period moving average
- 100-period moving average
- 50-period moving average
- 21-period moving average
- 13-period moving average

Selling Out-of-the-Money Put and Call Credit Spreads

What Is This Trade About?

An out-of-the-money spread is a spread that I sell in order to collect a credit in my account. I trade this spread specifically at levels that are out of the money, choosing strike prices that I believe are outside where I think the price movement of that trading instrument will be. This strategy is about collecting premium and waiting until the contract expires by staying well away from the price level at which the stock is being traded.

Why Choose This Setup Versus Another?

An out-of-the-money spread takes advantage of markets that have already had a big move, or a slow trend without too much movement, or a sideways market. Out-of-the-money spreads will provide less profit than at-the-money spreads, but they can be less stressful because the point of this type of trade is to stay outside of the current market price as opposed to relying on a big move.

This type of trade will spread the risk by selling a certain number of contracts at one strike price while also buying back the same number of contracts with a lower strike price with the same expiry as protection. When traders use a spread, they are able to calculate how much their maximum loss and maximum gain will be prior to entering the trade.

Trading Rules and Look-Fors: Selling Out-of-the-Money Spreads

1. Slow, grinding, or sideways market (trend appears but doesn't have large movements either up or down)
2. High premium (might be a result of high volatility)
3. Strong levels of support or resistance to protect the sold strike

Trade Setup Steps

1. Choose a stock that you might trade.
2. Use Foundations indicator on a 60-minute chart and see how many white versus black circles are displayed.
3. Look at levels of support and resistance on weekly, daily, and 60-minute charts to see whether the trading instrument is trending slowly or moving sideways.
4. Determine levels on the charts that are outside support or resistance.
5. Move to the options chain to look for the amount of credit available at a strike price that is out of the money and at a point where you believe the price of the stock will not expire.
6. Calculate the risk/reward ratio.
7. Decide whether the maximum gain and maximum profit are in line with your MY TRADE plan.
8. Place the trade.

Example of Out-of-the-Money Trading Setup

In this example, Goldman Sachs (GS) is in a downtrend on the daily and 60-minute charts, as shown in Figure 5.16b, but the trend is not a strong trend, and price is not moving consistently lower. In Figure 5.16a, GS is consolidating in a range on the daily chart.

It is for this reason that I would sell an out-of-the-money call credit spread. I can capitalize on the time decay and any potential weakness with GS, and my trade can still be profitable if price moves sideways or up slightly.

The decision to sell the out-of-the-money spread will protect me to some degree from a small, unfavorable move in GS. The moving averages are on the daily chart (Figure 5.16a), they will act as resistance as GS approaches the $160 level. By placing the trade outside that level, I am giving myself the best chance for the trade to work in my favor. Selling the monthly contracts slightly above the resistance at $160/$165 gives the trade some time to retrace if the key moving averages are broken. If you look at the options chain in Figure 5.16c, you can see that the $160/$165 spread is trading for a credit of $1.05. This trade aligns with the risk parameters I have outlined in my trading plan, so I would place this trade.

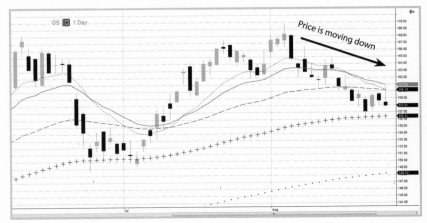

FIGURE 5.16a *(Source: MultiCharts.)*

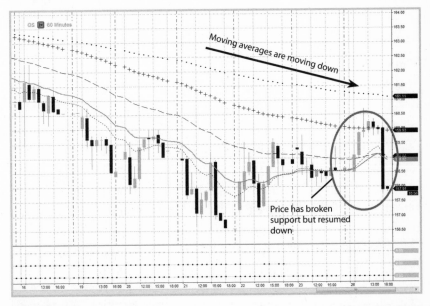

FIGURE 5.16b *(Source: MultiCharts.)*

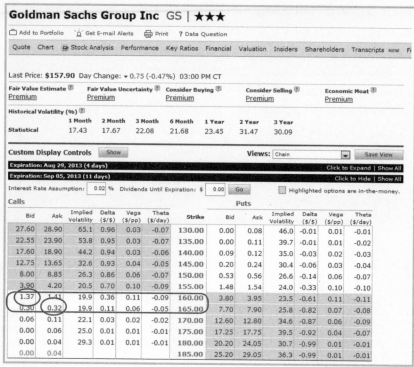

Call credit spread 1.37 – 0.32 = 1.05

FIGURE 5.16c

(Source: MultiCharts.)

Selling At-the-Money Put and Call Credit Spreads

What Is This Trade About?

This strategy is used when your trading assumption is that you believe that the price of the option will move higher by or before the option expires. I will place a put spread at the money if I believe that the market is moving up and a call spread at the money if I believe that the market is moving down. By selling an at-the-money call spread, my assumption is that I am placing a trade right around where the stock is trading at the time with the expectation that the trading instrument will have a big move.

Why Choose This Setup Versus Another?

An at-the-money spread takes advantage of markets that have momentum with an expected big move. An at-the-money spread takes advantage of having insurance if price moves in the opposite direction. A trader will spread the risk by selling a certain number of contracts at one strike price while also buying back the same number of contracts at a lower strike price with the same expiry as protection. When traders use a spread, they are able to calculate how much their maximum loss and maximum gain will be prior to entering the trade.

Trading Rules and Look-Fors: Selling At-the-Money Spreads

1. Good momentum
2. Trading assumption that price will move to target by expiry
3. High implied volatility
4. Enough time/days before expiry for the option to move

Trading Setup

1. Choose a stock to look at that you might trade.
2. Use the foundations indicator on the 60-minute chart and look to see how many white versus black circles are displayed.
3. Look at levels of support and resistance on the weekly, daily, and 60-minute charts to see whether the trading instrument is trending and has good momentum.
4. Determine if price has room to move without hitting major resistance.
5. Look at the options chain for the amount of credit you can receive at a strike price that is at the money.
6. Calculate the risk/reward ratio.
7. Decide whether the maximum gain and maximum loss are in line with your MY TRADE plan.
8. Place the trade.

Example of an At-the-Money Trading Setup

As you can see, Chesapeake Energy (CHK) is in an uptrend on the daily chart (Figure 5.17*a*) and on the 60-minute chart (Figure 5.17*b*). CHK has good momentum.

Figure 5.17*b* also shows that CHK has pulled back to the 21-period EMA and has bounced. I think this is a bullish setup with momentum. Figure 5.17*c* shows the options chain for the trade.

FIGURE 5.17a   *(Source: MultiCharts.)*

Using the 21 EMA as my support, I look at the options chain to see the credit I can collect. If I sold the $26/$25 put credit spread with this week's expiry, it would allow me to take in a credit of $0.33. Now, $0.33 is not a lot of premium to collect, so I need to weigh whether I think it is worth the risk to place this trade. I expect that the price will continue to move down, so I'm comfortable selling at the money. This trade aligns with my trading plan so I would place this trade.

Buying Directionals

What Is This Trade About?

Trading directionally is about buying the trading instrument in anticipation of a big move. The risk is that your option will expire worthless if the stock does not make the anticipated move.

FIGURE 5.17*b*   *(Source: MultiCharts.)*

Why Choose This Setup Versus Another?

I would choose a directional trade when I anticipate a large move in the stock. By choosing a directional, I am not limiting the profit potential of the trade like with a spread. A deep in-the-money directional will move almost dollar for dollar with the price of the underlying.

Trading Rules and Look-Fors: Directionals

1. Good momentum
2. Trading assumption that price will have a large move by expiry

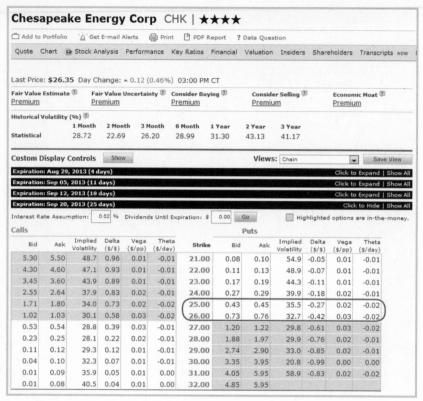

Chesapeake Energy Corp CHK | ★★★★

Add to Portfolio   Get E-mail Alerts   Print   PDF Report   ? Data Question

Quote   Chart   Stock Analysis   Performance   Key Ratios   Financial   Valuation   Insiders   Shareholders   Transcripts NEW

Last Price: **$26.35** Day Change: ▲ 0.12 (0.46%) 03:00 PM CT

Fair Value Estimate	Fair Value Uncertainty	Consider Buying	Consider Selling	Economic Moat
Premium	Premium	Premium	Premium	Premium

Historical Volatility (%)

	1 Month	2 Month	3 Month	6 Month	1 Year	2 Year	3 Year
Statistical	28.72	22.69	26.20	28.99	31.30	43.13	41.17

Custom Display Controls   Show   Views: Chain ▾   Save View

Expiration: Aug 29, 2013 (4 days)	Click to Expand | Show All
Expiration: Sep 05, 2013 (11 days)	Click to Expand | Show All
Expiration: Sep 12, 2013 (18 days)	Click to Expand | Show All
Expiration: Sep 20, 2013 (25 days)	Click to Hide | Show All

Interest Rate Assumption: 0.02 % Dividends Until Expiration: $ 0.00 Go   ☐ Highlighted options are in-the-money.

Calls   Puts

Bid	Ask	Implied Volatility	Delta ($/$)	Vega ($/pp)	Theta ($/day)	Strike	Bid	Ask	Implied Volatility	Delta ($/$)	Vega ($/pp)	Theta ($/day)
5.30	5.50	48.7	0.96	0.01	-0.01	21.00	0.08	0.10	54.9	-0.05	0.01	-0.01
4.30	4.60	47.1	0.93	0.01	-0.01	22.00	0.11	0.13	48.9	-0.07	0.01	-0.01
3.45	3.60	43.9	0.89	0.01	-0.01	23.00	0.17	0.19	44.3	-0.11	0.01	-0.01
2.55	2.64	37.9	0.83	0.02	-0.01	24.00	0.27	0.29	39.9	-0.18	0.02	-0.01
1.71	1.80	34.0	0.73	0.02	-0.02	25.00	0.43	0.45	35.5	-0.27	0.02	-0.02
1.02	1.03	30.1	0.58	0.03	-0.02	26.00	0.73	0.76	32.7	-0.42	0.03	-0.02
0.53	0.54	28.8	0.39	0.03	-0.01	27.00	1.20	1.22	29.8	-0.61	0.03	-0.02
0.23	0.25	28.1	0.22	0.02	-0.01	28.00	1.88	1.97	29.9	-0.76	0.02	-0.01
0.11	0.12	29.3	0.12	0.01	-0.01	29.00	2.74	2.90	33.0	-0.85	0.02	-0.01
0.04	0.10	32.3	0.07	0.01	-0.01	30.00	3.35	3.95	20.8	-0.99	0.00	0.00
0.01	0.09	35.9	0.05	0.01	0.00	31.00	4.05	5.95	58.9	-0.83	0.02	-0.02
0.01	0.08	40.5	0.04	0.01	0.00	32.00	4.85	5.95				

Put spread 0.76 – 0.42 = 0.34

FIGURE 5.17c   *(Source: Morningstar.)*

3. Low implied volatility
4. Enough time/days before expiry for the price of the underlying to make the anticipated move

Trading Setup

1. Choose a stock to look at that you might trade.
2. Use foundations indicator on the 60-minute chart and see how many white versus black circles are displayed.
3. Look at the levels of support and resistance on the weekly, daily, and 60-minute charts to see if the trading instrument is trending and has good momentum.
4. Determine if price has enough room to move before hitting major resistance.

5. Move to the options chain to look for the amount of premium at strike prices that are deep in the money.

6. Look at the delta column on the options chain. Pick a strike that balances premium paid and delta.

7. Decide whether the risk is in line with your MY TRADE plan.

8. Place the trade.

Example of Directional Trading Setup

AAPL is in a strong uptrend on the daily chart (Figure 5.18*a*) and the 60-minute chart (Figure 5.18*b*). The price is making higher highs and appears to have strong momentum. The Foundations indicator is confirming the trend.

FIGURE 5.18*a*   *(Source: MultiCharts.)*

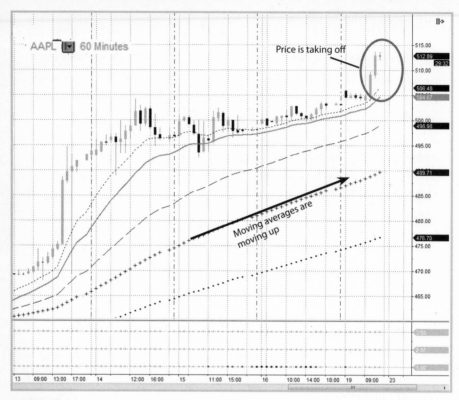

FIGURE 5.18*b*

(Source: MultiCharts.)

Since AAPL is trading at around $513, I move to the options chain (Figure 5.18*c*) to see how much it will cost to buy an option at a strike price that is deep in the money. Then I look at the delta. I need to balance high delta with the cost of the option. I could buy the $505 call for $12.15 or the $500 call for $15.70 with this week's expiry. This trade aligns with my trading plan so I would place this trade.

BUILDING YOUR OPTIONS WATCH LIST

It's important to create a watch list of stocks and ETFs whose behaviors you are going to become familiar with because there are just so many trading instruments to choose from. In order to focus your attention on placing trades instead of sifting through stocks, a watch list will help you

Apple Inc AAPL | ★★★★

☐ Add to Portfolio ☆ Get E-mail Alerts 🖶 Print 📄 PDF Report ? Data Question

Quote | Chart | 📊 Stock Analysis | Performance | Key Ratios | Financial | Valuation | Insiders | Shareholders | Transcripts NEW | Filings | Bonds | **Options**

Last Price: **$513.05** Day Change: ▲ 10.72 (2.13%) 10:21 AM CT

Fair Value Estimate | Fair Value Uncertainty | Consider Buying | Consider Selling | Economic Moat
Premium | Premium | Premium | Premium | Premium

Historical Volatility (%)

	1 Month	2 Month	3 Month	6 Month	1 Year	2 Year	3 Year
Statistical	28.29	25.43	22.76	25.76	31.08	29.27	27.52

Custom Display Controls [Show]   Views: [Chain ▾] [Save View]

Expiration: Aug 22, 2013 (4 days)   Click to Hide | Show All
Interest Rate Assumption: 0.05 % Dividends Until Expiration: $ 0.00 [Go]   ☐ Highlighted options are in-the-money.

Calls / **Puts**

Bid	Ask	Change	Change (Price)	Change (IV)	Change (Time)	Implied Volatility	Delta ($/$)	Vega ($/pp)	Theta ($/day)	Strike	Bid	Ask	Change	Change (Price)	Change (IV)	Change (Time)	Implied Volatility	Delta ($/$)	Vega ($/pp)	Theta ($/day)
23.75	24.05	▲8.73	▲8.89	▼1.28	▼1.18	30.6	0.90	0.10	-0.31	490.00	0.92	0.95	▼1.87	▲1.82	▲1.53	▼1.17	31.4	-0.10	0.11	-0.34
23.80	24.30	▲8.80								490.00	0.88	1.00	▼1.87	▲1.82	▲1.54	▼1.17	31.5	-0.10	0.11	-0.34
19.45	19.80	▲7.93	▲8.07	▼1.59	▼1.42	31.1	0.84	0.14	-0.45	495.00	1.56	1.59	▼2.75							
19.30	19.85	▲7.68	▲8.07	▼1.49	▼1.42	30.7	0.84	0.14	-0.44	495.00	1.51	1.63	▼2.73	▲2.63	▲1.65	▼1.40	31.1	-0.16	0.14	-0.45
15.50	15.70	▲6.85	▲7.10	▼1.39	▼1.56	30.8	0.77	0.18	-0.57	500.00	2.54	2.62	▼3.77							
										500.00	2.51	2.65	▼3.82	▲3.62	▲1.65	▼1.56	31.0	-0.23	0.16	-0.57
11.95	12.15	▲5.75	▲6.03	▼1.61	▼1.56	30.9	0.68	0.22	-0.67	505.00	4.00	4.10	▼4.95							
11.90	12.25	▲5.73								505.00	3.95	4.10	▼4.93	▲4.69	▲1.66	▼1.56	31.0	-0.32	0.22	-0.67
9.00	9.10	▲4.03	▲4.94	▼1.53	▼1.45	31.1	0.57	0.24	-0.73	510.00	6.00	6.10	▼6.10							
8.90	9.15	▲4.55	▲4.94	▼1.45	▼1.46	31.0	0.57	0.24	-0.73	510.00	5.95	6.15	▼6.10	▲5.78	▲1.54	▼1.46	31.3	-0.43	0.24	-0.74
6.55	6.65	▲3.45	▲3.92	▼1.27	▼1.28	31.4	0.47	0.24	-0.75	515.00	8.60	8.70	▼7.13							
6.45	6.70	▲3.50	▲3.91	▼1.32	▼1.26	31.3	0.47	0.24	-0.75	515.00	8.45	8.65	▼7.73	▲6.70	▲0.81	▲1.42	31.4	-0.53	0.24	-0.75
4.65	4.75	▲2.54	▲3.03	▼1.09	▼1.06	31.8	0.37	0.23	-0.72	520.00	11.60	11.80	▼8.15	▲7.68	▲1.12	▲1.06	32.1	-0.63	0.23	-0.72
4.55	4.80	▲2.51	▲3.03	▼1.06	▼1.06	31.7	0.37	0.23	-0.72	520.00	10.90	13.70	▼8.15	▲7.47	▲1.15	▲1.28	34.7	-0.62	0.23	-0.79
3.25	3.35	▲1.75	▼2.33	▲0.85	▲0.87	32.5	0.28	0.20	-0.66	525.00	15.15	15.40	▼8.95	▲8.38	▲0.87	▲0.87	32.6	-0.72	0.20	-0.66
3.20	3.35	▼1.74	▼2.33	▲0.84	▲0.86	32.4	0.28	0.20	-0.65	525.00	14.45	17.00	▼9.18	▲6.08	▲0.65	▲1.13	34.8	-0.71	0.21	-0.72
2.31	2.35	▲1.19	▼1.79	▲0.68	▲0.70	33.5	0.21	0.17	-0.58	530.00	19.20	19.45	▼9.50							
2.22	2.37	▲1.21	▲1.75	▲0.70	▲0.68	33.3	0.21	0.17	-0.57	530.00	19.05	19.50	▼9.50	▲8.95	▲0.71	▲0.69	33.5	-0.79	0.17	-0.58
1.63	1.66	▲0.81	▲1.37	▲0.55	▼0.56	34.5	0.15	0.14	-0.49	535.00	23.45	23.80	▼9.88	▲9.35	▲0.59	▲0.56	34.8	-0.84	0.14	-0.50
1.56	1.68	▲0.76	▲1.37	▲0.53	▼0.56	34.4	0.15	0.14	-0.49	535.00	22.75	25.00	▼9.95	▲9.13	▲0.52	▲0.74	36.5	-0.83	0.15	-0.55

FIGURE 5.18c   *(Source: MultiCharts.)*

to be more efficient. After all, it's placing trades that will make you money, not just calculating trades.

What every trader must realize is that trading isn't an exact science. It's important to understand that different trading instruments and setups will have a feel. This nuance for the market can only be developed over time as you trade longer. Therefore, to help this process, create a watch list that you will review on a regular basis. Get to know a short list of stocks really well. You will begin to notice the subtle nuances of how the stocks you track behave over time. This will allow you to make any necessary tweaks and adjustments in your strategy to refine your trades.

This chapter has covered a lot of information. It has reviewed many options trading terms along with strategies for placing trades. For some, this may feel like a lot of information, whereas others may now be tweaking their trading plan to personalize these strategies based on their own risk/reward parameters. Over time, much of this information will become automatic and so engrained in your everyday habits that you won't need to cognitively process each individual piece of information. Let's finish this chapter on a light

Sarah's Trading Tips

I add to and refine my watch list on a regular basis. I like to keep my watch list small and limited to stocks and ETFs that I trade often. Currently some trading instruments on my watch list are Baidu.com (BIDU), iShares Treasury Bond ETF (TLT), SPDR S&P 500 (SPY), MasterCard (MA), Visa (V), Priceline.com (PLCN), Chipotle Mexican Grill (CMG), Rackspace Hosting (RAX), Green Mountain Coffee Roasters (GMCR), and Google (GOOG). To find out more about trading instruments I'm currently considering, you can join the Corner-LOT. More information is available at www.shecantrade.com.

note. Take a look at the following recipe for trading options, and remember to always take time to enjoy the results of your trading.

Recipe to Trade Options

Trading options can be thought of much like cooking. Some people cook by following a recipe step by step, whereas others improvise. The result from this recipe will include the know-how to actually place trades for yourself. Every options trader should always have these ingredients at her trading platform ready to use.

Ingredients
- 3 market internals
- 3 strategies to trade
- 3 time frames on charts
- 1 Foundations indicator (optional but nice to have)
- 3 moving averages
- 1 MY TRADE plan

Directions to Trade

Measure each ingredient based on your taste, but always stick to the ingredient amounts that you have determined for yourself. Measuring will be very important; do not stray too far from the ingredients list for the most success. All the ingredients listed should be part of your trading plan but can be substituted for different amounts, provided that the amounts chosen always align with your trading plan. The trading plan cannot be removed from any trading decision. Add more ingredients slowly, and allow the mix to rise prior to attempting implementation. Add more market internals and strategies to taste, but ensure that things don't get too spicy. Consume a healthy amount; don't overindulge or undernourish yourself. Most important, enjoy your trades, but trade wisely.

> **Sarah's Trading Tip**
>
> *This chapter has reviewed many concepts. In order to make sure that you can take this knowledge and make it most practical for you, make a checklist of sorts for yourself. In one column, write down characteristics or look-fors for each trade setup you want to use. As you are going through trades, use this checklist to make sure that you are finding quality trade setups.*

KEY TAKE-AWAYS

- Options provide many ways to trade. Even though they may seem overwhelming to new traders, the basic strategies to trade are used by many. What are considered more advanced strategies are simply basic trading strategies used in combination.
- Trader terminology basics are clearly defined and then applied to a trading example. Many terms can seem overwhelming, but certain terms are necessary for every trader to understand in order to trade options.
- Options provide ways to trade directionally or with spreads. Options traders will place trades based on the market direction and their risk/reward profile. Different traders can have the same trading assumption but place different trades because they have different risk/reward parameters. One trader might sell a spread trade, whereas another might buy a directional trade.

- Each trader will have to align her own risk/reward parameters with the types of trades she places. Write down steps to help you choose what type of trading setup to use.
- My top three options trading strategies step by step: selling at-the-money spreads, selling out-of-the-money spreads, and buying directionals.

6

SARAH'S FUTURES STRATEGIES

Illustrated by Noble Rains

> **Key Chapter Concepts**
>
> - *Understand what trading futures is all about.*
> - *Review the advantages/disadvantages of futures.*
> - *Begin to understand the personalities of the different futures markets.*
> - *Detail the tools needed to trade futures.*
> - *Understand Sarah's top three futures trading strategies step by step.*
> - *Examine examples of trading scenarios.*

Many traders are lured to trading futures because of the appeal of making a lot of money quickly. Futures markets generally move fast and have a large amount of leverage. This chapter outlines some specifics about the *when*, *what*, *why*, and *how* of trading futures so that traders at all levels of expertise can have an understanding of the market and a jumping-off point to set up trades. By the end of the chapter, you will have reviewed some advantages and disadvantages of the futures markets, learned some of the language specific to futures trading, begun applying your market analysis and trading assumptions to the selection of a futures trade, and examined three trading setups. This chapter intentionally focuses on what you need to know to actually trade futures. I want to help you to answer any questions you have about futures trading so that you can incorporate futures trading into your MY TRADE plan and begin to implement a futures trading strategy for yourself.

WHAT IS TRADING FUTURES ALL ABOUT?

Futures contracts represent an underlying asset, whether it is corn, cattle, oil, or the value of a stock index. These contracts are traded back and forth with an assumption that the value of the asset is going up or down over time.

Trading futures is most associated with agriculture and is used by farmers to lock in prices of crops at the end of the growing season. Over time, the futures market has expanded beyond agriculture and now provides many other contracts to trade. It is possible to trade any product from gold, to crude oil, to foreign exchange, to lumber. By far the most popular contracts are bonds, equity indexes, and foreign-exchange pairs.

The range of markets provides flexibility for futures traders not only to find markets that look optimal to trade that day but also to find specific markets that match their personality. Some traders choose to trade multiple markets in futures, whereas others decide to trade just one. Futures markets provide opportunities to find time to trade around other commitments because there is a market open to trade somewhere in the world 24 hours a day.

Futures trade much like stocks, but they have a few key differences. First, unlike stocks, futures are leveraged instruments. For every $1 you invest, you control much more capital in the market. For the E-mini S&P 500 Index (ES), a $500 investment can control around $80,000 in the markets.

Unlike stocks, futures contracts expire every quarter or every month. A trader can be assigned the underlying asset at expiry. Most often futures traders don't hold contracts to expiry; they will often get out of a trade or roll a trade over to the next contract prior to expiry to avoid assignment of the underlying product.

Another difference is that futures are subject to day and overnight margin. *Day margin* requires less capital than if a futures trader wants to hold the trade overnight. If you plan on holding your positions overnight, then you will need to be aware of the need for increased margin.

One of the interesting facts about futures is that they can move only so many dollars or points in one day (this is referred to as limit up or limit down). Once those limits are reached, trades cannot be placed below or above them. Agricultural products such as corn and soy beans frequently go limit up or limit down, whereas bonds, metals, and the equity index rarely have a limit move. This is of concern to traders if they place a trade near a limit and get locked into a trade until the next day.

Futures-Specific Trading Language

The terms discussed in this section are specific to futures and will need to be understood in order for you to trade futures. If these terms are new to you, I would recommend that you spend some time copying the definitions down and keeping them close to you while you are reading the rest of this chapter.

Sarah's Story

It's 10:38 a.m., and the S&P 500 and the Dow have been trending down all morning. You place your hand on your mouse, and enter six contracts that get traded immediately. Your depth of market (DOM) is automatically set to take you out in thirds. In less than 15 seconds, your first trigger is fired, and suddenly you are down to four contracts with profit in your pocket. You breathe and continue to watch as the market continues short, taking you out to two contracts. Now you move your stop to cost plus 1 and comfortably trail your stop lower and lower. This is now an all profit—a free trade. You patiently trail your stop 30 more ticks of profit until you exit your final position. Congratulations, you followed your plan beautifully, and you have proven that you can trade.

(If you don't know what you just read, don't panic. What I just described is a dream futures trade setup and execution. We will get into the details later, and by the time you finish reading this book, not only will this trade setup make sense, but you will also know how to execute this trade yourself if you choose).

Contracts/cars/lots. This is the term that futures traders use to label one unit of the trading instrument (a contract is similar to a share of a stock). It refers to the minimum size of the trade that can be placed in that instrument. One contract is simply one unit of the futures instrument you are trading. A contract, a car, and a lot all mean the same thing.

Depth of market (DOM). This is a tool used to enter and exit trades. A futures trader will look at a DOM screen to watch the movement of each market and to place trades. Because futures trading is like an auction, the DOM is where a trader places her bid or ask at the level she is looking to buy or sell. Traders will also pay attention to the price movement of the instrument on the DOM and on the charts.

Expiry. A futures contract has a limited life; contracts expire on the third Friday of each quarter (or month). Traders will want to exit or roll over their trades before the trades expire (unless they would like to own a train car full of, say, corn).

Rollover. This refers to moving a trade over to the next expiry. For electronic contracts, the convention is to roll over to the next contract eight calendar days prior to expiration. Information about when a contract expires or rolls over is available from the exchange.

Settlement. Once a futures contract expires, it can be settled and delivered in various ways. Traders need to make sure that they are not assigned the underlying product and expected to take delivery.

Tick. This refers to the smallest change in price a futures contract can make. Each level the price moves is considered one tick. Every tick a contract moves is worth a certain dollar amount in value. Different trading instruments are worth different prices per tick. Each futures contract has its own minimum move and dollar value per move. For example, one tick in the E-mini S&P 500 futures contract (ES) is 0.25 and worth $12.50. A tick of movement on the DOM shouldn't be confused with TICKs, the market internal.

Day versus overnight margin. A specific amount of money will be set by your broker that has to be in your account called a *margin*. Futures contracts that are held overnight are subject to higher margin requirements. For small-account traders, it is most likely that you are trading only during the day and not holding your trades overnight. Every trader should know his margin requirements.

Limit move. Futures contracts are allowed to move only a certain amount each day. The maximum amount they can move is called a limit move. Once this maximum is reached, the contract effectively stops trading until the next day, and you cannot exit your position until trading resumes. The grain markets have narrow ranges and go limit up and down quite often, whereas contracts such as the ES have large ranges and never really reach their limits.

Minimum dollar move. Every time a futures contract moves by one tick, the value changes by a specific dollar amount, and every futures contract is different. The minimum dollar move of the ES is $12.50. This means that every time price changes by 0.25, the dollar amount of the move is $12.50.

Of course, there are many more terms in futures trading, but the preceeding terms are most common and very important, and ever trader needs to understand what they mean. These terms will be applied throughout the rest of this chapter.

Sarah's Story

Futures is the market where my trading experience began. It's where I learned how to read charts, apply my trading knowledge, and refine my trading strategy. Futures appealed to me because they just seemed simpler. I only needed to worry about trading with an assumption that the market is going up or down. I was placing a trade by going either long or short.

Futures also offered me the flexibility to trade at different times during the day; for example, the EUR/USD Futures contract (6E) is actively traded from around 4 a.m. Eastern Standard Time (EST). This was especially helpful when I was trading before I went to my full-time job. When I was trading part time, I would wake up early before I started my full-time job to trade the 6E contract before having breakfast and getting to the rest of my day.

WHAT INSTRUMENT DO YOU PREFER?

Each futures market has its own distinct personality and behavior. Some markets trend, whereas others ebb and flow. Ideally, a futures trader will choose to trade a market that matches his trading personality. Determining how you react to the ups and downs of a market will help you to decide which market best suits your personality.

I have categorized some of the futures markets in Table 6.1 in an effort to help traders pick a market that might better align with their personalities or trading styles. Read through this section to help you begin to think about what market might be best for you. Or if you already trade, take some time to think about how the personality of the various futures markets might help you find a market that is better suited to your trading style.

The chart in Figure 6.1*a* moves like a tide; it does not move straight up or down. It trends with many pullbacks against the prevailing trend.

TABLE 6.1. Market personalities

Tidal Markets	Trending Markets
A tidal market is just like the ocean. Picture the tide coming in on a beach. The water progressively moves farther up the beach, but it does not do this all at once. The water pushes up, pulls back a little, and then pushes up again. A trader will trade these markets by analyzing a pullback and getting in to ride the wave. But just as with a real tide, there will be times when an incoming tide turns around and becomes an outgoing tide.	Trending markets such as gold (GC) will have much shallower pullbacks to the prevailing trend when compared with a contract such as the E-mini S&P 500 (ES). When such markets begin to trend, they will move strongly in that direction.
S&P 500 (ES) Russell (TF) Dow (YM)	Gold (GC) Corn (ZC) Bonds (ZB)

Notice that price is moving up from left to right on this chart, but it pulls back and breaks some of the moving averages. These trading instruments behave differently from trending markets such as gold, corn, and bonds.

Figure 6.1b looks more like a downtrend. Notice that price on this chart has some shallow pullbacks to the moving averages but from left to right this chart is in a downtrend. When the markets are trending, the charts will appear to be making higher highs and lower lows.

Organizing markets into trending and tidal behaviors is a good way to begin to think about what futures market you might be interested in trading. When you trade futures, you will want to develop a feel for the market that you are trading. This can happen most quickly when you focus your attention on learning one or two markets at a time. Trading setups also will be personalized and tweaked depending on which market you prefer to trade.

FIGURE 6.1a   (Source: MultiCharts.)

FIGURE 6.1b   (Source: MultiCharts.)

Sarah's Trading Tip

Neither type of futures market is better or worse to trade. It just depends on your trading style and which market you have most success with. You will only learn this by trying different markets and comparing your profitability in each. The "Trading Personality Quiz" in Chapter 2 also may help you.

Time Is on Your Side

Now that you know about the personalities of various markets, you will also need to factor in the amount of time you want to dedicate to trading. Some markets and trading styles require more time at the computer, whereas others are about setting your entries, exits, and stops and then checking up on them at the end of the day. You can trade most markets 24 hours a day, but most professional traders trade when there is the most volume, which means trading during the U.S. session from 9:30 a.m. to 4:15 p.m. EST.

Sarah's Trading Tip

Using volume will help you to know the quiet times for the market you are trading. I'm not suggesting that you avoid sleep to trade; I'm suggesting that you find a market that fits your schedule and time zone. I believe that you have to be in front of the computer screen in order to watch a futures market for a good entry and exit, there is always a market that is trading somewhere regardless of the time of day. I am writing based on New York time.

Times to Trade Futures for the Part-Time Trader

Not everyone has the ability to begin trading as a full-time career. Some traders trade around other work commitments or have the flexibility to trade at different times. The following subsections describe times in the markets that a part-time trader might want to consider.

After you Drop the Kids Off at School

If you have time to trade during the day, you might want to consider day trading futures. This day-trading market opens and is active during the day. When I'm trading futures, my typical trades these days are between 10 a.m. and 12:00 noon EST and 2:30 to 3:30 p.m. EST. These two time frames provide opportunities for a trend to appear in the market and provide an opportunity to use the three trade setups discussed later.

Early Riser

For those of you who like to wake up early, currencies might be a market for you to consider. The EUR/USD futures contract (6E) and the GBP/USD futures contract (6B) are good options to trade early in the morning. If you want to get up early before work begins or before the kids get up, this might be the time for you. These markets are usually active anywhere after 4 a.m. EST. If your rooster rises early, this might be a market to consider. The euro and pound are great candidates for the in-fashion and va-va-voom trade setups.

Red Eye

European or Asian markets trade while we are sleeping in the Eastern time zone. Markets such as gold and the yen are also active later in the evening or at night. These markets usually have good volume after 10:00 p.m. If you don't mind staying up late or missing your favorite late night show, then this market is worth watching. These markets will set up opportunities to trade in-fashion and va-va-voom trade setups.

Combo Pack

Many traders scour multiple markets looking for one or two setups that they can trade in any market. This can be very profitable as long as you are patient and have the time to analyze the markets. There will be times when various markets are correlated, and there will be other times when they are not. Having the flexibility to check the markets throughout the day and trade different markets can offer advantages. One market might not be offering any trades, whereas another market you are watching might have a very tradable move. All three of the trading setups will work in various markets. However, don't try to trade every market. If you are going to trade a few different times or markets, outline which ones and when you will follow them in your MY TRADE plan. For example, outline the trade setups you will use in the 6E, and then articulate the trade setups you will use later in the day for trades in the E-mini Dow (YM).

Sarah's Trading Tip

I typically choose to avoid entering a futures trade during lunchtime. (12 noon to 2 p.m. EST) When the market slows, I stay in a trade if I'm already in it, but if I haven't entered already, I either choose not to trade or wait until the afternoon before I place my trade. The same is true when getting out of trades; I prefer to be out of my trades before 3:45 p.m. EST. Not only does this help me to create a good work/life balance, but I'm also out of the markets before the market closes and any big move that may occur around that time.

HOW TO TRADE FUTURES

Now that you have an idea of the markets on which you will focus and the time of day during which you will trade, let's begin to discuss how to actually trade futures. In the futures market, a trader is either *buying* or *selling*. The difference in price at which a trader buys or sells a contract is the *profit* or *loss*. Trading futures is similar to buying or selling a house. All buyers in the housing market are looking for a good deal, and a house that will appreciate in value so that when the buyer sells, it will be worth more. Conversely, someone selling a house is hoping to cash in on his investment to make money on the sale of his house. The seller wants to sell for more than what he bought the house for. The same idea is true in futures. A trader can buy contracts in a market, hold them for a short period of time to appreciate in value, and then sell them for more money because the value has increased. The same is true when a trader sells a futures contract. The trader will sell a contract based on a trading assumption that the market is going down. This trader sells at what she believes is a high price and then buys back the contract at a lower price once the value has gone down, thus making a profit. As a futures trader, you buy when the market is going up, and you sell when the market is going down.

Futures trading is pretty straightforward. Put most simply, if a trader has gathered market evidence about the market direction (as discussed in

Chapter 4) and believes that the market is moving up, he will place a trade by buying a contract in that market, hold onto it for a short period of time, and then sell it once it moves high enough to meet his profit target. If a trader has gathered evidence from the market and believes that the market is moving down, she will place a trade by selling a contract and buying it back when the market moves lower to collect a profit.

Let's work through two examples together to illustrate the idea of buying or selling in futures. The first example highlights how a trader will look at a chosen trading instrument [for this example we are using the E-mini Dow (YM)] to determine the direction of a trend across various time frames. This information will help the trader to determine whether he will buy or sell futures.

As discussed in Chapter 4, trading assumptions begin by formulating an opinion about the market direction from a trader's charts. A trader will begin this process by applying her own chart analysis. The following examples highlight how a trader would begin to determine whether the market is trending up or down. Specifically for futures, this would determine whether the trader is going to buy (because there is an uptrend) or sell (because there is a downtrend).

Using the charts, a trader can work through "Sarah's Simple Steps":

1. *Pull up a chart of the E-mini S&P 500 (ES) to represent the overall market. Is the ES moving in the same direction as the E-mini Dow (YM)?* Let's assume for this example that both the ES and YM are moving in the same direction.
2. *Look at the market internals. Are they indicating strength in the market or weakness?* Let's assume there is strength in the market.
3. *Based on the information you have gathered so far, what is your assumption about the trend of the overall market at this time?* The trend is long.
4. *Now move to the specific trading instrument you are considering.* Notice in Figure 6.2a the YM daily chart, look at the support and resistance levels created by the moving averages. Figure 6.2a is showing a long trend. The bars on the chart have all been moving up and holding above the moving averages since July.

5. *Move to the 60-minute chart to see if this trend continues on a shorter time frame.* Figure 6.2*b* also shows a trend up, but it is important to notice that the bars have broken through some of the moving averages. The 100- and 200-period EMAs are holding as support.

6. *Move to the shorter-term time frame to look for a trend.* Figure 6.2*c* is also moving up. Price is moving up and making higher highs.

7. *Look at the 21-period EMA on the 5-minute chart.* The solid line in Figure 6.2*c* shows that the bars have broken the 21-period EMA but have reestablished by staying above the 21 EMA later in the day.

8. *The Foundations indicator* on Figure 6.2*c* is primarily white dots all throughout the day, supporting my analysis that there is a trend and a trading opportunity.

9. *Determine your market assumption.* Based on the evidence gathered from various time frames, my assumption is that there is a long trend. Based on this assumption, I will use the 5-minute chart to look for an entry.

10. *Determine an entry* using the moving averages as support and resistance and the Foundations indicator. I would place a trade to buy the YM. I believe the YM will continue to move up so I will place the trade in the same direction.

FIGURE 6.2*a* (Source: MultiCharts.)

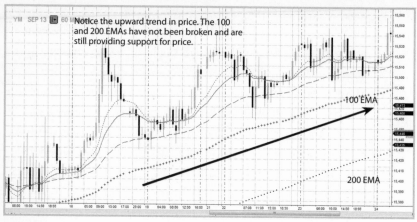

Notice the upward trend in price. The 100 and 200 EMAs have not been broken and are still providing support for price.

100 EMA

200 EMA

FIGURE 6.2b

(Source: MultiCharts.)

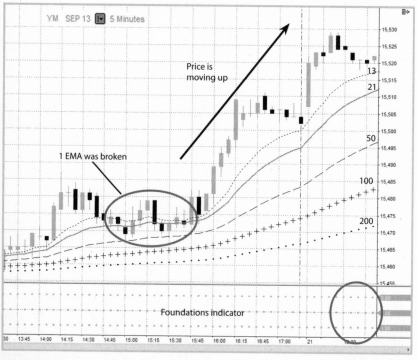

Price is moving up

1 EMA was broken

13
21
50
100
200

Foundations indicator

FIGURE 6.2c

(Source: MultiCharts.)

Conversely, the following example illustrates when a futures trader would sell because the market is going down. Let's apply Sarah's Simple Steps again.

1. *Is the ES market moving in the same direction as Gold Futures (GC)?* For this example let's assume it is moving in the same direction.

2. *Are the market internals moving up or down?* Assume the TICKs are negative.

3. *What is your assumption about the overall market at this time?* My assumption is that the overall market is moving down.

4. *Pull up long- and short-term charts for the instrument you want to trade.*

5. *Using the GC daily chart (Figure 6.3a), look at the support and resistance levels created by the moving averages.* Figure 6.3a is showing a short trend. The bars on the chart are all moving down and are below the moving averages and have done so since April.

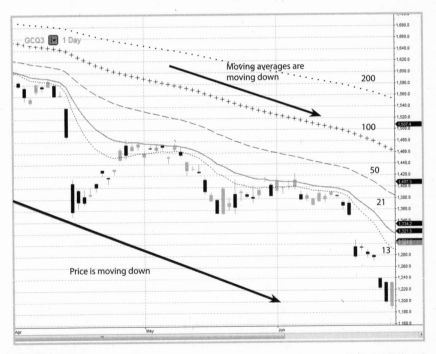

FIGURE 6.3a (Source: MultiCharts.)

Using the GC 60-minute chart, look at the support and resistance levels from the moving averages. Figure 6.3b also shows a long trend down, and the EMAs on this chart are all moving down.

FIGURE 6.3*b*

(Source: MultiCharts.)

6. *Move to a shorter-term time frame.* Figure 6.3*c* is also moving down. The bars on the chart have moved below some of the moving averages on this chart. The 13 and 21 EMA have been broken several times throughout the day.

FIGURE 6.3*c*

(Source: MultiCharts.)

7. *Look at the 21-period EMA on the 5-minute chart.* The solid line in Figure 6.3c shows that the 21-period EMA has been holding from about 1 p.m.

8. *Look at the Foundations indicator* in Figure 6.3c to see if there are white dots supporting an entry at this time or black dots that caution the trader away from trading at this time. The foundations indicator in Figure 6.3c is showing a good trading opportunity between about 1 and 2 p.m.

9. *Determine your market assumption.* The evidence gathered suggests that the GC contract is in a trend down. Hence, a trader would sell a futures contract.

10. *Determine an entry.* I would have sold the market around 1 p.m.

This is an example of when a futures trader would place a trade to sell with an assumption that the market will continue to move downward. The trader would place a trade short and take profits once the market had moved downward to a profit target.

SOME TOOLS OF THE FUTURES TRADE

In order to place trades based on the market trend, traders use specific tools. The tools I use to trade futures include a depth-of-market (DOM) screen to execute trades, market internals, support and resistance on charts as indicated by moving averages, the Foundations indicator to pinpoint entries and exits, and trading rules for each trading strategy. These pieces of information will help to form my trading assumption, to determine whether I think the market is moving up or down that day, and to decide where to place trades.

Tool: Depth of Market (DOM) to Enter and Exit a Trade

When ready to place a trade, many traders will use a tool called a *depth of market* (DOM) to execute and monitor their trades.

The DOM shows the price where the contract is being traded at the moment and where there is interest to buy and sell around the area of the

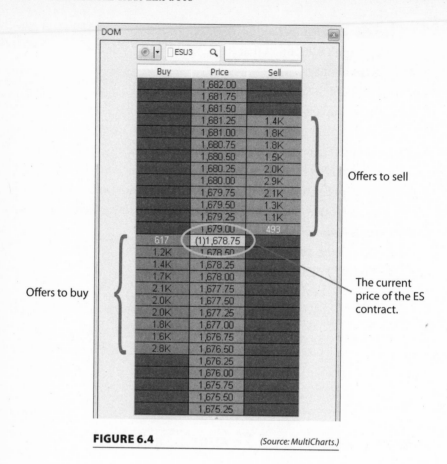

FIGURE 6.4 (Source: MultiCharts.)

price action. The DOM is also a great visual to show where there is the most interest or price action. Keep in mind, however, that the interest above and below the price action consists of just offers. Traders can cancel or move their offers at any time. Figure 6.4 is an example of a DOM.

To place a trade using the DOM, some traders push the buy market or sell market buttons on the DOM. This means that the trader will buy at the current price or sell at the current price. Other traders use the DOM a little differently by placing a bid at a certain price to enter a trade. Using the DOM in this manner allows a trader to wait for a price that he believes is a good deal and then exit when he feels that his profit targets have been met.

For every trade I place in futures, I place an entry, a profit target (my exit), and a stop (a level that will automatically exit me from the trade if the market moves against me) on the DOM. Traders can use other tools to place trades in futures, but this tool is what I—like many other professional futures traders—like to use to execute trades.

Therefore, going back to the preceding example and trading in its simplest form, a trader would enter one contract on the DOM at a specific price, let's say 1,222 (this level is just above the 21-period EMA as support on the five-minute chart in Figure 6.5), and place another contract lower down on the DOM, where she wants to exit the trade to collect profits. In this example the exit is at 1,202. A trader also can add a stop above the entry so that if the trader is wrong and the trade moves against her, the trade will exit at 1,225 for a loss. (I will discuss actual trade setups in more detail at the end of this chapter; this example shows only how to apply the use of the DOM and how to enter and exit trades.)

FIGURE 6.5   (Source: MultiCharts.)

Tool: Support and Resistance for Entries and Exits

A futures trader will pay specific attention to the levels of support and resistance on the various time frame charts to determine specific entries and exits. Many traders use a short-term chart to determine an entry or exit point and will typically look at the 21 EMA as support or resistance.

Traders will take advantage of the behavior of these moving averages as natural places to use to enter and exit trades. Some traders will enter trades right at the level it is being traded at the time, whereas others will be more prone to waiting for what is called a *pullback* to *support* before placing this trade. Because traders are always looking for a deal, most often they will place a trade at a specific level on the DOM and wait for it to be triggered.

Sarah's Trading Tip

I pay particular attention to clean charts when I trade futures. This means that I am very focused on where the moving averages are on each of the time frames I use (daily, 60-minute, and 5-minute charts). I look to see what moving averages are acting as support and what might provide resistance at the time. I want to see charts that ideally all show a trend moving in the same direction and without any major moving averages acting as resistance. If the moving averages have crossed, I will typically wait until they have all realigned before placing a trade. If I can't find clean charts, I will then consider any scalping opportunities using the va-va-voom set up or switch my attention to options that day.

Tool: Foundations Indicator

This tool is an indicator that I created to help me understand the direction of a market without having to have multiple screens open at the same time. Owing to the faster nature of the futures markets versus options, I have found that the foundations indicator is very helpful in saving time and informing entries in trades. The indicator gathers information about what has happened in previous time frames and compiles the information to identify the strength of a trend. I use the indicator on the screen I use to determine my entries. In futures, the indicator sits on my 5-minute chart. (Figure 6.6)

This indicator can be added to any trader's charts to provide them with an idea of the direction of the market. The best part about this indicator is that if you are new to understanding how to read many of the market internals, this can summarize similar information all on one screen. The indicator visualizes the short-, medium-, and long-term trends of the market on a trader's primary trading chart. This indicator is useful in both futures and options markets because it helps you to determine the market direction and gives you confidence in your trading assumption. Every trader still needs to make his own decision about what trade setup is best to use in conjunction with the other specific trading tools he uses. (This indicator is available for purchase at www.shecantrade.com.)

FIGURE 6.6 A 5-minute chart of the ES with the Foundations indicator.

(Source: MultiCharts.)

Tool: Market Value

Some traders choose to focus on specific markets to trade at all times. They may choose to focus only on trading the YM and not worry about other markets, whereas other traders look through various futures markets to see which market has the best opportunities to trade at that time

Sarah's Trading Tip

To initiate a trade in futures, I begin with my market analysis, which is detailed in Chapter 4. I begin by looking at and analyzing the market. I look for evidence to help me decide my trading assumption about where the market is moving. Then I look specifically to decide which trading instrument looks the cleanest on various time frames. Using support and resistance levels and the foundations indicator on a 5-minute chart, I look for entries at which to place a trade and place my exits.

to maximize their trading potential. The congruence of multiple markets provides opportunities for a trader to be choosy about which market to trade. When a trader sees similar patterns in more than one market, he now has a choice as to which market he will choose to trade to maximize his profits and limit his risk.

To help you decide which market to trade, three factors such as commissions, the minimum dollar move, and the average tick movement in each market should be weighed so that you can choose which market offers the best risk/reward ratio to trade.

Let's review them.

Commissions for Each Market

Obviously, commissions to the brokers will cut into any profits. Most often the commission structure will be different for each market. Pay attention to how much it will cost you in commissions to trade to each market. If the Russell 2000 Index Mini Futures (TF) and the E-mini S&P 500 (ES) are behaving similarly, a trader should consider which market provides the best commission structure.

Minimum Dollar Move

A trader should be aware of the minimum dollar move and average tick movement in a market to help determine the risk/reward in that market. Each futures contract has a unique dollar value per tick, known as a *minimum dollar move*. This movement is unique to each contract. It will influence how much a trader can make or lose per tick in each market. For example, as shown in Figure 6.7 the (YM) moves in one-point increments that are valued at $5. This means that if the YM moves one tick, from 15,442 to 15,443, a trader will make $5. Compare this with the ES, as shown in Figure 6.8, which moves in 0.25-point increments. Each tick of movement is worth $12.50. This means that if the ES moves from 1,600.00 to 1,600.25, a trader will make $12.50. Therefore, if a trader compares the minimum dollar move between the YM and ES, with every tick of movement, the ES can make or lose the trader more money per tick. You would have to decide what market you prefer to trade.

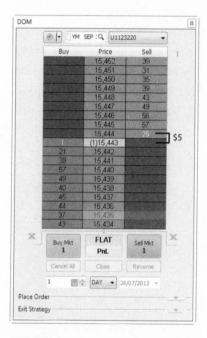

FIGURE 6.7 DOM showing that a one-tick move for YM is $5.

(*Source: MultiCharts.*)

FIGURE 6.8 DOM showing that a one-tick move for ES is $12.50.

(*Source: MultiCharts.*)

Average Tick Movement

The average tick movement should be considered in combination with the minimum dollar move. Each market will move a different amount; for example, the TF might move ten ticks for every four ticks that the ES moves. Just because the minimum dollar move in the ES is a larger amount of money per tick, the amount it is moving can affect which market might be the best choice to trade. For example, one day the ES is down 28 points and the TF is down 20 points. The dollar value for the move in the ES is $50 × 28 = $1,400, whereas the dollar move for the move in the TF is 20 × $100 = $2,000. On that day, a trader could have made more money in the TF even though the TF didn't move as much as the ES.

The average true range indicator (ATR), is especially helpful for visualizing the range of movement in the market. The ATR works when used on a short time frame (typically the chart used to decide entries). The ATR will help traders understand the average range of price movement for each market. Figure 6.9 shows the ATR in the ES. The longer the line, the larger is the range of price movement.

The dollar value of the moves is very different for each market. When a trader combines her commission structures to trade each market and the value per tick of movement and is aware of how much each market is moving that day, she can be sure that she is trading the market that is most aligned with her risk/reward parameters.

FIGURE 6.9 Image of average true range for the ES.   (Source: MultiCharts.)

Sarah's Trading Tip

Markets are intertwined and at times will follow or lead each other. The most traded equity index is the E-mini S&P 500 (ES). Most traders watch the ES as a gauge to the movement of the markets as a whole, because it is widely traded around the world and has the largest volume of the equity indexes.

Use the ES as a means to look for patterns to see whether the market you are trading is behaving in the same way. Often the Russell 2000 Index Mini Futures (TF) will lead the (ES), so before you place a trade in the TF, take a glance at the ES to see if it is behaving similarly. If the trends in both markets are congruent, this will help to strengthen your trading assumption about the direction of the market.

Tool: Your Futures Trading Rules

Along with learning how to read charts and implement trade setups, traders need to develop some trading rules for their trading, especially in futures, because the trades can be very fast. These rules will be outlined in your MY TRADE plan but should go beyond what your stop loss is; they will help to guide your decisions to maximize your trading potential and control the emotional connection that sometimes can interfere with sound trading decisions. Trading rules also should include whether you trade around economic news releases, what time of day you trade, and whether you trade futures rollover Thursday or Friday. I've detailed some of my trading rules below.

Five of my futures trading rules include:

1. I don't trade the open or close.
2. I don't trade immediately before or after economic news events.
3. I always set a stop.
4. If I see that the charts are not in a trend, I won't trade.
5. I don't chase big moves.

Open and Close

You won't find me entering a futures trade right at the opening bell or at the end of the day. The market behaves differently at the open and close. At the morning bell, if you watch the futures market, usually there will be a big move. This move is generally caused by trades that were placed when the market opened, brokers who are liquidating positions, or major institutions that have big trades. I will not place trades until the market has settled into a rhythm for the day.

The close is also a time of day when things can get unpredictable. At the end of the day, the same influence of large orders that must be executed regardless of price can cause unpredictable moves in the market.

Now, there are traders who make their bread and butter trading the open and close. I want to be clear that this is one strategy, but I feel that this strategy should be reserved for more experienced traders. Because most small-account traders can't hold their positions overnight in futures, it's best to trade when there is lots of time left during the day to be able to exit your positions rather than losing your shirt in a trade because you ran out of time and got automatically liquidated by your broker at the close of the market.

Trading Near Economic News Releases

There are many places online to gather information about when these news events will occur. News events are posted on many websites. Make it part of your daily routine to check the news before you begin to trade that day. The timing of these events should be kept in the back of your mind and be part of your decision as to whether or not to place a trade that day.

As part of your risk/reward parameters for futures, you will need to decide whether you are going to trade around the economic news releases that come out a few times per week. News events can cause big swings in the futures markets. For example, corn futures can have big moves on the days that corn crop reports are released, and the ES can have large moves on Federal Open Market Committee (FOMC) news releases and unemployment numbers. As a trader, you will need to decide ahead of time whether you want to trade near the time that news events could move the market. Regardless of your plan, you will notice that if you choose to be in a trade during a news event, you must realize that there may be a large move. You will need to decide whether you will let your stop take you out or whether it's better to avoid the trade altogether.

Sarah's Trading Tip

I have always had a hard rule about trading economic news releases. I initially decided that I wouldn't trade the news because of the unanticipated moves the market could make during these events. Even though I thought that once I had gained more experience I might start trading the news, I have maintained this rule for myself. Today I still don't trade futures during news events. I have watched the market have big moves during news events and heard about too many people getting hit hard in their trading accounts when the move goes against them. I prefer to line up as many probabilities as I can in my favor when I trade futures. Because I choose to trade with a conservative approach, I watch these moves from the sidelines. Sure, it's enticing when someone on Twitter announces the big money they collected on a news event in a particular futures trade, but chances are that same person may not be sharing their losing trades that might have been bigger than their one winner, or they may not be truthful about the trade. Make your own decision about the news based on your own risk tolerance.

Always Set a Stop

Every trade I enter always has a stop. I believe that if my trading assumption is wrong, then it's up to me to get out of the trade, regroup, and reevaluate before entering into another trade. The stop controls my losses and removes any emotional desire that might make me want to stay in a losing trade. I don't touch my stop once it's placed. This is a hard rule for me. I set my futures and options stops differently. In options, I have a mental stop, but because futures trade faster and have narrow bid/ask spreads, I actually set an automatic stop with my broker.

No Trend, No Trade

My trading style stresses the importance of trading with the prevailing trend. If I don't see a trend in the market I'm trading, I won't trade it. It's that simple. Instead, I will focus my attention on a different market or go and look at the options markets. Because I prefer to trade in the direction that the market is moving, trading only when there is a trend has been a rule that has kept me out of trouble.

Don't Chase the Move

There will be times when you are trading futures when you will feel that you have missed a move in the market because you didn't make your trade in time. This is normal, but it's how you react to this feeling that will determine your success as a trader. When a move is missed in the markets, it's best to always wait for a pullback before you reenter the trade.

Sarah's Trading Tip

I have to admit that there are times when it is hard to sit on my hands and avoid trading even though a setup might look lovely but doesn't align with my trading rules. You can decide how strict you want to be with your trading rules, but I choose to stay quite firm with mine. I have tried breaking my rules and have realized that I'm better off in the long run following my trading plan. I also find that it is useful to take time away from futures during the day to focus on other things in order not to get sucked into trades that may not be ideal. Statistically, I'm always looking for the best trade of the day, not many average trades. This means that I have had to be patient and always follow my trading rules until a trade sets up nicely. There are days when I don't trade at all but will always open my screens and watch the markets.

CREATE A MORNING ROUTINE

A good routine for scanning the markets for trades is very important. This should become second nature to all traders. A trading routine helps to establish good trading habits. Now that trading can occur anywhere there is an Internet connection, this has changed the working environment for many traders. What was once a career that required an office or a seat on the exchange now can be done in the comfort of one's own home. However, this means that creating a good trading routine is even more important to staying focused and disciplined as a trader. The next section is an example of my own morning routine. I believe that all traders need to create a routine to review their MY TRADE plan, review the overall markets, look for news events, and decide on an area of focus for the day.

My Morning Routine

Step 1. I begin the morning by looking online to see if there are any news events. I record any times that meaningful news events occur that day. www.forexfactory.com is a great resource for this information.

Step 2. Once the market opens, I watch the ES, YM, and TF to see how the market opens at 9:30 a.m. EST. I do not trade during the morning open until things settle down and begin to get into a nice rhythm.

Step 3. I look at the ES to begin to create my market analysis from my charts (from Chapter 4) and focus on what happened in the markets overnight.

Step 4. I review any options positions I'm currently holding to make sure that nothing needs attention.

Step 5. I begin to look through various futures markets and look at the multiple time frames (daily, 60-minute, and 5-minute). I'm looking for what I call *clean charts*. These are charts where price is moving cleanly in one direction with enough room to place a trade at support without running into major resistance. Based on this information, I will choose one or two markets to watch more closely during the day. If I can't find a futures market with clean charts that day, I will move my attention to options.

Step 6. Once I've decided on what markets I will focus on that day, I begin to decide if there is a trade setup in those particular markets. It is here that I'm beginning to think through my trade setups to decide which one might be appropriate for that day. I'm also gathering information to decide how strong the market is that supports my trading assumption.

Step 7. Wait. The market open is not the time to jump right into a trade (according to my personal trading rules). I observe the market internals and the support and resistance levels on the chart and use my indicators to help me pinpoint an entry. I also complete some notes on the "I Do, I Dunno, I Don't" chart (the template and instructions are listed in the Appendix).

Step 8. Once the market has settled in for the day, I enter a trade following the trade setup I have chosen.

Step 9. I look through the market internals and monitor the trade until it's time to exit according to the trade setup that I chose.

Step 10. I will usually focus only on futures in the morning and then move to options in the afternoon.

Sarah's Trading Tip

I pull up the ES every morning. Looking at the ES chart helps me to decide what markets I will focus my attention on during the day. I also use the ES to help with my options trades. It is a good gauge of the overall markets to help me understand whether the market is trending up or down that day. Generally, when I'm deciding what market to focus my attention on that day, I look for a market that is correlated with the ES and does not have resistance in the direction of the move. I look through the ES, YM, and TF and make my decision about which one I will focus on. Whichever market has cleaner charts will be my market of choice for that day. If I look at all three and I can't see a nice trend, then I will focus all my attention that day on options instead of futures. Yes, there are days when I don't trade at all. If I don't like the charts that I'm seeing, I can wait to watch to see what happens, but because I am typically a trend trader, I will wait on the sidelines until a trend appears before I enter the market.

Pulling It Together

So is this all there is to know about the futures markets? No. The information I have presented here is the information I had when I started trading. Keeping it simple is often best when you begin. This chapter gives you some foundational knowledge about the various markets, times to trade, and market personalities. Let's continue building on this knowledge and work through my specific trading setups.

Let's get into some trade setups, but before we do, I want to be clear. I am sharing my experience, my trade setups, and the perspectives that have worked for me. Please read the following disclaimer and reflect on it. It is important that you consider your risk before you place any kind of trade.

Disclaimer

Trading futures involves substantial risk of loss and is not suitable for all investors. You should carefully consider whether trading futures is suitable for you in light of your circumstances, knowledge, and financial resources. You may lose all or more of your initial investment. Consult your registered financial representative before investing any of your money. No investing recommendations are being made in this book. Always trade following your own plan.

You need to modify the trade setups discussed here when you create your own MY TRADE plan.

Trading in Fashion (Trading with the Trend)

This trading setup can be added to your trading toolbox. You can apply this strategy to the market and timing that you like, but it must be personalized to match your own risk/reward parameters. This is one of my favorite trade setups and is the one I use most often.

I typically use this trade in the ES, YM, and TF, but it has also worked for me in the 6E. This trade setup is pretty versatile for a trending market.

Trading-in-Fashion Trading Setup Look-Fors
- Good volume
- Clear levels of support and resistance
- Strong trend

What Is the Trade About?

This trade is about identifying a trend in the market and then placing a trade in the direction of the trend. If my trading assumption is that the trend is up or long, I look to buy. I place a buy order at a level where I think there is a pullback to a level of support. This trade is most successful in a trending market.

Why Choose This Trading Setup over Another?

This trade setup is helpful when the trends on the time frame I am looking at all are moving in the same direction, there's a similar trend in the ES, and market internals are supporting the direction of the trend.

When to Enter This Trade

This trade is a setup that I will use once a trend is established. I will not use this trade setup if I feel that the market is about to reverse directions. I use this trade setup during the day when there is good volume in the market.

Trading Tools for This Trading Setup

I begin by looking to find a market that is trending. I use market internals as well as the ES to determine whether there is a well-established trend. The market internals I review include:

- TICKs
- ADD
- ATR
- ES and the Foundations indicator

I look at all these market internals together to determine whether I believe that there is a trend in the market and whether it will continue long or short. I look for solid signs of evidence about the market direction by determining:

- Whether the TICKs is staying well below or above zero.
- Whether the ADD is positive or negative.

- What the range of the ATR is.
- What is happening in the ES and what the Foundations indicator is showing.

Then I move to the charts. I often look through the ES, TF, and YM to decide which market is the cleanest that day. I typically decide to trade only one futures market per day. I choose a market to focus on after quickly reviewing the charts from three time frames, including:

- Daily
- 60 minute
- 5 minute with the Foundations indicator

Each of my time frame charts has levels of support and resistance. These levels are:

- 200-period moving average
- 100-period moving average
- 50-period moving average
- 21-period moving average
- 13-period moving average

How to Enter/Exit the Trade
Once I believe that a trend is established and I have identified an entry point from the 5-minute chart, I will place a trade in thirds. Here are the steps in detail:

Step 1. Watch for a strong trend on various time frame charts.
Step 2. Determine if the internals and price are moving in the same direction.
Step 3. Using the Foundations indicator and support and resistance levels, look to enter a trade in the direction of the trend when it pulls back to a level of support.
Step 4. Enter a trade in thirds.

Step 5. Exit in thirds. Place the first exit about 6 ticks above the entry level (this may need to be adjusted based on the average true range that day) for the YM and 3 ticks for the ES.

Step 6. Place another exit at about 18 ticks above the entry level for the YM (this may need to be adjusted based on the average true range that day) and 6 ticks for the ES.

Step 7. To exit the last third of the contract, place the exit below where the price action is in order to trail the stop. Exit the contract when your profit target is hit, but always protect the profits already made by moving the stop close to the price action as it continues to move in your favor.

Trading-with-the-Trend Example

Begin by following Sarah's Simple Steps to determine the market trend, and choose which market you will use to trade. In this example, I have chosen to trade the YM.

Step 1. Watch for a strong trend in various time frame charts. Figure 6.10*a* shows that the YM has a nice uptrend.

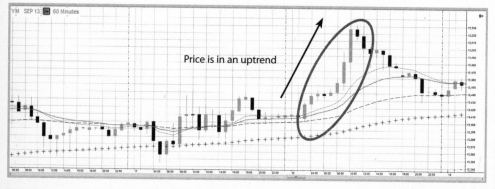

FIGURE 6.10*a* A 60-minute YM chart with trend.   *(Source: MultiCharts.)*

Step 2. Determine if the internals and price are moving in the same direction. For this trade setup, I'm paying close attention to the TICKs, ADD, ATR, and the broad market (the ES). I'm watching to make sure that these market internals are moving in the same direction. In this example, I'm looking for market internals that are supporting a long move.

Step 3. Using the Foundations indicator and support and resistance levels, look to enter a trade in the direction of the trend when it pulls back to a level of support. Figure 6.10*b* shows a great example of an in-fashion trade at 10:25 a.m. I believe that there is a trend long and, as such, will place a trade to buy. The Foundations indicator is also showing all white dots, supporting the decision to enter the trade.

Step 4. Enter the trade in thirds. In this example, I am using three contracts to keep the example simple. Please note that the number of contracts that a trader enters is a personal decision based on the trader's risk/reward parameters and account size.

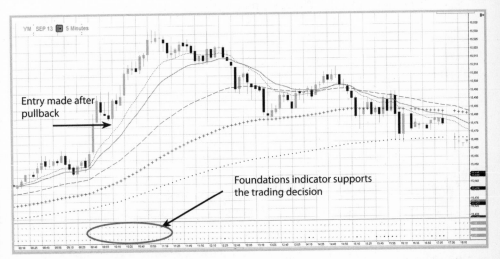

FIGURE 6.10*b* A 5-minute YM chart with trend. (Source: MultiCharts.)

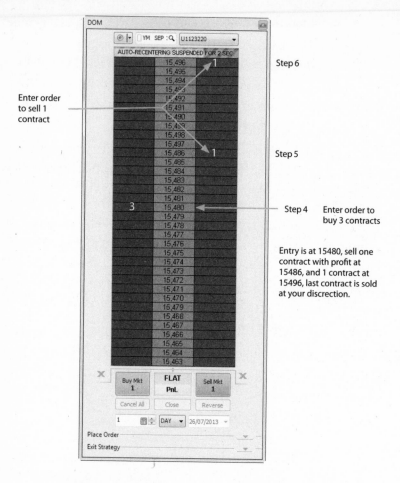

FIGURE 6.10c YM DOM.   *(Source: MultiCharts.)*

Step 5. Exit the trade in thirds. Place the first exit about 6 ticks above the entry level (this may need to be adjusted based on the average true range that day).

Step 6. Place another exit about 16 ticks above the entry level for the YM (this may need to be adjusted based on the average true range that day).

Step 7. To exit the last third of the contracts, place the exit below where the price action is in order to trail the stop. Exit this contract when your profit target is hit, but always protect the profits already made by moving the stop close to the price action as it continues to move in your favor.

Coffee-Break Trade

This trade setup is about focusing on the reaction of the markets around 10:30 a.m. EST. It takes advantage of a change in market trend that usually happens around this time (this is when I'm joking that other traders have all gone for a coffee break after the morning open).

What Is the Trade About?

I enter this trade if there is a trending market, but the market has had a quick move at the open in the opposite direction. I use the market internals to confirm that the direction of the trend is still valid prior to entering to make sure that the move isn't a reversal as opposed to a retracement. I have noticed that retracements against the trend will resolve themselves in the direction of the internals after the market open, usually around 10:30 a.m. EST. Then I look to exit once my profit target is hit. I am usually out of this trade by 11 a.m. EST when the market will pick back up again in the direction of the trend.

Why Choose This Trading Setup over Another?

This trade takes advantage of a natural break in the market when the market seems to relax after the morning rush.

When to Enter This Trade?

This trade is about time. Watch for reversal signs in the internals between 10:30 and 11 a.m.

Look-Fors

- Internals indicating that the opening move might reverse
- Levels of support or resistance where a reversal in trend could happen
- Strong up or down move at the open against the trend with internals not confirming the move

Trading Tools Used for This Trading Setup

The market internals are important for this trade setup. I use the TICKs, ADD, VIX, and the Foundations indicator. Because this trade is more about the time of day, I look for a move against the trend that might be appearing first thing in the morning but then focus my attention on the clock and indications that the trend may be reversing.

Charts I Use for This Trading Setup

- Daily time frame
- Five-minute time frame

Support and Resistance Levels Used for This Trading Setup

Each of these levels of moving averages is seen on all three of the time frame charts I use:

- 200-period moving average
- 100-period moving average
- 50 period moving average
- 21-period moving average
- 13-period moving average

How to Enter/Exit This Trade?

This trade is entered in the same direction as the prevailing trend when there is a retracement against the prevailing trend. The trade is placed at levels of support or resistance where the trend will change and is placed in alignment with the internals, waiting for the price to correct.

Step 1. Watch the ES for a trend after the market opens.

Step 2. Watch for internals and price to be opposite, for example, uptrend with weak internals.

Step 3. Using the Foundations indicator and support and resistance levels, look to enter a trade in the direction of the trend when the market begins to retrace.

Step 4. Enter the trade on the DOM.

Step 5. The trade can be exited in thirds, or place a profit target based on the momentum of the market internals and before any level of major resistance.

Here is an example of this trade setup:

Step 1. Watch the ES for a trend after the market opens. The daily chart in Figure 6.11*a* shows that the ES has been in a long trend overall. All the EMAs are acting as support and are below the price action. There is a long-term upside bias in the market.

The market opened with a move down, but the internals and daily trend were indicating that the market should be moving higher. The contrasting information from the daily trend and the internals at the open indicated that the initial push lower is most likely a retracement short that will end up reversing to match the long bias, as indicated by the internals and daily trend. They are both in opposition. This information is letting me know that a Coffee-Break trade is probably setting up.

Step 2. Watch for internals and price to be opposite, for example, uptrend with weak internals. Figure 6.11*c* shows the VIX. The VIX is moving down. When the VIX is moving in one direction, the overall market is usually moving in opposition, this confirms that the Coffee-Break trade is setting up. I will be thinking about placing a long (buy) trade when the market signals that price is once again moving to the upside.

Figure 6.11*d* shows the TICKs. This market internal is moving back and forth around zero. There isn't a clear direction. The indecision of the TICKs supports the idea that a reversal in trend is possible.

Step 3. Using the Foundations indicator and support and resistance levels, look to enter a trade in the direction of the trend when the market retraces. Figure 6.11*e* is the 5-minute ES chart. The reversal begins at around 10:05 a.m. You can see that the chart begins to move up. A more aggressive entry might be to enter now or wait for confirmation from the Foundations indicator. At 10:15 a.m., the Foundations indicator shows three white dots.

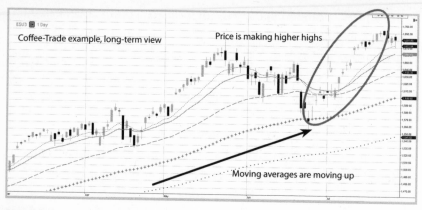

FIGURE 6.11a Daily ES chart.

(Source: MultiCharts.)

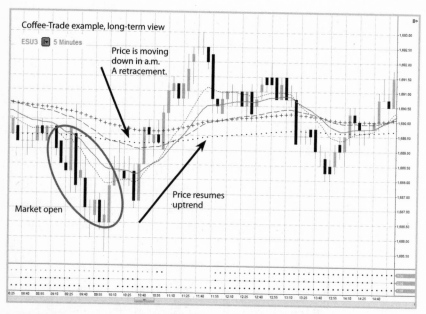

FIGURE 6.11b A 5-minute ES chart with Foundations indicator.

(Source: MultiCharts.)

Step 4. Enter trade on the DOM.

Step 5. The trade can be exited in thirds, or you can place a profit target based on the momentum of the market internals and before any level of major resistance.

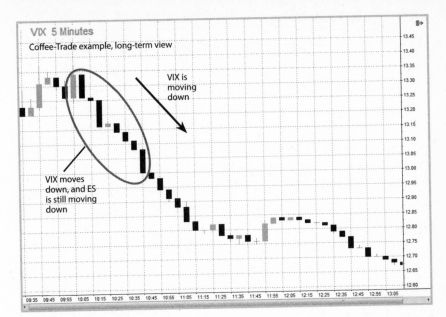

FIGURE 6.11c The VIX. *(Source: MultiCharts.)*

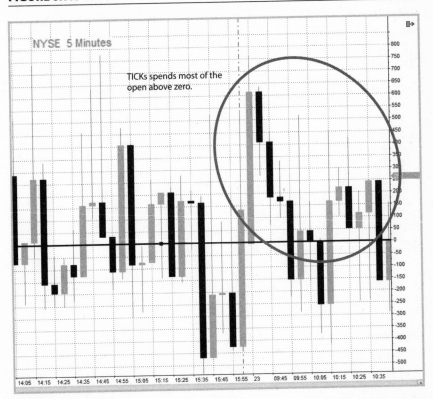

FIGURE 6.11d The TICKs. *(Source: MultiCharts.)*

Va-va-voom Trade Setup

The goal of this trade setup is to expect only a few ticks per trade. It takes advantage of how often price moves toward a major level of support and resistance because, generally, price will gravitate to levels of support and resistance.

I enter this trade in the direction of the market trend, with the assumption that price will continue to move in the same direction until it reaches a major level of support/resistance. I will capitalize on the movement by entering the trade as price gets attracted toward support and exit at support. This trading setup is similar to scalping in that I'm not looking for big moves; I'm looking for a few ticks of movement.

What Is the Trade About?

Because I'm using support or resistance levels as a guide for this setup, it doesn't matter if all time frames all aligned, but if they are aligned, that is even better. I enter and exit this trade with the idea that the market will move in and touch major levels. I use this movement to my advantage. Markets will be drawn to major levels because of momentum that is usu-

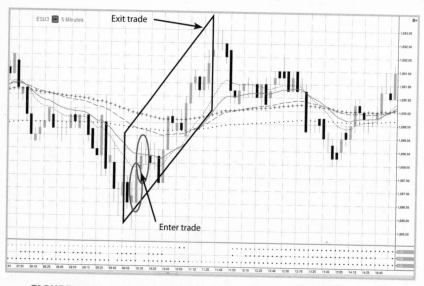

FIGURE 6.11e A 5-minute ES chart with Foundations indicator. *(Source: MultiCharts.)*

ally associated around each of the support and resistance levels. As such, I am able to take some small profit here. Just as in real life, it's hard to stop a train when it's moving at top speed; hop on the train, and take advantage of the momentum. Va va voom! When price is moving toward a level of support or resistance, the levels of support or resistance will tend to attract price.

Why Choose This Trading Setup over Another?

This trading setup is ideal in sideways markets, especially if the market isn't making big moves in either direction. It takes advantage of the movement between levels of support and resistance. This is also a good setup if you prefer to trade more often with smaller profits per trade.

When to Enter This Trade?

This trade can be entered at any time during the day; the more volume and momentum of a move, the higher the probability is that this trade will profit. Remember, the goal of this trade setup is to place a trade as price is moving into resistance or support; it isn't about a big move. The goal is to enter and take quick profits more often throughout the day off the major levels of support and resistance.

This trading setup can work in lower-volume markets, but with less probability. However, I look for consistent profits when I trade, so I like to find times when there is good volume because I feel this trading setup will work the best and trigger quickly in such situations.

Look-Fors

- Good volume
- Price action near major resistance support levels
- TICKs confirming the same direction of the movement into the EMA

Trading Tools Used for This Trading Setup

This trading setup will work in sideways markets and moving markets. Because this trade is made using the information from the charts, the only market internal I look at is the TICKs. The TICKs helps me with which direction to place the trade, either short or long.

Charts I Use for This Trading Setup
- 60-minute
- 5-minute

Support and Resistance on the Charts Used for This Trading Setup
- 200-period moving average
- 100-period moving average
- 50-period moving average
- 21-period moving average

How to Enter/Exit the Trade?

Step 1. Watch price movement, and observe where the 21-period EMA is on various time frame charts.

Step 2. Look for price to be moving close to a major level of support or resistance but is at least 10 ticks away.

Step 3. Look at the TICKs to ensure that the TICKs direction is the same as the current direction of price movement.

Step 4. Enter trade on the DOM in the direction of price movement.

Step 5. Exit the trade just before any level of major resistance.

Here is an example of this trading setup:

Step 1. Watch the market movement, and observe where the 21-period EMA is on various time frame charts. I look at the 60-minute chart (Figure 6.12*a*) and notice that there is an uptrend.

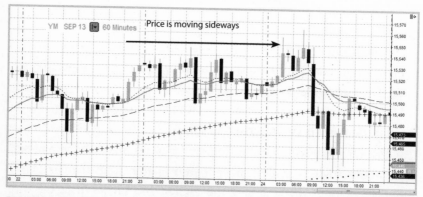

FIGURE 6.12*a* The 60-minute YM chart.   *(Source: MultiCharts.)*

Step 2. On the 5-minute chart (Figure 6.12*b*) I look for momentum moving close to a major level of support or resistance, but the current price must be at least 10 ticks away. I generally use the 21-period EMA as the level of resistance that will attract price. You can see that at 10:30 a.m., the market is forming a bottom, and price is being attracted to the 21-period EMA.

FIGURE 6.12*b* The 5-minute YM chart.   *(Source: MultiCharts.)*

Step 3. Look at the TICKs chart to ensure that the direction is the same as the current direction of price movement. The TICKs chart in Figure 6.12*c* confirms that price is heading lower, but at the same time that price looks like it is making a bottom, the TICKs is pushing higher and pushes above 0 for the first time that day, just as price makes its move back up to the 21-period EMA before a retracement of the downtrend.

Step 4. Enter the trade on the DOM in the direction of market movement.

Step 5. Exit the trade just before any level of major resistance.

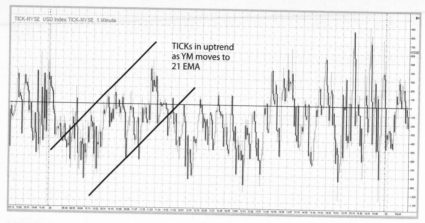

TICKs in uptrend
as YM moves to
21 EMA

FIGURE 6.12c

(Source: MultiCharts.)

About My Three Favorite Trading Setups

Following specific steps can be tremendously helpful in painting a bigger picture. These trading setups can be used step by step, but I would encourage you to add your own flare to them. Think of them as starting points that should be refined to match your trading personality.

I've shared these three trading setups with you because it's important that you walk away from this book knowing some steps to take to actually place a trade in the futures markets if you choose to. If this is your first time trading futures, I would recommend that you begin trying these setups in a paper account so that you can tweak them based on your risk/reward parameter and MY TRADE plan. These trading setups have worked for me after careful tweaking and reflection on my performance. Spending the time refining these trading setups to work for you will help you to make sure that you understand how to enter, manag e, and exit the trades.

Sarah's Trading Tip

Trading in the futures market can be fast, and as such, you will need to have an established plan before you place a trade. Any futures trade can move in your favor or against you quickly. In order to maintain your emotional control, make sure that you have written out your trading setup in your MY TRADE plan so that you are able to follow through on your trade in the heat of the moment.

Key Take-Aways

- Futures have many markets that can be traded. The futures market is characterized as a fast market that can be lucrative for some traders, but it can also go against traders quickly. Futures provide the flexibility to be traded almost 24 hours a day, which means that part-time traders can take advantage of trading before or after any other job.
- Futures trading should be tailored to your trading personality to ensure that your trading potential is met.
- Futures traders have specific trading rules and trading routines that need to be established in order to ensure that each trade is taken responsibly and with precision.
- Detailed steps are provided so that you can understand how I trade futures. My three futures trading strategies can be applied step by step to many markets but always should be tailored to meet your risk/reward parameters. The three trading setups include the Coffee-Break trade (after the morning rush), the In-Fashion trade (trading with the trend), and the Va-va-voom trade (momentum scalp).

7

HOW TO TRADE *SMART*

Illustrated by Noble Rains

Key Chapter Concepts

- *Develop the skill of trading with a MY TRADE plan.*
- *Understand how to create a trading plan with risk parameters with which you are comfortable.*
- *Understand risk and reward ratios.*
- *Understand how to complete your own MY TRADE plan.*
- *Discuss tracking systems to optimize your trading performance.*

Everyone needs a trading plan, period. Your trading plan outlines all the essential information you will need to inform your trading and anchor your trading performance. By writing down your trading rules, setups, and risk/reward parameters, you will be defining how and when you will trade. Everyone needs goals, and it isn't enough to just to think about these goals. In order to bring any goal to reality, you need a clear plan with steps to get there. The steps to meet your eventual goals should be tracked and celebrated along the way. Regardless of what your trading plan looks like, you need one!

Most important, you need a plan that you implement and review regularly. A trading plan is the manual that you will follow that outlines the information you will need for your trading setups. As you read through this chapter, make some notes or begin to complete the MY TRADE plan. The template for this plan is found in the Appendix at the end of this book and is available for download by e-mailing support@ shecantrade.com. I have developed the MY TRADE plan to help traders set goals and articulate their trading plans.

Successful trading requires systems to be in place for you to track and monitor your trades. Each trading strategy should include a plan that outlines the markets you will trade, how you will decide on your trading assumptions, steps to outline your trading setups, and a means to review your progress. This chapter will review a MY TRADE plan that can be used in any market so that you can spend time planning your trades, implementing your trade setups, and creating a trading journal to evaluate your performance.

DEVELOPING THE SKILL OF TRADING

Trading is a journey. Be cautious of any course that claims to teach you everything about the markets so that you'll be an overnight success. Just as with any other skill in life, you will need to learn, allow time to apply your knowledge, and then refine your plan so as to become a successful trader. Your MY TRADE plan will be the foundation of your trades, market analysis, and evaluation of your trading performance.

Developing your skills as a successful trader goes beyond just placing trades. It also includes understanding how to manage winning and losing trades, how to control your emotions, and refining how you analyze the markets you trade. Developing a trading plan will help you to stay on target and react to the markets in a manner that is reflective of your trading personality. Your MY TRADE plan will help you to articulate all these aspects of trading so that you are developing your skills to reach your trading potential.

Creating and reviewing your MY TRADE plan will serve to increase your confidence in your trading ability. If you are trading based on your own thoughts, analyzing the markets based on your own chart analysis, and forming your own trading opinions and assumptions, your confidence in your trading ability will increase. Your perspective on the markets will shift to one that is incredibly empowering. As you track your trading progress and review your plan, you will begin to develop your trading mindset. Trading will start to become second nature, and you will find that trading becomes almost automatic. Much as when you first started to drive an automobile, at first, every action and reaction required thought; as you gained more experience driving, these actions became more automatic.

Along with a MY TRADE plan, a trading journal will help you measure your progress. It allows you to understand how to leverage your strengths and support your trading needs in the most efficient way. Rather than just hoping that your trading will improve, your MY TRADE plan and journal will begin to reveal areas that you can continue to refine and highlight other areas of your trading plan that are working well. In trading, it is always better to concentrate on what is working rather than on what is not working in order to leverage your strengths to compensate for areas that still need improvement.

Anyone has the ability to make money in the markets—I've made this point throughout this book—it is the consistent application of this knowledge that makes a skilled trader. You need a plan, you need to monitor your plan, and you need to refine your plan as your knowledge and experience grow. This is true for all skills in life—and is also true for trading.

Sarah's Trading Tip

I love hearing from others and staying connected with both new and experienced traders. When people meet me, they will often tell me stories of how they tried to invest in the stock market, but it didn't really work out for them. As they tell their stories, some common themes emerge. Many of these people are referring to one of their first trades or trades they copied because they heard about some great trading tip. Each of these stories usually ends with how much money they lost and their feelings that trading is too complicated for them.

These stories are the reason why I wanted to write this book. It's important to acknowledge that in today's educational climate, specifics about trading education are rarely discussed in detail. Even university and college degrees in finance speak little of actual day- or swing-trading strategies for the average person. Your MY TRADE plan will help you begin to set up your plan so that you feel empowered to make your own trading decisions and understand how to create a trading assumption. I'm hoping that this book will bring me one step closer to reducing the number of people who come to me feeling helpless about trading.

How to Set Up a Trading Plan with Risk Parameters

My best advice about deciding on your risk parameters involves two main factors:

1. Your motivation to trade
2. The amount of money you begin trading with

These two factors will have an impact on your risk parameters. The reality is that all investing involves some degree of risk. How much risk you are willing to take on will vary from trader to trader, but all traders need to be aware of the risks of each of their trades (Figure 7.1).

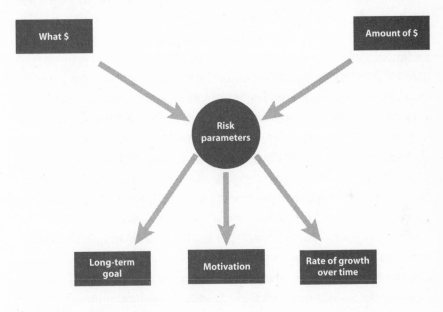

FIGURE 7.1 Risk parameters.

There are many ways to limit your risk when you invest. You can adjust your trading to be anywhere along the risk spectrum. You need to be aware of and comfortable with the way you are investing and make sure that it matches your risk limits. Understanding your risk parameters will help you to set up your trading plan. Once you have established your motivation to trade and determined the amount of money you will trade with, you will be able to use this information as you set up your trading plan.

First, what money are you trading with? This question supports some reflection about the money you are actually trading with. If you are trading with some extra money that you have saved up or that you got from a work bonus, your emotional attachment and expectations may be different from what they might be if you are trading with your retirement money. Each of your emotional attachments will support the way you will think and react to trading decisions. If you are trading from your 401(k), your trades should reflect a more conservative approach to trading. Ask yourself, can you afford to lose this money?

The second main factor is how much money you are trading with. Regardless of whether you are trading with $10,000 or $500,000, the size of the trades you place in your account should always stay aligned with the amount of money you have in your account. It just isn't a realistic goal to say that in 30 days you will make $5,000 trading a $10,000 account. Think about how you would feel if you lost everything in one trade.

Most people will naturally think about how great it feels to make all sorts of money with the account they are trading, but they do not think about how they would feel if they lost the money. Your profits will help you to dream and create goals to work toward, but you also need to consider what might happen if you lose the money. The reality check of creating your risk/reward ratios based on what you can afford to lose will help you to keep your ratios realistic. Your goal should be rooted in a steady increase in the size of your account over time. A good rule of thumb is to risk no more than 3 to 5 percent of your account in any one trade. In this way, no one loss will make a huge difference in your account.

More questions to consider connected to risk include:

- What is your long-term goal while trading?
- What is your rate of expected growth over time?

These questions should help you to understand how much of your money you will be comfortable trading at one time. In order to have a steady growth rate over time, it is obvious that you can't have 100 percent of your account in trades at one time. By having all your capital tied up, you are also unable to place further trades and take advantage of new opportunities. New trades will emerge throughout the week, and you need to keep some "powder dry" to make those trades. Your expected rate of growth should not be based on your total account size; it should be based on the capital you are putting to work every week.

These factors are the key to successfully managing your risk parameters. Understanding these parameters will help you decide how much money you are comfortable putting into trades at one time. This is a personal decision and one that should be thought through carefully.

> **Sarah's Trading Tip**
>
> *I have found that it's most helpful to place smaller trades relative to my account but and trade more often. I prefer to follow a more conservative slow and steady approach as a trading style. I don't ever risk my entire account. Individual trade sizes are always below 5 percent of my trading account. I started small but have grown my account size and now have the ability to place more trades. You will need to make your own decision about your trading risk parameters based on your trading personality and motivation.*

UNDERSTANDING RISK/REWARD RATIOS

Risk/reward ratios are important in trading; they help you to manage your profitability. Your profitability as a trader should be defined by your risk/reward ratios rather than by your percentage of profitable trades. In order to be successful as a trader, all your trades need to add up to more profits than losses. Thus, for example, if you have five great trades where you make $50 in each of the five trades but one bad trade that loses $250, you are left with no profits. In fact, you will owe money to your broker in commissions. Always be aware of your trading setups and their risk/reward ratios to help guide your trading strategy.

Figure 7.2 is a good visual to help explain how your win/loss ratio will affect you as a trader. People will fit into one of the four quadrants, but successful traders will fall into either the first or fourth quadrant.

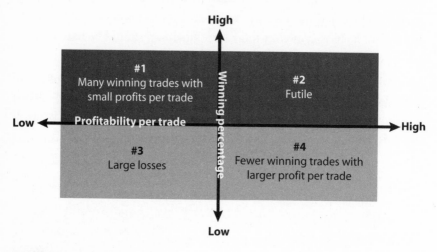

FIGURE 7.2 Risk/reward quadrants.

Picture a quadrant; on the horizontal axis is dollar profit per trade, and on the vertical axis is percentage of winning trades. Most new traders' goal might be initially to strive to be in the top right-hand quadrant (#2). New traders often think that professional traders would fall into this category. This quadrant however is futile. It implies that traders set up big trades to make a lot of money every single time. This is an unrealistic goal (quadrant). To assume that every single trade is going to have huge profits will only set you up for disappointment. The reality is that some of your trades will do well, but others may only make small gains or have losses.

Conversely, the quadrant to avoid is the quadrant where you lose a lot of money on a high number of trades. This quadrant is located at the lower left side of the image (#3). If a trader finds herself in this quadrant, she will deplete a trading account quickly. People will most often fall into this quadrant when they are trading by wishing and hoping rather than by following a solid trading plan. Logically, this leaves two remaining quadrants of risk/reward. These two quadrants are where most successful traders find themselves. It is these two quadrants that enable traders to be profitable over time. The first quadrant involves making a little profit per trade but on many trades. This type of trader looks for many small trades where both the reward and risk are lower but the probability is higher. This quadrant will also influence how you place your stops. If you prefer to take small profits you will also need to have smaller stops to ensure that one bad trade does not erase many profitable trades.

The fourth quadrant to be discussed involves making a large profit on a few trades. This type of trader patiently waits and watches the markets until she finds a setup she really likes; then she places a trade that will provide an opportunity for a larger profit. This type of trader will have wider stops but will be willing to let winning trades run without exiting early and taking partial profits. Letting your winning trades run can be more difficult than it sounds, especially when you are new to trading. In order to be successful in this quadrant, a trader must be able to stay calm as her trades move in the anticipated direction until her profit targets are hit. If this type of trader is constantly exiting trades once they have made a little bit of money without reaching their targets, she cannot be profitable. This type of trader will also have to watch profitable trades turn into losers as the ultimate profit goal of the trade has not been reached. Watching winners turn to losers is very tough on the psyche of a trader. You need to have confidence in your plan and know that you will find big trades and have the patience to let them develop fully.

Each of the trading styles just described will require traders to develop their trading plan in a specific way. As a trader, you need to figure out where you fall on the chart and trade according to the quadrant that best reflects your preferred trading style. This is where your trading plan is so helpful because it prompts you to keep your emotions in check and allows you to execute trades based on your plan and not on your emotions. The goal is to help you to overcome two of the biggest hurdles for traders—taking profits too early and staying in losing trades too long.

Setting Stops

I believe that everyone should be trading with stops, whether the stops are in your head or is an actual stop order placed with your broker when you initiate a trade. *Setting a stop* refers to where a trade will be exited if it goes against you. Conversely, *setting a profit target* is where a trade will be exited because it has met your profit target.

Trading with or without stops is a widely debated topic, with different opinions based on different traders' perspectives and depending on the market you are trading. Personally, I believe that everyone should be placing appropriate stop levels or levels where you exit a trade regardless of what you are trading. The stop levels should be specific to the market you are trading.

Other books about trading might discuss placing stops at predefined levels and establishing targets based on your account size or the number of contracts traded, but they neglect to mention that trading style also contributes to risk/reward parameters. I would argue that stops and targets should be adjusted for each trade taken based on your risk quadrant in combination with the volatility of the market and dollar value of the trade will determine an appropriate stop level.

I believe that stops need to be set based on four factors:

1. Size of your account and the percentage of your account you are willing to risk on each trade.

   If you are willing to place riskier trades, then you will also need to realize that trades will go against you. Ensure that you have designed your trading plan to reflect the profit and loss targets that will still equate to a positive sum. Even aggressive traders will need stops that are aligned with the amount of money they are willing to risk on each trade.

2. The instrument you are trading (e.g., volatility of the trading instrument).

   If you are a trader who likes to take quick profits, then you need to adjust your stops accordingly and take small losses. Contrast this with a trader who is able to hold winning trades; this trader can also have larger stops because his winners are larger as well. A stop level will be set differently in each market and to accommodate different trading instruments because some stocks are more volatile than others. I would not try to trade Baidu Inc. (BIDU) in the same manner that I trade IBM or gold. When you create your trading plan, you need to make accommodations for the volatility of the instrument you are trading.

3. The trading style or risk quadrant you relate to.

   When you are able to identify the quadrant of risk that you are most comfortable with, your stop loss levels should also reflect that quadrant. Someone who trades often with small profit targets should also have a small stop loss. A trader using a strategy of trading less often with larger profit targets will have to place a relative stop that provides enough time for the target to be achieved without being stopped out too soon.

4. Anticipated targets for the trade. (e.g., support and resistance).

   In order to overcome any temptation to undermine your target and stop decisions, you need to set targets and stops not based on what you hope to make in profit but rather based on how you have seen a trading instrument move in the past. Support and resistance are important when determining a stop level. Stop levels that coincide with support levels are much more likely to hold. This becomes even more important for options trades that last longer and have more volatility. For futures, stop levels also need to be aligned with market movement based on an indicator such as the average true range (ATR).

Setting stops provides an automatic way for a trader to control trading losses so that accounts don't get wiped out. Make sure that your stop is mathematically related to your profits. A trader's goal is to consistently make money and control her losses. It just doesn't make sense to set stops at a level where, even if four out of five trades work in your favor, the fifth trade will wipe out all of your profits from the previous trades.

You cannot base your stops on dollar value alone; you need to also base the size of the stop on the volatility of the instrument you are trading. If you trade a volatile instrument with tight stops, you might be right on the trade, but you will be whipsawed in and out of the trade. It can be very frustrating to have the correct assumption about a trade but still lose money because your stops were set too tight.

Remember that markets change on a daily basis and even faster on an intraday basis; it is for this reason that your stops will have to be constantly evaluated as part of your trading considerations before you place a trade. For example, the S&P 500 might be moving 6 to 8 ticks per 5-minute bar in the morning and quiet down and move only 3 to 4 ticks per 5-minute bar in the afternoon. Determine your stop levels based on the price action you are seeing at the time you place a trade.

It will take time to develop a good eye for setting stops based on the four factors just mentioned as well as time to develop the confidence to trust your stops and targets. Experiment in your paper trading account until you have found a stop-loss strategy that incorporates all four factors.

Sarah's Trading Tip

Interestingly, in my experience, most traders are better able to take a stop than wait until their profit targets are hit. What happens is that traders will use a wide stop and let that stop be hit before exiting the trade but will exit the trade with a few ticks of profit just to protect what they have made. This creates a risk/reward ratio biased to the downside. New traders often get excited when a trade is moving in their favor and quickly exit the trade before their profit target is hit. Be aware of your response to both managing your losses and hitting your profit targets when you trade.

MY TRADE PLAN

Once you have identified your risk parameters, which include your motivation to trade, your comfort with stops, your rate of growth, and your risk quadrant, you can apply this information by answering each of the following questions to complete your MY TRADE plan. The MY TRADE plan is organized into specific categories and has two parts. Each of the categories is listed in Figure 7.3.

MARKETS

YOUR GOALS

TRADES

RULES

ACTION

DRAWDOWNS

EVALUATE

FIGURE 7.3 MY TRADE plan.

The categories from the MY TRADE plan will help you answer these questions:

- What market will you trade?
- What are your trading goals?
- What trading setups will you use?
- What rules will you follow for yourself?
- What will you do as you enter, manage, and exit trades?
- What are your drawdowns, including stops and losses?
- How you will evaluate your trading performance?

The questions from the first section of the MY TRADE plan will help you to articulate your trading goals, trading strategies, risk parameters, and progress. The second part of the plan supports the articulation of measurable and achievable action statements. These statements outline what a trader will actually do to trade.

Whether this is your first time writing a trading plan or you are reviewing an existing plan, these questions will help you to reach your trading potential. A template of the MY TRADE plan is available in the Appendix and is available to download from www.shecantrade.com.

Purpose of MY TRADE Plan

Figure 7.4 is a representation of the cyclical nature of a MY TRADE plan. These reflective questions are part of the process to develop a solid trading plan that is individualized based on your own trading personality and style.

FIGURE 7.4 Implementation of a trading plan

MY TRADE Plan Is Smart

Even though it is often talked about, very few traders will actually share their personal trading plans. The MY TRADE plan not only helps you to think through vital information, but it also helps you to establish goal statements that are written using language that is specific, measurable, attainable, realistic, and timely—most commonly in the business world known as S.M.A.R.T. language. Many large organizations have created their organizational goals in what is referred to as S.M.A.R.T. language because of the positive effects it has on the ability to help people meet goals. S.M.A.R.T. language is designed to help everyone be able to articulate and formulate an action plan. You can search for information about S.M.A.R.T. language and its benefits online; my goal in bringing this up is so that you can apply some of these ideas to a trading plan that becomes most beneficial for you. The S.M.A.R.T. language in your MY TRADE plan will be articulated as you create your measurable and achievable action statements.

Look specifically at each of the sections in Figure 7.5. This is an example of my action statements. By the end of this process of writing a MY TRADE plan, you should have something similar that specifically outlines how you will trade a market. You will need to create a separate plan for each market that you intend to trade. For example, if you will be trading futures and options, you will need two copies of the MY TRADE plan because the setups, goals, and trades will be different. If you are trading using many trading setups, you also might find it helpful to separate the setups and work through the questions for each. Whatever way you choose to fill out the plan, it needs to work and make sense for you. Once you have reviewed all the questions, you will create a one-page summary of your goals that is written in language that is observable, measurable, and attainable for your trading.

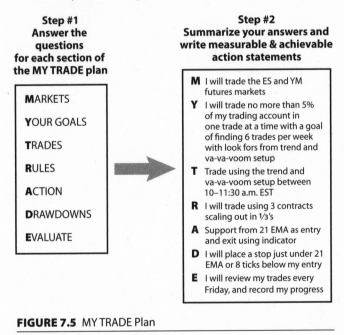

Step #1
Answer the questions for each section of the MY TRADE plan

MARKETS

YOUR GOALS

TRADES

RULES

ACTION

DRAWDOWNS

EVALUATE

Step #2
Summarize your answers and write measurable & achievable action statements

M I will trade the ES and YM futures markets

Y I will trade no more than 5% of my trading account in one trade at a time with a goal of finding 6 trades per week with look fors from trend and va-va-voom setup

T Trade using the trend and va-va-voom setup between 10–11:30 a.m. EST

R I will trade using 3 contracts scaling out in ⅓'s

A Support from 21 EMA as entry and exit using indicator

D I will place a stop just under 21 EMA or 8 ticks below my entry

E I will review my trades every Friday, and record my progress

FIGURE 7.5 MY TRADE Plan

Answer the MY TRADE questions—Step #1

Begin by writing down the answers to the questions under each section of Table 7.1. Each set of questions will pertain to specific areas of your trading. These questions are designed to help you think through what market you want to trade, your goals, how you will trade, specific trading rules you will follow, how you will manage risk and evaluate your performance.

TABLE 7.1 MYTRADE Plan reflective questions

M is for Markets
This section focuses on what you will do in each market you trade. Questions you need to answer in this section include: • What broad markets will you use to inform your overall assumptions about the direction-of-the-market?   • What specific markets will be on your watch list?   • What trading instrument will you trade in each market?   • Where will you gather information about economic news events (economic reports, earnings)?

Y is for Your Goals
This section focuses on the goals you would like to achieve. Questions you will need to answer in this section include: • What are some goals you would like to achieve given your account size?   • What timeline will you set out for yourself to meet at least three small steps leading to a larger goal?   • What will your rewards be along the way?   • How will you track your progress?

T is for Trades
This section focuses on the tools you will use to trade. Questions you will need to answer in this section include: • What will you trade?   • What setups will you use?   • How will you decide at what level to enter a trade?   • What time will you trade?

R is for Rules

This section focuses on the rules you will follow when you trade. Questions you will need to answer in this section include:

- What time will you trade?
- What contract size will you use when you place trades in specific markets?
- Where will you place your stops/targets for each trading strategy you use?
- What is your pre/postmarket routine?
- What percentage of your account will you actively have in the markets at any time?

A is for Action

Questions you will need to answer in this section include:

- What criteria will you use to enter a trade?
- How will you monitor your trades once you are in?
- What is your exit strategy?
- What indicators will you use?

D is for Drawdowns

Questions you will need to answer in this section include:

- What will you do if a trade is going against you?
- What information will you gather to determine your exits?
- How will you identify how your emotions are influencing your trading actions?
- When will you reduce/increase your position size?

E is for Evaluate

Questions you will need to answer in this section include:

- How will you review how your trades went?
- How will you record how you felt before, during, and after a trade?
- When will you review your trades?

Taking the Plan to Action—Step #2

Once you have completed answering the questions in Table 7.1, each section will need to be summarized and broken down into statements that are measurable and achievable to form your plan. To write your action statements follow these steps.

1. Review your answers from each section of MY TRADE.
2. Summarize the information, and write one sentence as an action statement for each section using your answers from the Market section, then write a sentence that outlines which market you will trade.
3. Write each action statement using words that include *I will* with *what* and *how* you will do specific to each section. Notice that the examples shown in Figure 7.6 link to the questions that are written in each section of the MY TRADE plan.

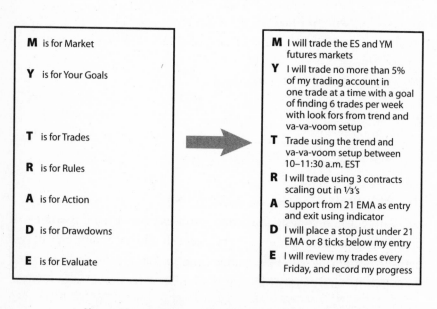

M is for Market

Y is for Your Goals

T is for Trades

R is for Rules

A is for Action

D is for Drawdowns

E is for Evaluate

M I will trade the ES and YM futures markets

Y I will trade no more than 5% of my trading account in one trade at a time with a goal of finding 6 trades per week with look fors from trend and va-va-voom setup

T Trade using the trend and va-va-voom setup between 10–11:30 a.m. EST

R I will trade using 3 contracts scaling out in ⅓'s

A Support from 21 EMA as entry and exit using indicator

D I will place a stop just under 21 EMA or 8 ticks below my entry

E I will review my trades every Friday, and record my progress

*Your action statements should be written in language
that is positive and focused on action.*

FIGURE 7.6 Example of action statements from Sarah's MY TRADE plan.

There will be one action statement for each section of the MY TRADE plan. This means that your MY TRADE plan will include an action statement to answer:

- What market will you trade?
- What are your goals?
- What trading strategies will you use?
- What trading rules will you follow?
- How will you inform your trading decisions?
- What are your parameters for money management?
- How will you evaluate your progress?

These action statements should be accessible and close to you when you are trading; this will help to inform your trading decisions.

Once you have completed your action statements, your trading plan is complete. However, it will need to be updated and reviewed regularly. Your trading will continue to improve and be refined the longer you trade. As a result, your trading plan will also need to be adjusted accordingly.

Monitoring Your MY TRADE Plan

A new trader will solidify her learning over time, whereas an experienced trader will always be looking for ways to refine his trades to increase his profits. This is why every trader, regardless of experience, should have a method to monitor his or her MY TRADE plan.

Tracking Your Trades Throughout the Day

I certainly wouldn't be the first trader to write about the importance of tracking and analyzing trades. Every trader should have some type of system for monitoring this. Information from your trades should be gathered so that entries and exits can be improved and refined. Some traders choose to use a spreadsheet where they monitor the entries, management of their trades, and exits of each trade, whereas others have quick checklists to gather information throughout the day. While many traders may have a system to monitor their progress, I will share how I monitor my trades in the short and long term.

During the trading day, I use a three-column chart with a column for "I Do," "I Don't," and "I Dunno" to track my trades, as shown in Table 7.2. This tracking chart template is printed in the Appendix and is available to download at www.shecantrade.com.

TABLE 7.2. I Do, I Don't, I Dunno tracking chart

	I Do	I Don't	I Dunno
In Fashion Setup 10:20	Volume Resistance/ support levels Congruence in S&P	Trend	Trend

I write down the specific market internals I use on the left-hand side of the chart. Before I enter a trade, I check off whether these variables are aligned with my trading plan (the "I Do" column), the variables that are not aligned (the "I Don't" column), and most important, the variables that I'm not sure about (the "I Dunno" column). I also use the "I Dunno" column when there are times that I *think* the market is about to do something but it isn't yet aligned with my trading plan. If everything is checked off in the "I Dunno" column, then this indicates to me that I shouldn't be trading at this time.

Even if I don't actually enter a trade, I always mark down on this quick checklist the name of the trading setup and the time. At the end of the month, I look at all of my quick three-column charts as part of my review analysis. This system has allowed me to collect great data in order to refine MY TRADE plan and improve my trading statistics.

TRADING JOURNAL

Trading journals allow you to measure the longer-term success of your trading setups and execution. A trading journal provides an opportunity to reflect on your experience over a period of time and record details of market evidence and performance before, during, and after a trade. It also provides an opportunity for you to track the market conditions, your market assumptions, your emotions, and the trading setups you used. The information you are tracking over time will help you to refine your entries and exits so that you can maximize your profits. Whether you choose to fill out your trading journal by jotting down point form notes that make sense to you or you choose to write a few paragraphs, you should carve out some time to reflect on your trading performance at regular intervals.

As you write in your journal, be mindful of the language you are using to describe your performance. Keep track of your emotions—what you are feeling—along with your performance. Be careful to write down both positive and negative thoughts. Every trader has areas of strength and areas of weakness. Even the most successful traders have areas that they would like to improve. Your goal should always be to build your trading account and refine your trades to maximize your profits. Notice that I have never mentioned anything about being a perfect trader. One hundred percent isn't the goal you should be striving for because this is completely unrealistic. Many factors will influence your trading performance. Factors like your emotions can be controlled with practice. Other factors like the direction of the markets can't be controlled; you can only control your ability to react to what you see happening in front of you. Figure 7.7 is an example of my trading journal. A template of this journal is in the Appendix and is available to download from www.shecantrade.com.

All too often people can be really hard on themselves. This is why it is important to be mindful of your own personal feedback and make sure that it always remains constructive. Take time to reflect on things that went well and things that need improvement. You need to spend just as much time considering what you do as you do considering things that you *didn't* do. Empower yourself by realizing your weaknesses but also consider ways to leverage the strengths that you identify from your review.

Date	Summary of Trade Impressions	Analysis of Action Factors	Commitment
	How has your trading gone? • Summarize your performance from your daily I Do, I Don't, and I Dunno	How did your decisions from chart analysis correlate to your trade assumption? • What comparisons can be made between the trade you planned to initiate and what actually happened? • What trade setup is most profitable for you?	What will you be mindful of moving forward? • What tweaks might need to be made in your MY TRADE plan?
Dec. 5–7	• Good week of trading. Executed mostly in Fashion trades this week in ES. The I Do, I Don't, I Dunno chart shows I am identifying market intervals like ATR and TICKs well. This helped me get in and out of trades consistently for profit.	• I may have gotten in too early on Tuesday in Fashion trade. • I will wait for price to pull back to support before I enter. • Overall good execution in Fashion trades were most profitable this week.	• I need to remain patient. • Overall it was a great week. I feel good. I made strong decisions based on my market analysis in the ES.

FIGURE 7.7 Trading journal example.

251 at the top

Sarah's Trading Tip

There are three ways to help you consolidate your trading so that your feedback remains helpful:

1. *Discuss any new learning you have about your trading with another trader you trust. Ask another trader just to listen, really listen, to you without offering his or her own commentary. The opportunity to talk through one of your own findings will help you to feel more confident. It is particularly helpful to have a trading coach so that you will able to build your potential. Coaching services are available from www.shecantrade.com.*

2. *Label times on your calendar to review your trading plan. Many of us are good at saying that we will review our trading plan some time in the future. In order to ensure that the future becomes reality, you need to dedicate time in your schedule to review your trading plan. Without dedicated time, you are less likely to sit down and review it.*

3. *Isolate areas for improvement but also areas that you have applied well. For example, if you had a losing trade because you moved your stop and ended up losing more than you had originally planned, acknowledge that you didn't follow your trading plan, and review why you made the decision to move your stop. Did you make this decision based on your emotions because you were scared to get stopped out? What are two things that you did during this trade that were in your favor? Were you able to stabilize the trade? By focusing on what you did well and what needs improvement, you will be improving your trading confidence.*

USING TRACKING SYSTEMS

The three ways to track your trades include, the MY TRADE plan, the I Do, I Don't, I Dunno chart, and the trading journal. Each of these three tracking systems connects to the next one. All three should be constantly reviewed and adjusted, but all three should align. The MY TRADE plan is the anchor of your trading decisions. It informs what you will do and how you will react to the markets. The "I Do, I Don't, I Dunno Chart" is a quick system to track trades during the day while you are trading. It provides a quick and easy way to track the variables you are looking at to make your trading assumption and decisions. Your trading journal is used on a regular basis after market hours or during a time when you aren't focused on the markets. The trading journal is a place to summarize your long-term progress.

The more all three systems are used, the more information you will have to help improve your trading.

Sarah's Trading Tip

I use all three systems when I trade. I keep the action statements from MY TRADE plan posted by my computer screen at all times. During the day, I jot quick notes in the "I Do, I Don't, I Dunno Chart" each time I'm considering a trade. I review those notes at the end of the week and use the information to write in my trading journal. Friday afternoons is my time to review my weekly trades and MY TRADE plan. There are some weeks when I review everything quickly and other weeks when I will spend more time and actually tweak the MY TRADE plan. I review the MY TRADE plan thoroughly at the end of every month. To be honest, since I have developed this routine, there are days when my notes are very brief, whereas other days have more information. I do think it is important to track your trades, but there are times when I don't write everything down as well as I should. I want you to know that I try to stick to this routine, but life does happen and sometimes gets in the way of every detail. Try your best to collect as much information about your trades as you can.

KEY TAKE-AWAYS

This chapter has reviewed trading systems to monitor and inform your trading. I believe that it is important to devise a plan that anchors and identifies your trading actions and your daily trading decisions and monitors your progress.

- Trading is a skill to be developed over time. Any new trader cannot expect to master absolutely everything in a day. Trading is like learning any other skill; in fact, many experienced traders would say that they too are still refining their trading. The markets do have patterns but will always keep any trader on his or her toes.
- All traders need to identify the risk parameters with which they are trading. These risk parameters will help to inform their trading decisions so that they stay in line with their account size.
- Align your risk parameters with your trading behavior to maximize your trading potential. Work with the strengths that you have, and identify your trading needs.
- There are three tracking systems that you can use to set up and analyze your trades. There are many benefits to tracking and monitoring your trading success. The paperwork establishes clear guidelines for trading and a system to continue to maximize your trading potential.

8

BECAUSE YOU CAN

Illustrated by Noble Rains

Key Chapter Concepts

- *Understand trading psychology.*
- *Learn the five most important lessons every trader should know:*
  - *Trading myths.*
  - *Character traits of a successful trader.*
  - *Common strategies that fail traders.*
  - *Rookie mistakes to avoid.*
  - *How to manage your trades and take profits.*
- *Differentiate between trading with (simulated trading) and the real thing (cash).*
- *Common answers to questions traders typically ask me.*

Mastering the skill of trading goes beyond understanding technical trading setups. Our emotions play a significant role in our trading decisions and affect the results of our experiences in the markets. Experienced traders might even argue that developing the skill of emotional control for a new trader is more important than learning trading strategies and knowing how to analyze the markets. Without the ability to control their emotions, even traders with winning trading strategies will not be as successful as they could be. Each trading setup, regardless of how good it is, will always require tweaking and personalization based on the current market trend and the emotional response that a trader feels at the time. Rational decision making is imperative during times of winning and losing trading. A trader's success will be based on her ability to remain calm while in trades and make sound rational decisions quickly and calmly. Spending time consciously thinking about how emotions will affect your trading in order to develop strategies to deal with them will greatly improve your trading potential.

Every trader has walked down his own learning pathway and has accumulated many lessons learned in the process of becoming a professional trader. This chapter reviews some of the barriers to entry, addresses psychological obstacles to overcome, debunks some trading myths, and provides solution strategies for the problems that many traders have worked through.

TRADER PSYCHOLOGY

Trading should be approached by your remembering that it involves both emotional and physical obstacles. Your perspective and your ability to manage your emotional response in the markets will be powerful tools to improve your trading performance. All traders should be able to identify areas of strength and areas of improvement in terms of their emotional control and response in the markets. In order to succeed in trading psychology, traders will need to be able to identify strategies for these six psychological obstacles:

- Trading focus and follow-through (TFFT)
- Trading commitment to overcome barriers (TCOB)
- Realistic and positive self-talk (RPST)
- Balanced self-confidence (BSC)
- Emotional self-control (ESC)
- Celebration of successes (CS)

These six areas of focus will help you to overcome common barriers resulting from the psychological aspects of trading. Along with developing the physical skills of trading and market analysis, working through each of these obstacles will provide you with a resilient response to any bumpy terrain on your trading journey that may be affected by trading psychology.

Sarah's Trading Tip

As each of these psychological aspects is discussed, create a self-assessment to evaluate your responses. Your assessments can be combined to become part of your MY TRADE plan or your trading journal. As you come across areas that need your attention on your personal trading journey, spend time thinking about ways to improve them. Remember to always leverage your strengths to overcome your weaknesses.

Trading Focus and Follow-Through (TFFT)

Focus and the *ability to follow through* refer to your commitment to your trading performance—your ability to perform when you are in trades and manage multiple positions while you are in the moment during the trading day. Your focus on the markets, market internals, market sentiment, and your ability to respond to changing market conditions will ensure that you are doing more than just having a successful and profitable trade but are actually improving your entries and exits so that each trade helps you realize a maximum profit. Ask yourself:

- What is my trading vision?
- How would I describe my focus?
- How would I rate my ability to follow through on the steps in the MY TRADE plan I designed?

Trading Commitment to Overcome Barriers (TCOB)

Every trader should be committed to trading success and overcoming any trading barriers that may hinder performance. Your commitment is supported by:

- Your motivation to trade
- Attaining your dreams of becoming a successful trader
- Maximizing your trading potential
- Setting clear goals and achieving them
- Remaining open to learn and improve
- Loving what you do

Even though a trader may be committed, there will be days when trading won't go as planned. A trader's ability to manage any barriers and stay on course will be crucial. The days when trades go against you are the days when you might begin to question whether a particular trading strategy is really the best for you. You begin to experience self-doubt and lack of motivation. Every trader will have days like this, especially new traders. When you experience days like this, return your thinking to your trading commitment to overcome any barriers. Remember that every trader goes through this cycle of overcoming barriers. The more you work through this process, the easier it becomes. Assess how strongly you are committed to TCOB, and articulate a response to the following questions and steps to take action on any answer that needs attention. Ask yourself:

- What is my trading vision?
- What would it look like if I were meeting all my trading goals and excelling in my trading performance?
- What would meeting my goals look and feel like?
- What is a barrier that needs improvement?

Use these reflective questions to refocus your commitment and develop a strategy to overcome any barrier that you have identified for yourself.

Realistic and Positive Self-Talk (RPST)

This strategy is helpful for two types of self-talk: unrealistic expectations and/or negative self-talk. Both of these types of self-talk will debilitate a trader. Because many of us trade on our own, working in solitude will often make us more susceptible to disillusionment if our self-talk is self-deprecating. Some traders have great dreams but are unable to turn their dreams into realistic goals. Each trader should create both long- and short-term goals. A trader's short-term goals should always be set in a manner that is realistically achievable, whereas long-term goals can be bigger, broader goals that will take many small achievements to reach. Be careful to ensure that your goals are realistic and that your self-talk keeps you motivated. Be sure to acknowledge the progress and successes you have experienced. Ask yourself:

- What is my trading motivation?
- What conclusions can I draw from what I envisioned and what actually happens when I trade?
- Where on my trading journey am I?

As you become more aware of what is actually being said as part of your own self-talk, you will be able to assess how positive or negative your trading outlook actually is. Positive self-talk will ensure that you are performing at you best. Your performance is linked to what you do, what you think, and how you have gathered evidence to create a trading assumption. You may even want to create a script for yourself that you rehearse or review to help build positive self-talk. Relying on a script can help to establish a new routine and outlook until you are able to think of something to say in the moment that is more positive.

Balanced Self-Confidence (BSC)

Confidence is important, but overconfidence can be detrimental to a trader. If a trader becomes too cocky, she can lose sight of the follow-through required based on her own trading plan. Cocky traders make decisions without gathering evidence because they momentarily feel that they are better than the markets. Traders with too much confidence will be schooled by the market—guaranteed. Traders need to remain balanced but self-confident in their ability. You will need to check in with yourself regularly to monitor your self-confidence. Ask yourself:

- What are my trading areas of strength and weakness?
- How do I leverage my strengths to support the weaknesses I have identified?

Your confidence will fluctuate in cycles very similarly to the markets if you are not able to keep yourself balanced. If you are not able to keep your self-confidence in check, the markets will do this for you. It is much easier to keep yourself in check than to rely on the costly lessons that the market can teach. Check in with yourself about your BSC throughout the trading day, especially as you are reviewing charts and deciding your trading strategy each day.

Emotional Self-Control (ESC)

Trading can be intense and intoxicating; it can pull you into the markets. Traders need to be able to balance their enthusiasm and excitement in order to stay relaxed and focused. Maintaining self-control must be realized in your day-to-day trading routine. You will experience a range of emotions, including excitement, pride, disappointment, and frustration. Traders also need to keep things in perspective; there will always be a bigger fish in the pond than you. When traders get too cocky and think that they can move the market, they will get eaten by those bigger fish. Always be mindful that you are trading with other professionals, mixed in with institutional traders and large funds. They will have more weight in the market. Keep your perspective in check, and you will be able to remain in control of any overexcited emotions as you trade. Ask yourself:

- After a successful trade, what might I do?
- After a losing trade, what might I do?

We all want winning trades; this can be a great feeling, especially when you meet all of your trading targets. As traders develop a trading routine and are able to meet their goals, the emotional side of trading shifts more to a routine. Even though we all experience pride and/or disappointment, emotional self-control is very important so that decisions are always made rationally and according to your MY TRADE plan.

Sarah's Trading Tip

If you catch yourself saying something like, "I should just hold on because I can feel it in my heart that I just shouldn't sell," this means that you are probably making decisions in an emotional state and not necessarily a rational one. Especially as you evaluate trades, look at the evidence from the markets, and ask yourself how realistic it is that the markets will move in your favor. If the market internals and charts confirm your position, then you have probably made a good trading decision. If you can't find evidence to support your actions in a trade (specifically if it is going against you), then you should be aware that you could be making a decision based on emotions.

Celebration of Successes (CS)

Many traders are successful because they are able to reflect on their trading performance and are motivated to continue to improve. Internal drive and motivation are huge strengths for any trader, but if you fail to stop along your trading journey to measure your growth, you will fail to celebrate the journey and barriers you have overcome so far. Setting measurable goals and acknowledging your successes will help you to stay focused and motivated. These celebrations can be as simple as acknowledging the great days in the markets; it doesn't mean that you are throwing yourself a party every day. Ask yourself:

- Have I identified timely profit targets for myself weekly, monthly, and quarterly?
- Whom will I share my success and any new learning with?
- How might I ensure that I have a trading network?
- How will I share my achievements and lessons with my network?

Sarah's Trading Tip

My goal in writing this book is to help traders maximize their trading potential in the markets by empowering them with clear and concise trading knowledge. When I began trading, I spent many days feeling lost and overwhelmed. Researching information about trading online can lead to endless hits from a Google search, with all sorts of traders claiming to teach trading skills, but too much information can be just as overwhelming as having none. It can be difficult to decipher which traders are delivering real content versus those who are focused on marketing and gimmicky trading systems.

This is why I wrote this book—to help traders with great starting points so that they have a solid foundation to trade from. This is the book that I wish had existed to support my trading journey, so I'm so glad that this book is helping you on your trading journey. I have overcome many of my own psychological trading barriers with time and much reflection. I believe that you have the ability to perform and move consistently toward your trading goals. Don't let any setbacks limit your trading journey.

Even acknowledging the psychological connection in trading can help you to remain cognizant of its impact. Continuous self-assessment of these psychological factors will promote great self-awareness of your performance. Your mental preparedness to address any psychological bumps along your journey will help to ensure that you pick a good path and vigorously pursue your goals.

FIVE TRADING LESSONS

As traders pursue their trading goals, they all have at least one thing in common: every trader wants to make money in the markets. In order to achieve this goal, each trader will have his own personal journey of lessons learned along the way. Regardless of where you are on your trading journey, below are five lessons that you will need to overcome and master to achieve your goals. Each lesson will identify a problem and a solution. Problems that must be overcome include breaking down trading myths, developing characteristics of a successful trader, strategies that fail traders, rookie mistakes, and managing profits.

Lesson 1: Trading Myths Exposed

There are many trading myths out there, and I believe that it is these myths that stop many people from learning to trade. Rumors and myths may not always be true but can quickly be considered as true the more widespread they become. As the saying goes, "Perception is reality." This is definitely the case in trading. Unfortunately, there are myths that seem to be widely accepted as truth that dissuade people from trying to trade on their own. Let's expose some of these myths to overcome any barriers that you might believe are reality when in fact they are only rumors. Don't let these rumors influence your trading ability or self-confidence in the markets.

Myth: You Need to Be Good at Math to Trade Successfully

The ability to problem-solve through sophisticated math equations to determine probabilities to trade is one style of trading, but it is not the only way to trade. Algorithmic trading systems do exist, but many professional traders do not rely solely on these systems to earn their living in the markets. The average trader may need to do some basic calculations, but with technology at our fingertips, there are very few trading calculations that a trader needs calculate on her own. Of course, if you want to calculate your maximum profit and maximum loss for a spread, you can, but most trading platforms will do it for you. Calculating premium is simple addition and subtraction. Your trading platform can alleviate any math barriers to entry.

Myth: Trading Is Too Complicated

Many people will not try trading because they believe that it is too complicated. Admittedly, it can certainly feel complicated, especially at the beginning, if you are just learning to trade. But just as with any other skill, it's important to bite off a little bit of trading at a time, master it, and then move to the next step. Think of it like a ladder that you need to climb. It is easier to climb one step at a time. Don't get caught trying to take too many steps at once. When a new trader looks at developing the skill of trading in small, measurable goals, one-step-at-a-time trading will feel much more manageable. When you are feeling overwhelmed, take a pause, and step back for a moment. Go back to something you understand, regroup, and then layer on the new learning.

Always use your trading plan as your anchor to guide you along your trading journey. Trading doesn't have to be complicated. Simple trading setups can produce quality trades. Sophisticated trading doesn't necessarily mean better results. Stick to strategies that you understand, and build on what you know over time when you feel ready. If you are just starting out as a trader, my best advice is to approach trading in the same way you would approach learning any new skill.

Myth: You Need to Be Wealthy to Trade

Any trader can lose or make money in the markets. Whether you have a large account or a small account, you should be trading based on the account size that is appropriate for you. A trader with a large account still can lose money and probably will be more likely to do so. The key is to understand what size trades to put on relative to your account size so that when you have a losing trade, it won't wipe out all your profits. Remember that you will need to have time to master trading. Time in the markets with good money management is important rather than the size of your trading account.

You don't need a huge account, but the size of your account will affect the number of trades that you can place at one time. The more money you have in your account, the more trades you can place. If the size of your account is only sufficient to place one or two trades at a time, then it might be helpful to use a paper account until you can save more. You want to have enough money to allow you to place multiple trades at once.

Trading using a paper or fake account can be a great way to master some of the skills behind trading while saving up enough money to trade with. Trading in a paper account is similar to but not exactly the same as trading with real money, and it will provide you with a great way to learn if you are still saving or afraid to jump right into the market.

Myth: Buying and Holding a Stock in a Long Market Is the Only Way to Trade

This is the most common way that people think to trade, but as we have discussed, there are many more ways. The market moves up and down at different times, and as such, traders need strategies to participate in the markets no matter what direction the market is taking. This rumor is probably perpetuated because most often the public hears from various financial shows about stock picks by fund managers and banks. Trading education and specific perspectives from actual traders sharing their knowledge with the general public about actual short-term trade perspectives can be more difficult to find.

Trading futures and/or options provides many trading opportunities beyond the buy-and-hold strategy. There are many more ways to trade, especially in both long and short terms in the markets. A well-diversified portfolio might include the purchase of some stocks in combination with other shorter-term trades may be a happy medium.

These myths and many others may prohibit people from trading but shouldn't. Trading is a journey that will take every person through successes and stumbling blocks. You must become skilled at overcoming barriers that are in your way to success.

Lesson 2: Character Traits that You Need to Be a Successful Trader

In my experience, there are some key characteristics that you will need to develop or be aware of to improve your trading potential. Even though these characteristics may not be seen physically, these traits must be developed and honed if you are to become a successful trader.

Self-Reflection

Learning to trade is the most effective and powerful way to get to know who you are and what your strengths and needs are. Trading is probably the most costly education you will invest in if you are not willing to identify your strengths and develop strategies to overcome your weaknesses. Trust me. You will get schooled over and over again until you become aware of how your weaknesses are limiting your potential in the markets.

Here's how to do this: Designate times during which you will review your MY TRADE plan on a regular basis. You need time to analyze your entries and exits and how you were feeling during the trades. As traders, we all have strengths, and we all have areas that need improvement. In order to overcome and diminish your weaknesses, you must be able to identify them and create supports to leverage your strengths. This process will be most successful when you spend time reflecting on your trading behaviors and performance. Every trader must develop a strategy to review and self-assess personal physical and emotional behaviors. Ask yourself these questions:

- Am I overreacting to a small movement in the markets?
- Am I too emotional or too relaxed while trades are on?
- What do I spend the most time focusing on while I am in a trade?

Patience

Patience is important in two respects. You need to be patient enough in your trades to let your profit targets get hit, and you need patience to grow your account over time and trade in a manner that is appropriate for your account size. Trading without patience will result in your being hypersensitive. Patience, in turn, will help you to establish self-control in the markets.

Here's how to do this: Create a personal trading mantra for yourself, and write this down:

- You need to have patience to build your account.
- You will miss trades.
- You need to be patient in order to grow your account.
- You must follow your plan.

Humility

You will need to learn that there are bigger trading fish in the sea than you. Don't get too cocky and think that you can outsmart the big players. Trading with humility requires that you accept your size and use it to your advantage by trading with the movement of the market.

Here's how to do this: In my opinion, it is better to trade with the overall direction of the markets than to try to anticipate a change in the market and guess at the future direction of price. Trade what you see happening with price now.

Discipline

It is one thing to create a trading plan, but it is another to follow it. You need to be sure that you have the discipline to follow through with your trading strategies and, most important, follow through on your entry and exit decisions.

Here's how to do this: The best way to develop or improve trading discipline is to remain committed to your MY TRADE plan and to select specific rules you will follow. Habits will include when you start your trading day, steps taken to evaluate and execute trades, self-reflection processes, and commitment to continuous improvement. These rules should address the physical and emotional aspects of trading. New traders will struggle with their ability to control their emotions as they trade, but once you develop a good trading routine and habit, these tendencies will be less prominent. Ask yourself:

- How might I rate my success at following my trading routines?
- What are some of the personal trading commitments that I have made for myself?

Decision Making

As a trader, you will need to be decisive. Your trading decisions will affect your profits and losses. You need to develop the skill to be able to look through the markets and then act on them. Your goal is to actually trade. Watching the markets in fear of placing a trade won't make a trader any money. In order to make money, you need to be able to make decisions and follow through with your MY TRADE plan.

Here's how to do this: Create trading rules. These rules should stay close to you at all times so that you can refer to them as you make your trading decisions. Over time, these rules will become ingrained and automatic. Your trading rules should address the actual steps you take during trades, as well as the ways you control your emotions. Trading rules strengthen your commitment to your overall trading goals. Trading rules also break down steps for you to be able to be more decisive without getting overwhelmed.

Developing good skills in trading will be part of any trader's journey. It is an endless road of sorts because every trader should always be developing new skills, whether hard or soft skills, to improve. As you pursue your trading goals, recognizing the ways you have grown throughout this process is very empowering. You know yourself better than anyone else, and therefore, you will know what your strengths and weaknesses are (or at least they will become evident to you as you hone your trading skills).

Lesson 3: Common Trading Strategies that Fail Traders

Many traders have taken the following types of trades, which have most likely resulted in a losing trade. It's best to avoid these strategies if you want to trade over the long term.

The Big Ticket

Some traders are only looking for "the one big trade." The trading tip they are searching for can come from anyone, regardless of that person's cred-

Sarah's Trading Tip

When I began to trade, I didn't realize that I would need to become so aware of my strengths and weaknesses. When I first began trading, I needed to learn about patience. I was able to learn to be patient in a trade, letting my profit targets get hit. This was only half the patience quality that I needed to learn. Even though I was able to let my profit targets get hit, I was trading with too many contracts for my account size. I wasn't being patient enough to let my account grow over time. The moment I had a trade that was successful, I would repeat the same strategy the next day with more contracts. My belief was that I had figured out a strategy that worked, so it was time to start making some real money. Unfortunately for me, I needed to realize the importance of trading only with a number of contracts relative to the size of my account. I started placing trades with too many contracts. Because I was trading beyond my account size, when I had a losing trade, it really affected my trading account. After reviewing my trading performance, I realized that I needed to be more patient. I needed to trade more often with a smaller size so that when I had a losing trade, it wouldn't wipe out my profits. Patience was a skill that I needed to be mindful of. It takes time to build up a trading account; remaining mindful of patience was one of my trading keys.

ibility. This type of trader hears promises of winning big on this trade, so he puts his money in the trade and hopes for the best. Unfortunately, chances are that his money will end up in someone else's pocket. Just like the lottery, your odds aren't very good.

Hoping-and-Praying Trades

This trading strategy is one in which someone places a trade (usually she buys a stock or a call option) based on a hunch that she thinks the market is going up. Without analyzing the markets to inform her trading assumption, she blindly enters a trade and hopes that it works in her favor. This trade is probably rooted in an emotional response without rational evidence to back it up. Such a trade will often end up losing money.

Roller-Coaster Trades

These trades occur when a trader calls the market so correctly that her profit targets are hit immediately. Instead of getting out of the trade, however, this trader moves her profit target and continues to stay in the trade to collect more profit. The emotional response of this trader has taken over her trade management. Unfortunately, the pattern may not continue and can reverse at the same rate. What was once a winning trade can just as quickly become a losing trade. This means that the trader can be left with nothing more than paying commissions and the frustration that comes from not cashing in her profits when she should have.

Rolling-the-Dice-Too-Often Trade

Rolling a trade is an options term that refers to rolling one option to another expiry because the trade went against the trader before it expired. Instead of getting out of the trade and moving onto the next one, this trader continually rolls his trades to the next month in an effort to avoid registering a losing trade. This strategy can get dangerous quickly because every time you roll, you will need the trade to move even more to cover your costs of rolling. Soon you are left with nothing more than lots of commissions to pay and a trade that has been rolled so often that the trade that once had potential is nothing more than a flattened pancake. Worse yet, the trade can continue to go against the trader for longer than she can afford to roll, magnifying the ultimate loss many times larger than what the original loss was.

Lesson 4: Rookie Mistakes to Avoid

It seems that all too many traders have experienced these rookie mistakes. At times, I wonder if these mistakes are a rite of passage because they seem to happen to so many new traders. I have listed them in hopes that you can avoid experiencing them and benefit from not having to pay for them out of your hard earned capital.

Putting on Too Large a Trade in One Position at a Time

New traders get excited when they find what they think is a perfect trade. They get lured into believing that they can make big money and end up trading with a position size that is too big for their account. Placing a trade with a large percentage of your account means that you may be risking too much per trade. This rookie becomes so sure of himself or is so desperate to make money that he puts too much of his account behind one trade. All traders should be aware of their potential for gains and losses and trading within their trading parameters. One or two of these trades might work in your favor, but when they don't, they can wipe out all of your account. Your position size in each trade should always be relative to your account size.

Placing a Small Trade by Copying Another Trader Placing a Large Trade

Some new traders will copy trades from other traders who may be placing trades that just aren't appropriate for small accounts or someone who is new to the market. This rookie trader believes that because a well-known trader or investment advisor is doing it, it must be a good trade. However, what might be good for one trader may be devastating for another trader, especially if you are trading with a different account size than the trader you are following. Traders with different account sizes will be able to support different entries and exits based on their own risk/reward parameters. Advice from a large-account trader might not be relevant to a small-account trader. It is very frustrating to watch professional traders exit a trade with profits while you get stopped out. Only place trades using strategies that you understand and ones that match your own risk/reward parameters.

Chasing a Big Move

Rookie traders will see a big move in the markets and want to jump in to trade, thinking that they can grab some of the move that they may have missed. Instead of waiting for another good entry, possibly on a retracement, the rookie trader enters the trade anyway, often paying too much to enter at the peak of the move. Many rookie traders don't understand that regardless how often you watch the markets or how experienced you are, every trader misses some moves. We all do. It's okay; we can't possibly be watching every single market, every single hour of every day. However, how a trader reacts to a missed move will differentiate between a rookie and a professional. If you have missed a big move, don't jump in at the top of the move only to have it retrace against you with the same amount of momentum. Don't chase the trade. Wait for it to come back to you, or find something else to trade.

Losing the Money in Your Account Before You Have Mastered the Trade
This is one of the crucial mistakes that traders make at the beginning of their careers. This type of trader loses her capital before she ever develops the skills of trading. As a new trader, you need to make sure that the money in your account lasts as long as it takes you to refine your trading plan. If you bet big and your account lasts only 10 trades, then you have not given yourself enough of a chance to learn how to trade. You need your account to last hundreds of trades in order to begin to gain real insight into trading. Trading is like golf; you will get better the more balls you hit at the driving range. Don't expect to be a master golfer after hitting only one bucket of balls.

Lesson 5: Managing Your Trades and Taking Your Profits
There are many theories about the best way to grow your account. The best way for each trader to grow her account will be directly related to her trading personality, what market and instrument she trades, and most important, the risk quadrant she identified for herself in Chapter 7.

I believe that it is better to trade and grow an account slowly over time than to hope for one big trade that will double your account in size. As you evaluate your MY TRADE plan, always keep in mind that even if you have some losing trades, the idea is to have an account that is growing over time.

There is a bit of a tug of war that happens with account growth. As your confidence grows, you will want to put on more trading size in order to make more money. This seems like a reasonable way to consider growing your account. The catch is that sometimes, as you realize success in the markets, you begin to follow your trading plan less, and what once was a small winning trade may turn into a large losing trade because you did not stick to your MY TRADE plan and trading rules.

Have a Process to Manage Each Trade Once You Are In: Breathe,
Analyze, Stabilize

Once a trader enters a trade, she will need a process to manage and/or monitor the trade before she exits the trade. Hopefully, everything goes according to plan, and there is nothing to manage. But there will be times, however, when trades do not react in the manner the trader anticipated. When a trader needs to manage a trade, he will need to remember to breathe, analyze, and stabilize these trades.

The manner in which you made a bad trade will affect how you manage it. When your trade has a large move in the opposite direction you anticipated very quickly or you place a trade in error, I believe you need to just get out of the trade and chalk it up to the wrong assumption. After all, we all make mistakes sometimes. If however the market moves in the opposite way you expected slowly, there may be some opportunity to analyze and stabilize it, once a trade begins to slowly move against you, follow these three steps to help make sure that you are making good management decisions.

1. Take a deep breath. You want to make sure that you are thinking clearly. Keep your emotions in check.
2. Analyze both the overall market related to the trades you've placed and the specific charts for the stock you have traded, the market internals, and your MY TRADE plan. Keep reviewing your trade to verify that the market conditions are still the same as your trading assumption. If you traded in the direction of the trend, go back to your charts to verify if levels of support are holding. Pay particular attention to what is happening on the 21 EMA on both long-term and short-term charts. If the market conditions have changed since you entered the trade, it may be wise to exit your position. Always keep in mind your risk parameters and how much money you are willing to lose on any one trade.
3. Just as in an emergency room, if there are trades that are in critical condition (i.e., getting closer to your stop loss), consider if it is worth getting out of your position early by closing it out.

If you are trading options, you will want to consider when this trade will expire and how much the trade is worth at that time. Deciding to get out of a trade earlier than you anticipated and taking some profits or a small loss can sometimes be a very wise decision. There is a delicate balance between when to intervene and when to let the trade go that every trader will learn over time. Just as an ER doctor won't perform surgery unless he has a full picture of the patient in front of him, try not to make impulse decisions, and continue to breathe, analyze, and stabilize as necessary. The stop you have placed for the trade is the final safety for you; always make sure that you follow through on it.

Stay Flexible When You Read the Markets

A predetermined bias about market direction can hurt you. Each day that you watch the markets is a new day and should be reviewed with an unbiased opinion. As part of your trading routine, create a list of key items that you will review that will help you to form your trading assumption for that day. Listen to the markets rather than trying to tell the markets what direction they should move. Trust me, the markets won't hear you. There are many large traders and organizations that are trading in the markets; if you are trading high-volume trading instruments, then it isn't likely that you are going to move the market. Instead, listen to what is happening, and stay flexible so that you can adapt to the movement of the markets. This concept can be quite contrary to what many people think. Some people believe that they need to know the reason why a market is moving; they may watch mainstream media, listen to an expert trader, or theorize based on economic factors. All these things are fine, but just make sure that you understand that it doesn't necessarily matter why the market is moving. If you have remained flexible as to what you see, you will be on the right side of the move regardless of why the move took place.

Learning to Trade Is a Process

We all want to have good returns in the markets. Every trader is constantly looking for ways to improve his trading strategy to maximize his trading potential. Most often traders will focus on the science of trading, the step-by-step process they will follow to enter, manage, and exit trades. This skill is very important, but there are subtle nuances in any market that also need to be mastered in order to achieve the best results. The art of trading is the ability to make small tweaks and adjustments based on what the traders are seeing in the markets at the time. This feel for the markets will take time for a trader to master.

Every trader should approach trading like someone who is running a marathon. Just like a marathoner requires appropriate training and good pacing in order to avoid injury, traders need to pace themselves in order to avoid losing all of the capital in their accounts. If a marathoner goes out too strong at the beginning of a race, she risks burning out which could result in dropping out before the race is complete. Racers will eventually learn the pacing required for them to complete the race. As traders spend more time in the markets, they will have the ability to notice the subtle art that is required to maximize the profit potential for each trade.

Throughout the process of learning to trade, you will no doubt come across a number of websites that claim to have a trading system that is a 100 percent guaranteed secret to success. Even though it might be tempting to listen to someone claiming to have a get-rich-quick market strategy, it may not be as successful as you may think. If it sounds too good to be true, it probably is. In the same way that some fashion may look good on the runway, it might not be a practical choice for everyday life. Connect with traders whom you trust and believe are also trading responsibly.

Ten Tips to Find Good Trading Resources

If you are learning to trade, it is important that you are learning from a trusted individual who is offering good trading education and resources. Below are my 10 tips to help ensure that you can find good resources to help you learn to trade.

1. *The person teaching a trading course sounds knowledgeable but isn't able to explain concepts so that you can understand them.* Some great traders are just that—great traders. Being a great

trader does not necessarily mean that the person will be a great teacher. Sometimes traders speak in such sophisticated language or get so wrapped up in the analysis that they are not able to articulate the actual steps they are looking for when placing a trade. Make sure that you understand how the trader is speaking in order to gain the most information from his or her teaching.

2. *Be wary of people who claim that they never have had a loss in the markets.* Of course, everyone would love this scenario, but chances are that every trader will have had a losing trade. A successful trader is usually one who knows how to manage her losses as well as her gains. If someone is claiming to teach you trades that are 100 percent profitable every time, be wary; that one big loss will be coming that can wipe out all that person's previous gains.

3. *Trading footprint.* In this digital age, it is easy to look up many traders online and learn more about their digital footprints. Take the time to learn about the person you want to learn to trade from to make sure that he is someone you trust. A trader who is teaching others to trade should have a reputable trading footprint.

4. *Trading scale.* Here is where I can sometimes get into a debate about who it is best to learn from. There many ways to trade the markets and many different sizes of accounts that people will use to trade the markets. Strategies that may work for large funds or institutions may not work for the trader trading a small account. If you are going to learn to trade from someone, make sure that she is teaching strategies that you will actually be able to use based on the size of your account and risk parameters you intend to trade with. It may be entertaining to watch someone trade 100 contracts, but if you cannot replicate what that person is doing in your account, then you are more than likely setting yourself up for failure.

5. *Advice to leverage small accounts.* Leverage is a double-edged sword. Just because it is possible to trade one contract of the S&P 500 (ES) for every $500 in your account doesn't mean

that you should. If you are directed to trade more contracts than seems reasonable for your account size, this may be a warning sign that you might lose more money than you can make or, even worse, blow up your trading account. It's hard for one trader to give advice to another trader about specific size for individual trades; this really should be a personal decision based on your own risk/reward parameters. Be cautious about someone giving you specific advice about leveraging your account.

6. *Overtrading is gambling not trading.* Trades should be well thought out. If another trader advises you to trade 10 to 15 times per day in multiple directions and with multiple instruments, this may be a warning sign that this person trades by gambling as opposed to a specific strategy. This type of overtrading may benefit your broker because of the commissions he will collect, but it may not be kind to your account balance. Overtrading can feel more like gambling and rolling the dice rather than making a trading decision grounded on evidence you gathered from the market.

7. *High-cost trading courses.* If the cost of the trading program is the same as a year of tuition at Harvard, this may be a warning sign. There are some trading courses out there that ask a very high amount of money and promise unrealistic results. I believe that you can expect to pay for a quality course, but within reason. If the price tag of a course seems too high, shop around. Make sure that the trader teaching the course actually makes money from trading, not just from charging enormous prices to teach a course.

8. *No trading mastery in under five hours.* Trading is a combination of learning and hands-on experience that will be acquired over time. Be cautious of trading courses that offer to share everything a trader needs to know in one course. It isn't reasonable to expect to acquire all the knowledge required to trade in one five-hour trading course. Five hours is certainly enough to get acquainted with trading and to place your first trade, but a master of trading it will not make you.

9. *Hiding losses with fancy strategy.* Even great professional traders will have losses. Granted, these loses will be relatively small compared to their trading accounts, but there will be losses nonetheless. If someone is spending more time teaching you how to hide your losses rather than how to place good trades, then this might not be the best way to set yourself up for success.

10. *Listen to your gut.* We are usually good at identifying people around us who are trustworthy and those who are not. Traders are real people, too, so connect with other traders whom you feel best relate to you. Every trader will have her own perspective on the markets and trading; one perspective is not necessarily better than another. Listen to your intuition about certain traders who promise to divulge a big trading secret or a plan to get rich quick.

TRADING WITH PAPER MONEY

Many, if not all, brokerages have paper or practice accounts that allow you to trade with fake money. Trading with paper provides many advantages; it not only helps you to experiment with new trading setups, but it also helps you to get used to a trading platform and allows you to get a feel for trading without using real money. However, trading with paper money removes one of the largest factors that influences trades—the emotional connection to money. As you trade with paper money, you are able to execute trades according to your trading setup without the fear or excitement that can sometimes interfere when trading with real money.

I always recommend that traders who are just beginning in the markets begin trading with paper money, but the catch is that such traders must trade in the same manner and with the same amount of money that they are planning to trade in their real-money account. The purpose of paper trading is to experiment and implement a trading plan without the stress of using actual money. It's devastating when a trade gets placed with real money in error because someone wasn't familiar with his brokerage platform.

Trading a paper account allows you to become familiar with the trading platform; it helps with things like navigating how to place and exit a trade. Using paper money also allows you to experiment with the implementation of your trading setups.

Trading with paper money has a role in trading, but it is not exactly the same as trading with real money. Paper trading has some disadvantages as well.

The timing of an entry and exit in a trade and the way in which a trade is filled are not the same as in a real trading account. You will always get filled in the paper account when it trades your price, but this does not always happen in real life because at the exchange your order has to stand in line behind all the other orders placed before yours.

Paper trading does not allow you to experience the element of your emotions and their impact on your behavior as you trade. Any trader will tell you that dealing with emotions is one of the most difficult challenges to overcome.

Sarah's Trading Tip

Trading will bring to the surface your best and worst emotions. There is nothing quite like the feeling when you make your first successful trade, and conversely, there is nothing more devastating than losing money on a trade. Trading will provide a metaphorical mirror and force every trader to see his own reflection, the good and the bad. For example, if you are someone who gets very excited very quickly or is impulsive, trading may bring out one of these characteristics tenfold. Without a solid trading plan and the discipline to follow it, this can cost you when a trade goes against you if you act impulsively without referring to your trading plan to enter, manage, or exit a trade. If you have trouble controlling your emotions, I would suggest that seeing a psychologist would be cheaper than trying to sort out your emotions in the markets.

A DAY IN THE LIFE OF A TRADER: FAQs

I really enjoy hearing from other traders, especially new traders. I have included some frequently asked questions (FAQs) that I get asked most often about trading.

Question: What does your typical trading routine look like?

Answer: I have met many traders over my trading career, but certainly when I began trading, I knew only a few. Over time, what I have learned is that every successful trader has his or her own trading routine that he or she will follow each day. It's important for all traders to develop a routine to review the markets and create routines to establish decisions about trading setups and to review their trading plan. Each trader's daily routines may be slightly different, but many share similar themes.

My daily routines have evolved over time. I have created trading rules for myself that help me to establish a work/life balance within and after my trading day. I can articulate what types of trades I typically place on specific days, when and why I use specific trading setups, and the trading rules I follow for each of my setups. I would encourage you to develop good trading routines in order to use your time most effectively during your trading day.

My days are different depending on the day of the week. Typically, I don't trade Mondays. I keep this day to coach other traders, work on my blog, or work on any extra projects that I'm involved in at the time. My days are pretty routine, just like anyone else who works full time. I've established a routine in order to ensure that I am productive each day. We all have days, though, that don't go exactly as planned. I'm sure you can relate, but I try my best to stick to this.

A trading day begins in front of the markets just before 9:30 a.m. EST. I like to make sure that I have my computer screens loaded and ready to watch once the market opens. I spend the first half hour watching the markets and making my decision about focusing on futures or options that day. Also, I review any options trade that I placed on previous days. I look online to see if there are any news events or earnings plays coming up. As the morning progresses, I trade futures if an opportunity presents itself but will aim to be out of the trade by 11 a.m. EST. I typically review my options watch list in the morning and decide on some possible trades that I might set up later in the day. The middle of the day is reserved time for coaching and teaching other traders. I also review some of the stocks and exchange-traded funds (ETFs) on my watch list to look for any options trades. The afternoons are spent focused on setting up new options trades. I also try to find time during the week to participate on Twitter @shecantrade and hear from other traders. Staying connected to a trading network is very important, especially if you are at home trading by yourself.

Fridays I rarely place any new trades. I am usually focused only on exits as opposed to entries into new positions. If I find a trade that I like, I will write it down and take a look at it on Tuesday of the following week. My busiest days of the week for trading are Tuesday through Thursday. Every day I also try to get outside to exercise. I find that because most of my day is spent in front of the computer screens, I need time away from my desk every day so that I don't get too sucked into the market.

Question: What has helped you the most to make your trading goals a reality?

Answer: Learning to follow through with a solid trading plan is what has helped me to become a successful trader. Interestingly, many traders I speak with don't have a detailed trading plan. This is what has helped me realize what types of trading setups work best for me, and what pieces of information in the markets I use to form my trading opinion. I work with my trading plan with great detail, and I stick to my trading rules. Even when I hear that another trader is doing something, I am able to restrain myself unless I evaluate the trade for myself and feel that it aligns with my plan. I am very comfortable with my trading plan and pull confidence from my ability to manage any trades that are not as profitable as I had hoped because I feel confident in my trading ability.

Question: How do you find winning trades?

Answer: The reality is that I don't pick winning trades every time. There are times that my trading assumption is wrong or, most often, my timing is off. When I have trades that go against me, I remain very careful not to get too emotional about it. Every trader has these days. I don't let losing trades get away from me. I'm confident pulling the plug on a trade that isn't working. Then I reevaluate it another time and look for another entry either that day or another day. I realize that a profitable trader does not look for 100 percent profitable trades. Instead, I look for a positive profit that is steadily increasing over time. I have a watch list and what I consider a short list of some of my favorite stocks to trade. I look through my short list almost daily to see if anything looks clean to trade; then I move to my watch list for other trading opportunities. I do find that the Foundations indicator helps to speed up my ability to scan for trading opportunities. There are days when I might like a chart but still won't trade it. I like to wait for a pullback to get a good price before I enter a trade. Experience over time also helps me to find trades to place, but honestly, it takes time to look through charts and decide which ones are worth trading at the moment versus which ones merit continued watching. My insights about my options trades are available at www.shecantrade.com.

Question: How do you get through some tough days in the markets?

Answer: We all have bad days, and we need to give ourselves a break to realize that this happens to everyone. We can't be 100 percent 100 percent of the time—it just isn't realistic. One thing I have realized is that every new trader will be involved in a trade in which she loses more than she anticipated. This lesson is very important and will most often be the marker to determine who will become a successful trader and who will end up losing her account.

I can remember my first big loss in futures. I began the day with a very profitable trade. I got too excited and entered another trade. Instead of walking away with the profits I made that day, I didn't reevaluate the market well and just entered a trade again. I got greedy. Well, the market schooled me that day. My next trade blew through my profits, and I made a mistake that I have never made again: I got rid of my stop. This was a huge mistake for me and something I have learned from and no longer do. This situation actually made me take a step back from the markets for a few days and decide whether this was something I really wanted to do. I overcame that day, though, tightened up my trading plan, and created a hard rule for always having stops in my futures trades. After this moment was when I also began learning about options. As I reflected on my experience, I also realized that I was ready to learn another trading instrument so that I could better diversify my trading. Even though that day hurt my trading account and my confidence, I was able to rebuild and improve my trading. As I have learned from other traders, everyone has a story like this when they begin trading; it's what they do with it during the days following that seem to have made the biggest difference in why some traders are able to persevere and become successful full-time traders and those who give up the trade.

Question: How did you get into trading?

Answer: My trading began very differently from many others in this industry. Unlike most traders, I don't have a financial background. I was always interested in and intrigued by the markets but didn't understand them. I began asking a lot of questions, trading with a paper account, and monitoring my performance. I approached trading the same way I approach training for a triathlon or other race. I knew it would take time to train and develop my trading ability. I began trading part time, but even then there were many days when I would wake up early before my full-time job began to watch the markets, but not to place a trade. It took time to develop my own style of trading that worked for me. I have always enjoyed a challenge and learning something new. Trading was a great challenge and one that I made a priority to master. Unfortunately, the skill of trading is very difficult to learn because there aren't formal educational institutions offering trading courses. I think many more people would trade if they understood it. This is why I feel passionately about helping to inform people about how to trade in a clear and concise manner. I remain committed to sharing information about trading by writing this book and posting events, information, and courses at www.shecantrade.com to help break down any barriers to the trading world.

Question: What advice do you have for a new trader?

Answer: Whatever your trading routine, it needs to work for you. My trading routine has changed since I moved from trading part time to trading full time. I used to get up early before I began my full-time job to trade. This limited the markets I was able to trade but helped me to establish good, efficient trading routines because I didn't have all day to trade. As I shifted my time to trading full time, I realized that the routines I had established were very effective at ensuring that I was maximizing the time I spent in front of my computer screens. I was less likely to get distracted because I had established a good trading routine. Regardless of when you trade, you should be able to articulate your trading routines to ensure that you are using the time you do have in front of your trading screens most effectively.

KEY TAKE-AWAYS

- All traders will develop trading setups and focus their energy on learning the markets. Traders also should be aware of some of the common lessons that other traders have already learned.
- Being aware of trading myths, how to avoid rookie mistakes, character traits of a successful trader, and establishing good trading routines will serve to help you avoid some setbacks in the markets.
- Remember that even though the psychological aspects of trading are often invisible, they certainly can affect your trading.
- Anyone can learn to trade, but it is a skill that needs to be developed, just like any other skill.

CONCLUSION

I wrote this book for anyone—for traders or for those who were wishing they could learn the skills to trade. No longer should trading feel like an impossible skill that is explained only to the precious few and closely guarded. I believe that trading should be a skill set that anyone is able to learn if they choose and hope that in time more institutions will offer real education to support people's quest to learn and understand the markets from the perspective of day traders and not just from the industry of investment advisors. This book has offered actual trading setups that I use personally while also helping to break down technical analysis and a MY TRADE plan to outline next steps. I congratulate you on your decision to trade—to feel empowered and in control of your ability to make money in the markets. Trading is incredibly rewarding and offers amazing rewards beyond monetary gain. A tremendous sense of pride and self-confidence can be gleaned from any day trader who trades professionally. Even though many traders' points of view may be personalized, we all approach the markets with a trading plan that matches our strengths. The variance in our trading opinions provides opportunities for each of us to trade with each other and leads to a healthy discussion about the markets.

When I was a young child, I remember someone asking me what I wanted to do when I grew up. I answered, "I want to make a difference." This is where my passion to help others learn about trading comes from. It's time that many of the walls in trading are broken down so that anyone can learn the skills to trade. I hope that in some small way this book will make a difference and help to empower people with knowledge to take whatever their next step might be.

I close this book with a quotation that I believe has gotten me to where I am today. I hope that it will inspire you to reach whatever goal you have for yourself.

The only difference between a dream and a goal is a timeline.

—Unknown

Trade smart!

APPENDIX

MY TRADE Plan

The MY TRADE plan is a trading plan template that I developed. It is organized into specific categories to ensure that traders have thought through all of the necessary information they will need to create a solid trading plan. The MY TRADE plan has two parts. The first section is designed to answer questions to many important areas for traders. The second part summarizes your answers into concise action statements. These action statements will be your personalized manual to help you trade. The first part of the plan will help you to articulate:

- The market you will trade
- Your trading goals
- The trading setups you will use
- The rules you will follow
- What you will do as you enter, manage, and exit trades
- Your drawdowns, including stops and losses
- How you will evaluate your trading performance

The second part of the plan supports your ability to:

- Articulate how you will use the information you gathered
- Define your measurable and achievable action statements
- Outline what you will actually do to implement your plan while you trade

Begin to complete your plan by answering the questions in each section. Next, write your action plan, You should have a statement for each section. Each action statement should be written using words that include I will with what you will do and how you will do it specific to each section. Your action statements should be written in language that is positive and focused on action.

> **M**arkets
> **Y**our goals
> **T**rades
> **R**ules
> **A**ction
> **D**rawdowns
> **E**valuate

MY TRADE Plan	Your Answers	Your Action Plan
M is for Markets *This section focuses on what you will do in which market. Questions you need to answer in this section include* • What overall markets will you use to inform the overall direction of your market assumptions? • What specific markets will be on your watch list? • What trading instrument will you trade in what markets? • Where will you gather information about news events (economic reports, earnings)?		

MY TRADE Plan	Your Answers	Your Action Plan *Smart* Goal
Y is for Your Goals *This section focuses on what goals you would like to achieve. Questions you will need to answer in this section include:* • What are some goals you would like to reach considering your account size? • What timeline will you set for yourself to meet at least three small steps to reach a larger goal? • What will your rewards be along the way? • How will you track your progress?		
T is for Trades *This section focuses on what tools you will use to trade. Questions you will need to answer in this section include:* • What will you trade? • What setups will you use? • What time will you trade?		

(continued on next page)

MY TRADE Plan	Your Answers	Your Action Plan *Smart* Goal
R is for Rules *This section focuses on the rules you will follow when you trade. Questions you will need to answer in this section include:* • What time will you trade? • What contract size will you use when you place trades in specific markets? • Where will you place your stops/targets for each trading strategy you use? • What is your pre/postmarket routine? • What margins relative to your account size will you trade with?		
A is for Action *This section focuses on your strategy. Questions you will need to answer in this section include:* • What will you use to form your trading assumption in order to enter a trade? • How will you assess your trades once you are in?		

• What is your exit strategy? • What indicators will you use?		
D is for Drawdowns *Questions you will need to answer in this section include:* • What will you do if a trade is going against you? • What information will you gather to decide your exits? • How will you identify how your emotions are affecting your trading actions? • When will you reduce/increase your position size?		
E is for Evaluate *Questions you will need to answer in this section include:* • How will you monitor how your trades went? • How will you record how you felt before, during, and after a trade? • When will you review your trades?		

I Do, I Don't, I Dunno Chart

This chart will help organize your thoughts to help you determine if you have enough market evidence to support your trading assumptions. Organize the market variables that you see at the point in time you are considering placing a trade. List all of the market variables like support and resistance, clean charts, market internals, trend, and so on in the appropriate columns below. Use the "I Do" section if the variables are present, use the "I Don't" section if the variables are not present, and use the "I Dunno" section to list variables that are causing you indecision at the moment.

Notes	I Do	I Don't	I Dunno

Example:

Notes	I Do	I Don't	I Dunno
In Fashion setup 10:20	Volume Resistance/support levels Congruence in S&P ADD	Trend	Trend

Trading Journal

This trading journal can be used as a template to help guide your thinking when you look back on your trading performance. Some traders will complete a journal every day, while others will use it weekly. Establish times for yourself when you will review your trading performance on a regular basis. The information from your I Do, I Don't, and I Dunno will include your notes from your insights in the moment, while this journal is more of a reflective tool. Complete the journal by answering the questions in the summary, analysis, and commitment columns.

Date	Summary of Trade Impressions	Analysis of Action Factors	Commitment
	• How has your trading gone? • Summarize your trades and performance from your daily I Do, I Don't, and I Dunno	• How did your decisions from your chart analysis correlate to your trade assumption? • What comparisons can be made between the trade you planned to initiate and what actually happened? • What trade setup is most profitable for you?	• What will you be mindful of moving forward? • What tweaks might need to be made in your MY TRADE plan?

INDEX

ABOUT THE AUTHOR

Sarah Potter trades options and futures using technical analysis to place swing and day trades. She writes a popular blog www.shecantrade.com where she shares real information for traders of all abilities. Sarah has a unique ability to explain the world of trading in a clear and concise manner that traders new and experienced appreciate. She has degrees in sociology, communication studies, a bachelor of education, and a masters of education. Her work has been featured in numerous publications including *Active Trader*, *TraderPlanet*, *SFO Magazine*, *Canadian Investing Magazine,* and more.

Sarah shares some of her current trading ideas with the members of the CornerLOT available from www.shecantrade.com. For a limited time, readers of this book are eligible to receive Sarah's trading ideas for a discounted membership rate. Just e-mail sarah@shecantrade.com and mention the "book special." Her trading idea service, The CornerLOT has one of the best performance track records of many trading newsletters available to retail traders.